Arizona MEMORIES

Arizona MEMORIES

Anne Hodges Morgan

AND

Rennard Strickland

EDITORS

The University of Arizona Press

Tucson, Arizona

About the Editors

ANNE HODGES MORGAN has written several books on Southwestern history and, with Rennard Strickland, edited *Oklahoma Memories*. She earned a master's degree in international affairs from Columbia University and a Ph.D. in history from the University of Texas. In 1980 she became vice president for programs at the Kerr Foundation in Oklahoma City.

RENNARD STRICKLAND, professor of law and history at the University of Tulsa, has written extensively on Indian art, history, and the law. His books include *Indian Dilemma: Rhetoric and Reality of Cherokee Removal* (with William M. Strickland) and *As In A Vision: Masterworks of American Indian Art* (with Carol Harolson and Ed Wade). He has S.J.D. and J.D. degrees from the University of Virginia and has taught at universities in the South and West.

Second Printing 1985
THE UNIVERSITY OF ARIZONA PRESS

Copyright © 1984
The Arizona Board of Regents
All Rights Reserved

This book was set in 11/13 Linotron Caledonia.
Manufactured in the U.S.A.

Library of Congress Cataloging in Publication Data

Main entry under title:

Arizona memories.

   Includes index.
   1. Arizona—Social life and customs—Addresses,
essays, lectures.   2. Arizona—Biography—Addresses,
essays, lectures.   3. Pioneers—Arizona—Biography—
Addresses, essays, lectures.   I. Morgan, Anne Hodges,
1940–   .   II. Strickland, Rennard.
F811.5.A75   1984   979.1'04'0922   84-8853

ISBN 0-8165-0869-0

To
H. Wayne Morgan

Contents

Preface

In this book, the men and women who settled Arizona tell the state's colorful history in their own words. Those who have "lived" history are often the best chroniclers. Although the professional historian performs an important task in analyzing, synthesizing, and summarizing information about the past, secondary works usually lack the sense of immediacy, the poignant anecdote, and the intensity of response to a particular event which can be found in letters, diaries, and. memoirs. In *Arizona Memories*, Arizonans tell their stories without the encumbering apparatus of formal historical scholarship.

The selections we have chosen are primarily memoirs written about the period from the first decade after the Civil War through the 1960s. These recollections are presented in chronological order, which provides the book's narrative structure. In most cases the selections are autobiographical or firsthand accounts. One of the pieces, "Advice to the Health Seeker," is representative of the literature that beckoned the frail and consumptive westward near the end of the nineteenth century. Another narrative, "Arrested for Polygamy," is the work of a daughter recording the events of her mother's life based on extensive family diaries.

In choosing material for this volume, we have attempted to include pieces that depict the occupational diversity as well as the cultural complexity of the state. We looked for memoirs that did more than merely record an historical event or episode. These are the recollections that reflected the rhythms and cadence of daily life, the contemporary social attitudes, and the lifestyles and occupations that were virtually swept away in the wave of modernization that reached Arizona after World War II. In bringing these selections together, we hope that others will be stimulated to collect and preserve the personal recollections and memoirs which are so valuable a part of every state's cultural heritage.

We have deliberately chosen not to clutter the text with footnotes or explanatory material. Spelling and punctuation have been changed to conform to current usage. For the reader who wants to delve further, there are several good general histories of Arizona, including Marshall Trimble, *Arizona: A Panoramic History of a Frontier State* (Garden City, N.Y.: Doubleday, 1977); Odie B. Faulk, *Arizona, A Short History* (Norman: University of Oklahoma Press, 1970); Bert M. Fireman, *Arizona, Historic Land* (New York: Alfred A. Knopf, 1982); and Rufus Kay Wyllys, *Arizona: The History of A Frontier State* (Phoenix: Hobson & Herr, 1950). Although written more than three decades ago, Wyllys' book remains the most provocative single-volume interpretation of the Grand Canyon State.

Jay J. Wagoner's two volumes, *Arizona Territory, 1863–1912* (Tucson: University of Arizona Press, 1970) and *Early Arizona, Prehistory to Civil War* (Tucson: University of Arizona Press, 1975), are essential for the reader interested in the period before statehood. In addition, Lawrence Clark Powell's *Arizona: A Bicentennial History* (New York: W. W. Norton, 1977) emphasizes the early era.

Some of the place names and geographic designations that appear in the selections have changed or disappeared. The reader may wish to consult Henry P. Walker and Don Bufkin, *Historical Atlas of Arizona* (Norman: University of Oklahoma Press, 1979); Byrd H. Granger, *Will C. Barnes' Arizona Place Names* (Tucson: University of Arizona Press, 1960); and James E. and Barbara H. Sherman, *Ghost Towns of Arizona* (Norman: University of Oklahoma Press, 1969).

In gathering material for this volume we traveled extensively throughout the entire state over a three-year period. We visited a variety of depositories, from large archives and special collections at major educational and cultural institutions to small public libraries, museums, and historical societies. Along the way we met scores of people who eagerly shared their resources and their knowledge of Arizona history. It is a pleasure to thank those who so graciously helped us. The staffs of the Northern Arizona Pioneer Historical Society, Inc.; the Museum of Northern Arizona; the Mohave County Historical Society; the Prescott/Sharlot Hall Historical Society; the Arizona Historical Foundation; the Arizona Collection, Hayden Library at Arizona State University; the Fort Verde Historic Park; the Fort Huachuca Recreation Services Post

xii

Library; the Arizona Department of Libraries, Archives and Public Records; the Maricopa County Historical Society; and the Chiricahua National Monument Library were consistently cooperative and cheerful. We are especially grateful to Dr. Louis A. Hieb, head of Special Collections at the University of Arizona Library, and his staff for their courtesies and service beyond the call of duty. David Hoober, archivist of the Arizona Historical Society, guided us to many of the selections included here and continued to respond to our inquiries long after our return home. Jan Thornton of the Special Collections staff at Northern Arizona University Library tracked down elusive materials and provided helpful insights into prospective sources in her part of the state. At the Yuma County Historical Society Robin Gilliam eagerly shared the Bill Keiser memoir on mining. Kay Benedict of the Casa Grande Historical Society offered her collections and her coffee on a bright, crisp December morning. Harwood Hinton, professor of history at the University of Arizona and editor of *Arizona and the West*, provided suggestions, sources, and indices. He was also an encouraging and sympathetic listener and luncheon companion.

We are grateful to Pat Sugg and Sue Dowling for their help in typing and their thoughtful suggestions which strengthened the book. And, as always, Rosemarie Spaulding typed the numerous drafts of the manuscript with patience and good humor.

Our greatest debt is to H. Wayne Morgan. He introduced us to the muted beauty of Arizona's deserts and the splendor of her high country and instilled in us his own profound fascination with the state's history.

Anne Hodges Morgan
Rennard Strickland

History Begins in the Heart

Anne Hodges Morgan
and Rennard Strickland

If geography is destiny, Arizona was marked for greatness. Only one boundary, the Colorado River on the West, was not man-made. Yet the people who determined Arizona's perimeters included within them some of the most varied and spectacular scenery on the North American continent.

Arizona is a land of dramatic and unexpected contrasts and contradictions. Forested mountains tower a mile high in relative proximity to a river that has eroded a multi-colored canyon almost a mile deep. In a state renowned for its tawny deserts, there is the country's largest stand of ponderosa pine. In the northeast region of the state, ancient forests have tumbled and turned to stone. In other areas vegetation has developed spiky thorns and prickly foliage to adapt to the arid land. Snowclad peaks send their runoff into the valleys below to nourish once-barren soil. Twentieth-century technology has transformed the Valley of the Sun into a modern cosmopolitan metropolis with a complex economic, cultural, and social environment. Yet less than two hundred miles away, ancient tribal rites still persist as the Hopis honor their Kachinas who lodge in the San Francisco peaks as they have for centuries. Indian, Hispanic, and Anglo cultures mingle yet remain distinct despite the homogenizing tendencies of modern life.

Archaeological evidence reveals that Arizona was the home of ancient peoples who constructed great dwellings and canals in the desert and lived in caves and cliffs in the higher elevations. These people attained a high degree of civilization in an age of stone and are among the ancestors of the state's present-day Indian tribes. Other than utensils and ruined dwellings, they left little.

The recorded history of Arizona begins with the Spanish, who came seeking treasure, souls, and empire more than four hundred years ago. Although their search for precious metals was lonely and futile, the explorers left some trails and a few place names. In the seventeenth century, missionary activities spread from other

1

regions of New Spain into Arizona, and as mission settlements grew, military personnel followed. Soon immigrants from the Mexican states began to flow into Arizona in increasing numbers to farm, raise livestock, prospect, and trade.

After the Mexican wars of independence, mountain men and traders passed through Arizona on their travels from Santa Fe south into Sonora and Chihuahua and west to the Pacific. Year by year more became known about this land called Arizona and its possibilities.

In the years between the Mexican Cession and the end of the Civil War, overland travel to California increased rapidly. While most travelers passed through Arizona on their way to the gold fields, some stopped at various points along the Gila River and established ranches and farms. In the two decades after the Civil War, Arizona Territory's population climbed upward as mining booms attracted large numbers of single workmen, but continuing Indian troubles discouraged families from following. With the extension of railroads into Arizona, travelers began to praise the natural beauties and soon tourism that began as a trickle became a steady flow. Health seekers who came for the dry air and the sunshine remained to enjoy their health as permanent residents. By the close of the nineteenth century, Arizona Territory had a viable economy based on the "Five Cs"—cattle, citrus, climate, copper, and cotton—with sufficient population to press vigorously for statehood.

From Arizona's admission into the Union in 1912 until the outbreak of World War II, the state's history paralleled the nation's. With the completion of Roosevelt, Boulder, and other large dams on the major rivers, irrigation and electrical power facilitated settlement in underdeveloped regions and permitted the extension of agriculture and other economic enterprises.

Within this broad framework of Arizona's history from the Civil War to the 1960s, countless human dramas transpired. Yet, for the most part, these stories have been ignored in state histories which have emphasized dates, wars, treaties, and political figures. The selections here deal with significant events and episodes in Arizona's history: Indian hostilities and military life, trade, settlement, the exploitation of natural resources and mineral wealth, health seeking, the struggle to control water, ranching, farming, the Great Depression, the change in life and attitudes after World War II. The difference between these selections and the standard

2

state history reader is that this collection is designed to show how historical events affected the lives of ordinary individuals.

The subject matter ranges from the harshness of military campaigns to the elegance of literary evenings; from the cacophony of Tucson's narrow streets echoing with the cries of peddlers to the silence of the mountain forests where a solitary ranger scanned the horizon. One selection chronicles the scientific discovery of a new planet while another glimpses the mysticism which sustained a Navajo soldier throughout the horrors of the war in the Pacific. Cowboy life on the Babbitt ranch is captured in vivid detail, and the anguish of a rancher's personal and financial loss in the Great Depression is almost palpable to the reader.

The major themes of Arizona history are illuminated through the personal lives of the pioneers—the struggle to subdue hostile Indians so settlement and development could proceed; the conflicts that ensued when Protestant settlers encountered Mormon families, whose religious practices seemed abhorrent as well as illegal; the burgeoning of wealth from the toil of the miners and laborers who freed the minerals and channeled the waters that propelled development in the twentieth century. The theme of racial tension is also explored through the memoir of a Hopi artist caught between two cultures and a woman confined because her Japanese parentage obliterated the rights her American citizenship should have guaranteed. Woven throughout these recollections is the theme of the majesty of the Arizona landscape, the contrast of deserts and mountains, the dazzling beauty and the punishing harshness of the natural environment. Upon this landscape, the story of the Arizona pioneers' resilience, strength, and tenacity was enacted.

In the following pages, men and women express their feelings and fears, their impressions and aspirations about the significant events which touched their lives. These memoirs reaffirm Willa Cather's conviction that "the history of every country begins in the heart of a man or a woman."

Old Camp McDowell

Martha Summerhayes

If the average American in the last half of the nineteenth century knew anything about Arizona, it was the territory's reputation as the battleground of a long, drawn-out war against the Indians. Tales of Apaches preying on isolated rancherías, miners, and commercial travelers filled the Eastern press. Generations later these stories entered the nation's literary heritage in the fiction of Zane Grey, Louis L'Amour, and scores of lesser Western writers.

For some years after the Civil War, preoccupation with national reconstruction distracted attention from the mounting Indian troubles in Arizona Territory. But by 1870, Apache warfare forced Washington to commit sufficient personnel and resources to subdue hostile Indians and confine them to reservations. Under George Crook, relentless hunt-and-kill operations finally forced the resisting Indians to capitulate. Yet another decade would be required to settle all Indian hostilities in so vast an area, and the Army's Eighth Infantry played an important role in these campaigns. Among the Eighth Infantry's officers' wives was Martha Dunham Summerhayes, whose recollection of army life in Arizona in the 1870s has become a classic.

Mrs. Summerhayes was born on Nantucket Island on October 21, 1846. As the daughter of a cultured New England family she was well educated and had traveled abroad. During a two-year stay in Hanover to study German music and literature, she lived with a Prussian military family. The splendor and romance of military uniforms, the apparent gaiety and stimulation of the professional soldier's life captivated her. Upon returning home, Martha married a fellow Nantucket resident, Maj. John Wyer Summerhayes, a former whaler, trapper and thrice-wounded Civil War veteran. Poised for a life of glamour and adventure, Martha Summerhayes quickly confronted reality.

5

Within a few days of her arrival as a young bride at Fort Russell in Wyoming Territory, Mrs. Summerhayes realized that military life might not be all "bright buttons, blue uniforms and shining swords." A few months later, in June 1874, her husband's regiment was ordered to Arizona, which she described as "that dreaded and then unknown land."

During her four years in Arizona, Mrs. Summerhayes learned to accommodate to days of 120 degrees, drinking water of 86 degrees, and butter that poured like oil. Inexperienced and frightened, she had her first child at Camp Apache, Arizona. She picked ants from her children's faces and searched their slippers and boots for scorpions and snakes. Despite the terrors and hardships of military life, Mrs. Summerhayes was inherently an optimist. When her husband was posted to Fort McDowell on the Verde River, Mrs. Summerhayes set about housekeeping with imagination, inventiveness, and little else because most of the family's household furnishings, clothes, and personal possessions had been lost in a steamship fire on the Colorado River.

With pluck and good humor, Mrs. Summerhayes set out to endure Arizona. As she journeyed by steamboat, military ambulance, on horseback, and on foot, she began to appreciate the desert's subtle beauty. Life in the military became less of a glittering pageant and more of a grand adventure, and in her old age she recalled the Arizona years with great affection.

6

We were expected, evidently, for as we drove along the road in front of the officers' quarters they all came out to meet us, and we received a great welcome.

Captain Corliss of C company welcomed us to the post and to his company, and said he hoped I should like McDowell better than I did Ehrenberg. Now Ehrenberg seemed years agone, and I could laugh at the mention of it.

Supper was awaiting us at Captain Corliss's, and Mrs. Kendall, wife of Lieutenant Kendall, Sixth Cavalry, had, in Jack's absence, put the finishing touches to our quarters. So I went at once to a comfortable home, and life in the army began again for me.

How good everything seemed! There was Doctor Clark, whom I had met first at Ehrenberg, and who wanted to throw Patrocina and Jesusita into the Colorado. I was so glad to find him there; he was such a good doctor, and we never had a moment's anxiety, as long as he stayed at Camp McDowell. Our confidence in him was unbounded.

It was easy enough to obtain a man from the company. There were then no hateful laws forbidding soldiers to work in officers' families; no dreaded inspectors, who put the flat question, "Do you employ a soldier for menial labor?"

Captain Corliss gave me an old man by the name of Smith, and he was glad to come and stay with us and do what simple cooking we required. One of the laundresses let me have her daughter for nurserymaid, and our small establishment at Camp McDowell moved on smoothly, if not with elegance.

The officers' quarters were a long, low line of adobe buildings with no space between them; the houses were separated only by thick walls. In front, the windows looked out over the parade ground. In the rear, they opened out on a road which ran along the

From Martha Summerhayes, *Vanished Arizona: Recollections of My Army Life* (Philadelphia: J.B. Lippincott, 1908), 196–207.

7

whole length, and on the other side of which lay another row of long, low buildings which were the kitchens, each set of quarters having its own.

We occupied the quarters at the end of the row, and a large bay window looked out over a rather desolate plain, and across to the large and well-kept hospital. As all my draperies and pretty crétonnes had been burnt up on the ill-fated ship, I had nothing but bare white shades at the windows, and the rooms looked desolate enough. But a long divan was soon built, and some coarse yellow cotton bought at John Smith's (the sutler's) store, to cover it. My pretty rugs and mats were also gone, and there was only the old ingrain carpet from Fort Russell. The floors were adobe, and some men from the company came and laid down old canvas, then the carpet, and drove in great spikes around the edge, to hold it down. The floors of the bedroom and dining room were covered with canvas in the same manner. Our furnishings were very scanty and I felt very mournful about the loss of the boxes. We could not claim restitution, as the steamship company had been courteous enough to take the boxes down free of charge.

John Smith, the post trader (the name "sutler" fell into disuse about now), kept a large store, but nothing that I could use to beautify my quarters with—and our losses had been so heavy that we really could not afford to send back East for more things. My new white dresses came, and were suitable enough for the winter climate of McDowell. But I missed the thousand and one accessories of a woman's wardrobe, the accumulation of years, the comfortable things which money could not buy, especially at that distance.

I had never learned how to make dresses or to fit garments, and, although I knew how to sew, my accomplishments ran more in the line of outdoor sports.

But Mrs. Kendall, whose experience in frontier life had made her self-reliant, lent me some patterns, and I bought some of John Smith's calico and went to work to make gowns suited to the hot weather. This was in 1877, and everyone will remember that the ready-made house-gowns were not to be had in those days in the excellence and profusion in which they can today be found, in all parts of the country.

Now Mrs. Kendall was a tall, fine woman, much larger than I, but I used her patterns without alterations, and the result was something like a bag. They were freshly laundried and cool, howev-

8

er, and I did not place so much importance on the lines of them, as the young women of the present time do. Today, the poorest farmer's wife in the wilds of Arkansas or Alaska can wear better fitting gowns than I wore then. But my riding habits, of which I had several kinds, to suit warm and cold countries, had been left in Jack's care at Ehrenberg, and as long as these fitted well, it did not so much matter about the gowns.

Captain Chaffee, who commanded the company of the Sixth Cavalry stationed there, was away on leave, but Mr. Kendall, his first lieutenant, consented for me to exercise "Cochise," Captain Chaffee's Indian pony, and I had a royal time.

Cavalry officers usually hate riding: that is, riding for pleasure, for they are in the saddle so much for dead earnest work. But a young officer, a second lieutenant, not long out from the Academy, liked to ride and we had many pleasant riding parties. Mr. Dravo and I rode one day to the Mormon settlement, seventeen miles away, on some business with the bishop, and a Mormon woman gave us a lunch of fried salt pork, potatoes, bread, and milk. How good it tasted, after our long ride! And how we laughed about it all, and jollied, after the fashion of young people, all the way back to the post! Mr. Dravo had also lost all his things on the "Montana," and we sympathized greatly with each other. He, however, had sent an order home to Pennsylvania, duplicating all the contents of his boxes. I told him I could not duplicate mine, if I sent a thousand orders East.

When, after some months, his boxes came, he brought me a package, done up in tissue paper and tied with ribbon: "Mother sends you these; she wrote that I was not to open them; I think she felt sorry for you, when I wrote her you had lost all your clothing. I suppose," he added, mustering his West Point French to the front, and handing me the package, "it is what you ladies call 'lingerie.'"

I hope I blushed, and I think I did, for I was not so very old, and I was touched by this sweet remembrance from the dear mother back in Pittsburgh. And so many lovely things happened all the time; everybody was so kind to me. Mrs. Kendall and her young sister, Kate Taylor, Mrs. John Smith and I, were the only women that winter at Camp McDowell. Afterwards, Captain Corliss brought a bride to the post, and a new doctor took Doctor Clark's place.

There were interminable scouts, which took both cavalry and infantry out of the post. We heard a great deal about "chasing

9

Injuns" in the Superstition Mountains, and once a lieutenant of infantry went out to chase an escaping Indian agent.

Old Smith, my cook, was not very satisfactory; he drank a good deal, and I got very tired of the trouble he caused me. It was before the days of the canteen, and soldiers could get all the whiskey they wanted at the trader's store; and, it being generally the brand that was known in the army as "Forty rod," they got very drunk on it sometimes. I never had it in my heart to blame them much, poor fellows, for every human being wants and needs some sort of recreation and jovial excitement.

Captain Corliss said to Jack one day, in my presence, "I had a fine batch of recruits come in this morning."

"That's lovely," said I; "what kind of men are they? Any good cooks amongst them?" (for I was getting very tired of Smith).

Captain Corliss smiled a grim smile. "What do you think the United States Government enlists men for?" said he. "Do you think I want my company to be made up of dish-washers?"

He was really quite angry with me, and I concluded that I had been too abrupt, in my eagerness for another man, and that my ideas on the subject were becoming warped. I decided that I must be more diplomatic in the future, in my dealings with the Captain of C company.

The next day, when we went to breakfast, whom did we find in the dining room but Bowen! Our old Bowen of the long march across the Territory! Of Camp Apache and K company. He had his white apron on, his hair rolled back in his most fetching style, and was putting the coffee on the table.

"But, Bowen," said I, "where—how on earth—did you—how did you know we—what does it mean?"

Bowen saluted the First Lieutenant of C company, and said: "Well, sir, the fact is, my time was out, and I thought I would quit. I went to San Francisco and worked in a miners' restaurant," (here he hesitated) "but I didn't like it, and I tried something else, and lost all my money, and I got tired of the town, so I thought I'd take on again, and as I knowed ye's were in C company now, I thought I'd come to McDowell, and I came over here this morning and told old Smith he'd better quit; this was my job, and here I am, and I hope ye're all well—and the little boy?"

Here was loyalty indeed, and here was Bowen the Immortal, back again!

10

And now things ran smoothly once more. Roasts of beef and haunches of venison, ducks and other good things we had through the winter.

It was cool enough to wear white cotton dresses, but nothing heavier. It never rained, and the climate was superb, although it was always hot in the sun. We had heard that it was very hot here; in fact, people called McDowell by very bad names. As the spring came on, we began to realize that the epithets applied to it might be quite appropriate.

In front of our quarters was a ramada, supported by rude poles of the cottonwood tree. Then came the sidewalk, and the acequia (ditch), then a row of young cottonwood trees, then the parade ground. Through the acequia ran the clear water that supplied the post, and under the shade of the ramadas, hung the large ollas from which we dipped the drinking water, for as yet, of course, ice was not even dreamed of in the far plains of McDowell. The heat became intense, as the summer approached. To sleep inside the house was impossible, and we soon followed the example of the cavalry, who had their beds out on the parade ground.

Two iron cots, therefore, were brought from the hospital, and placed side by side in front of our quarters, beyond the acequia and the cottonwood trees, in fact, out in the open space of the parade ground. Upon these were laid some mattresses and sheets, and after "taps" had sounded, and lights were out, we retired to rest. Near the cots stood Harry's crib. We had not thought about the ants, however, and they swarmed over our beds, driving us into the house. The next morning Bowen placed a tin can of water under each point of contact; and as each cot had eight legs, and the crib had four, twenty cans were necessary. He had not taken the trouble to remove the labels, and the pictures of red tomatoes glared at us in the hot sun through the day; they did not look poetic, but our old enemies, the ants, were outwitted.

We did not look along the line, when we retired to our cots, but if we had, we should have seen shadowy figures, laden with pillows, flying from the houses to the cots or vice versa. It was certainly a novel experience.

With but a sheet for a covering, there we lay, looking up at the starry heavens. I watched the Great Bear go around, and other constellations and seemed to come into close touch with Nature and the mysterious night. But the melancholy solemnity of my

11

communings was much affected by the howling of the coyotes, which seemed sometimes to be so near that I jumped to the side of the crib, to see if my little boy was being carried off. The good sweet slumber which I craved never came to me in those weird Arizona nights under the stars.

At about midnight, a sort of dewy coolness would come down from the sky, and we could then sleep a little; but the sun rose incredibly early in that southern country, and by the crack of dawn sheeted figures were to be seen darting back into the quarters, to try for another nap. The nap rarely came to any of us, for the heat of the houses never passed off, day or night, at that season. After an early breakfast, the long day began again.

The question of what to eat came to be a serious one. We experimented with all sorts of tinned foods, and tried to produce some variety from them, but it was all rather tiresome. We almost dreaded the visits of the Paymaster and the Inspector at that season, as we never had anything in the house to give them.

One hot night, at about ten o'clock we heard the rattle of wheels, and an ambulance drew up at our door. Out jumped Colonel Biddle, Inspector General, from Fort Whipple. "What shall I give him to eat, poor hungry man?" I thought. I looked in the wire-covered safe, which hung outside the kitchen, and discovered half a beefsteak pie. The gallant Colonel declared that if there was one thing above all others that he liked, it was cold beefsteak pie. Lieutenant Thomas of the Fifth Cavalry echoed his sentiments, and with a bottle of Cocomonga, which was always kept cooling somewhere, they had a merry supper.

These visits broke the monotony of our life at Camp McDowell. We heard of the gay doings up at Fort Whipple, and of the lovely climate there.

Mr. Thomas said he could not understand why we wore such bags of dresses. I told him spitefully that if the women of Fort Whipple would come down to McDowell to spend the summer, they would soon be able to explain it to him. I began to feel embarrassed at the fit of my house-gowns. After a few days spent with us, however, the mercury ranging from 104 to 120 degrees in the shade, he ceased to comment upon our dresses or our customs.

I had a glass jar of butter sent over from the Commissary, and asked Colonel Biddle if he thought it right that such butter as that should be bought by the purchasing officer in San Francisco. It had melted, and separated into layers of dead white, deep orange

12

and pinkish-purple colors. Thus I, too, as well as General Miles, had my turn at trying to reform the Commissary Department of Uncle Sam's army.

Hammocks were swung under the ramadas, and after luncheon everybody tried a siesta. Then, near sundown, an ambulance came and took us over to the Verde River, about a mile away, where we bathed in water almost as thick as that of the Great Colorado. We taught Mrs. Kendall to swim, but Mr. Kendall, being an inland man, did not take to the water. Now the Verde River was not a very good substitute for the sea, and the thick water filled our ears and mouths, but it gave us a little half hour in the day when we could experience a feeling of being cool, and we found it worthwhile to take the trouble. Thick clumps of mesquite trees furnished us with dressing rooms. We were all young, and youth requires so little with which to make merry.

After the meagre evening dinner, the Kendalls and ourselves sat together under the ramada until taps, listening generally to the droll anecdotes told by Mr. Kendall, who had an inexhaustible fund. Then another night under the stars, and so passed the time away.

The Sunday inspection of men and barracks, which was performed with much precision and formality, and often in full dress uniform, gave us something by which we could mark the weeks, as they slipped along. There was no religious service of any kind, as Uncle Sam had not enough chaplains to go round. Those he had were kept for the larger posts, or those nearer civilization. The good Catholics read their prayer-books at home, and the non-religious people almost forgot that such organizations as churches existed.

Another bright winter found us still gazing at the Four Peaks of the McDowell Mountains, the only landmark on the horizon. I was glad, in those days, that I had not stayed back East, for the life of an officer without his family, in those dreary places, is indeed a blank and empty one.

"Four years I have sat here and looked at the Four Peaks," said Captain Corliss, one day, "and I'm getting almighty tired of it."

13

A Stage Coach Robbery in the Desert

E. Conklin

The dime novel of the late nineteenth century and the motion picture of the twentieth century enveloped stage coach routes across the American West in legend and romance. In the Hollywood version, the leading lady alights at the end of a thousand-mile journey swathed in yards of damask, silk and furs. Her plumed millinery and veil are arranged at a fashionable angle, her gloves appear white and spotless. Her coiffure, nerves, and dignity are all in place.

In real life the scene played differently. Stage journeys were expensive, nightmarish marathons over primitive, boulder-strewn trails, up and down perilously steep grades, through swollen rivers or across them on flimsy rafts. Standard coaches, minus the plush velvet seats and draperies, accommodated nine people inside, provided the passengers locked knees. Extra passengers perched on the roof and held on for their lives. If the mail load was unusually heavy and weighed down the rear, passengers on the front seat fought to keep their balance. The results were predictable—no chance to rest and pains in the lower back.

Despite the high cost of a stage journey, passengers often had to walk and push if the terrain was steep. And on some routes across the desert, burros often were substituted for the coach at certain stages of the journey. The food was poor. The experienced traveler carried mustard to mask the taste of the mule meat which sometimes was substituted for jerky or venison. The physical discomforts of a stage journey were bad enough, with sleepless nights in a crowded coach with no shock absorbers. But the abuse to the nostrils must have been worse in the era of desert travel prior to deodorants, mouthwashes, and tourist accommodations with showers.

15

In addition to the physical discomforts, there was the constant threat of robbery and violence. Stage coaches were the principal mode of transportation from one town to another and frequently carried large sums of gold or silver as well as mail and some freight. Often, just as in the movies, the coaches and their passengers were robbed. In the following selection, a victim writes of the horror and the hilarity of being robbed in the desert at midnight.

We have said the men were there. How they came there in the position we now beheld them we could not tell. Like spirits of the deep springing up from the bowels of the earth by some invisible trapdoor, or dropped down from the heavens. They were simply there and that is all we knew—and enough. A very few moments elapsed between our seeing them and the commencement of the excitement which was to be the terror of our midnight ride. But in this moment a volume of horrible visions ran through my mind, the most terrible of which was that we were now in the hands of the highwaymen positively and securely, and barred out from all the world by a colossal wall of dreary mountains, upon a wide stretch of an arid, fruitless, uninviting desert.

I sat on the left of the driver. To the left of the horses' heads and facing us stood a goodly specimen of physical man with a large revolver levelled at our heads. It was about the size, I should judge, of those used by the "Horse Marines." To the left of the stage, on a range with me, was another "six-footer" with a hat, which, had it been mid-day, I would suppose was used to keep the sun off him, spreading out on all sides, and slouched down over his face. He held in his hands and levelled at my breast a rifle. In the next moment, what a volume, what a life of thought intervened! In the very stillness of the desert there was noise; your very soul talked aloud to you; and as for spirits—why, the whole world seemed to be composed of them. And then, breaking the silence, came the demand for "your money, or your life!" and the voices of these men seemed to echo from mountain to mountain. I was ordered to get down from the coach and stand before them; while the soldier inside was ordered "to the front" to hold the horses' heads. Being a soldier, and one of his essential duties being to "obey!" he was

From E. Conklin, *Picturesque Arizona* (New York: The Mining Record Printing Establishment, 1878), 363–380.

17

constrained, in his good judgment, to do so. Nobly did he perform his duty in this instance. Now, I had never been a soldier; yet, I obeyed orders in this case quite as well as he did. However, it was perhaps the stern force of "duty" that actuated him to obey, whereas mine was by force of persuasion. A rifle at your head and a six-shooter at your breast are terrible persuaders. I was thwarted, however, in my willingness to obey, by the "tucking in" that was done when leaving Desert station; and when I came to unloose myself from under the lap robe, it was obstinate, and I remem-'bered that the buckle of the strap which held the robe to the seat was broken and I had tied the ends together strongly and securely. This called forth execrations from the robbers.

"Why the D---l don't you get down off that coach?"

"Gentlemen," said I (which of course cut the grain acutely, but I swallowed it, and repeated), "gentlemen, don't shoot! And if you allow me I will explain--------"

"Hold up your hands!" interrupted one, with which command both Hill and I readily complied. And when once in this position again, I was instructed to explain "what the d----l" I was doing, and inquired of whether I had "any arms" at my side. Upon answering in the negative, I was allowed to proceed, and after extricating myself was ordered to "get down off of there."

Of course I complied. Once down, the following dialogue ensued:

Highwayman—"Who are you? What's your name?"

Having told him and after a silence of a moment he replied:

"Well! I'll take your money, and be quick about it or I'll blow your brains out."

I complied again: and at this instant, and while turning my possessions over to them, a "click" from the "Horse-Marine" pistol broke the silence of the desert. But fortunately it broke nothing else. It was either a "miss-fire" or the thing was done for effect— which, I am unable to say. At each interval the silence seemed to increase.

Our positions were now as follows: The soldier at the horses' heads to prevent them from running; the driver standing up on the coach, and I on the sandy ground at the left side of the coach. Still further to my left stood one of my molesters with his rifle; and in such a range that by simply elevating or lowering his piece either the driver or myself could be cleared of all responsibil-

18

ity in this life without it costing us one cent. In front of me and up at the side of the horses' heads where stood our soldier, was our other facetious friend, with his six-shooter still pointed at my breast. We had all been ordered to put our hands above our heads; and there we were, as if practicing calisthenics, and waiting for further drill. This is the common mode of the highwayman on our frontier, of securing your submission. With hands up, you can of course make no resistance; and if you take them down, nine to one, you will at the same instant be pierced with a bullet. No wiping of noses now, nor drying tears.

The first order given to the driver was to "Pass down Wells, Fargo & Co.'s express box!" The driver stooped, picked the box from beneath the seat, and threw it from the coach. It landed, with all its treasures, upon the sand directly in front of me with a heavy thump, which made my frame shudder and my veins contract like a headless chicken in its last death struggle. Each hair on my head was a porcupine quill. The next order was for the "United States mail sacks." These the driver also tossed upon the ground. There were three in number. They then ordered out some pouches of quicksilver, which were in the bottom of the stage; which demand the driver also complied with. This over, and fearing their booty would not reach their desires, they made a slight change of venue, and placing me in front of the treasure heap, demanded to know again who I was, and all about me. Having told them, there was a reign of silence—a terrible reign of about thirty seconds. Imaginations concerning this silence ran through my mind as rapidly as the reflections and thoughts of a drowning man are supposed to crowd themselves upon him; and as rapidly did I come to the conclusion that it must be they were disappointed in their man. They had expected someone else on this stage in my place. They then made a second demand, however, for all my papers, and any other "matters" I had about me, all of which I cheerfully relinquished. Had they known I was but a poor newspaperman, and, as they soon found out, all they were to get for their trouble was fifteen dollars, it seems to me they might have saved a good deal of valuable time and—"let me alone."

It was worth the amount, however, to get an excuse to take down my arms, which all this time had been held above my head in an upright position. This was an uncomfortable one, to say the least; and all the more so, as I stretched them high and straight to evince to

19

these "spirits of the desert" my disposition to obey orders. Having secured my money, and evidently taking it for granted that the driver and the soldier had none (or being now satisfied with what they had obtained) we were told to resume our places on the coach. Having done so, the fire-arms being kept steadily upon us the while, we were ordered to drive off; and as we did so, the two men cried out alternately, "Good-night!" "Good-night!"

I have been aroused by sudden changes; I have enjoyed the ecstatic effect of contrast; but never had any experience so forcibly struck upon such opposite sentiments in my nature as the contrast between these soft salutations "Good night!" "Good night!" and the terrible "halt" only a few minutes before. The former transactions were accompanied with sonorous tones of the deepest gutteral effort, and re-echoing as we fancied, in the distant mountains around. The latter tones were uttered in the gentlest simplicity and even savored of mellowness. It had such a pleasing and soothing effect upon us as to almost put us off our guard; and made me feel like turning around and saying: "Oh! you won't hurt us, will you?" I intimated to Hill, that if we should ask them now to give the things back, they would probably do so. I say this was the effect their "good night" produced upon me. But a moment's reflecting and a slight remonstrance from Hill convinced me that I was permitting my better judgment to be swayed by their blandness and apparent civility. A little consideration brought me to my senses and I was amazed at my own credulity, as the result of their words.

This whole affair was performed so quickly—began and ended so suddenly—was such a succession of surprises, that it was not until after all was over and we had resumed our journey that we thoroughly realized that anything had actually occurred. Now was the "winter of our discontent." As the horses began to trot off at a faster pace, Hill and I began to shake in our seats. We repeatedly looked around and wondered if they were coming after us. How often did we inquire of each other if we saw "anything of them?" We suffered more in the following few miles from an anticipation of a renewal of the attack than we did from the whole genuine affair. There was something so weird in our ride now. Every bush we approached, every cactus we saw, seemed to be possessed with life. When we stopped talking, the stillness increased. It increased until it actually became noisy; for the spiritual man then kept up a clatter with the mortal man, and talked to us of things we never knew (or

20

those that we had once known but wanted to forget), and in some respects annoyed us with its clatter. If one wants to get an idea of what a perfect quiet is, it seems to me he must go to Arizona to do it. These deserts, with nothing inviting, devoid of any noisy insects, or creatures whatever (except the coyote whose occasional distant whine or howl only contrasts with the stillness to make it greater), are suggestive of places for intense—for penetrative meditation.

"Well! Now then!" said Hill shortly afterward, as he spurred up his horses. "Now you've had it. Now you've had your robbery story better than I could have told you one, and I hope you're satisfied."

I did feel quite satisfied, and I wanted to know of Hill, whether this was the kind of sociable(?) Arizona tendered to strangers.

"Sociable!" quoted Hill. "That's pretty good."

"Yes!" rejoined I. "They are what I would term midnight sociables of the deserts."

Thus we rode along leaving these "spirits of the desert," we hoped, far behind. It was about 7 o'clock in the evening when our robbery took place. It was just before the time for the moon to rise, and the atmosphere wore that peculiar haze suggested by the old proverb, "'Tis darkest just before dawn."

Hill, who was an old pioneer in the stage business of our west, had many experiences (either personal or otherwise) to relate of the highways and the red man. I had one myself, having suffered a like engagement once before. Between us both, we consequently listened to many hair-breadth escapes and midnight revelries. We must have been intuitively prepared for this one from the systematic manner in which we went through the drill. At the very instant of the word "Halt!" and before we had been ordered to "Hold up your hands!" which is always the next command, my hands went up high over my head. Misery liking company, I looked to my right with one eye to see how it fared with my brother Hill, while the other I kept on my desert friends. Hill had his hands up, too. In short we wanted to get through with the midnight drama as quickly as possible. I remember how anxious I was to get back on my box after I had been robbed. But being commanded to "Halt!" with, at the same time, a click from the six-shooter, I allayed my impetuosity somewhat, and seemed to feel willing to stand there all night rather than attempt to get back to my seat again until I had been ordered to do so. I was encouraged all the way through by Hill's calm and polite manner in dealing with the case at hand.

This little narrative will give a general idea of the robberies of the overland stage coaches on our western highways. Of course, depredations are governed by no law, and these "sociables of the desert" are governed by no set or established routine. They take you how and where they find you and are governed in their actions accordingly. Many variations there are, then, to this system of aggression, although this is the average *modus operandi.* In a former robbery of a coach upon which I was a passenger, the coach was simply stopped by two men running out from behind a bush; and one grabbing the horses' heads, while the other stepped to the side of the coach and ordered the driver to "hand down Wells, Fargo & Co.'s express box." The driver having complied with the request, he was told to drive on, which he did; and the stage and its load drove off, and on to its destination as though nothing had happened—except that when we arrived there the box containing all the treasures was not with us. There is shooting at times, and often loss of life, but this is generally the result of disobedience to their commands or wishes; and if ever the reader has an occasion to fall into the hands of these "spirits of the desert," we would advise him to simply accept the situation with a calm and quiet grace, and obey as you had been taught to do in your youth. In nine times out of ten, you will come out of the battle unscathed, although it is admitted that there are men bloodthirsty enough to love to kill for the glory of it, and without any provocation.

Some, there are, who may not understand why resistance is not the better part of valor, and not oftener resorted to in these instances, on the part of the stage companies or the passengers. We simply say to those that to attempt to explain would be a thankless task, as they would only look at you as one trying to excuse your own cowardice, and vaunt their own bravery at you by asserting what they would do if they were "caught that way." Many have I had talk with me in this way while attempting to satisfy their curiosity as to the situation in such cases, and the conditions governing it. But when they are "caught" themselves, they are aggravated to find, in turn, that a no better portrayal of the situation can be found in them. The safest plan is never to carry but a mere paltry sum of money—enough to pay your way from point to point where you can replenish.

We reached Florence at 4 o'clock in the morning. It was on this occasion that I met the great prospectors, Capt. Charles McMillen and Josiah Flournoy. As we were about to leave Florence, two men approached the stage and took passage on it for Yuma. Their dress consisted of a pair of overalls, sand shoes, a huge blanket strapped across their back, a pair of large six-shooters—one at each hip; a bowie knife in their belt behind, a rifle strapped across their back, and a big slouched hat ornamented with holes, which covered the whole structure from rain. They greeted me in true frontier style wanting to know if I was the man who had been robbed out on the desert—whether I was hurt any, and whether I had any money left. When I had answered their questions, and informed them that all my money had been taken, each put his hand in his pocket and passed carelessly over to me a twenty-dollar gold piece, telling me they guessed that would see me through to Yuma, and that the twenty dollars would be as good to them at some other time. When I offered to give them "my note," they looked displeased that human nature had fallen so low, that a piece of paper was worth more than a man's honor, and said: "A man's word is his note in this country, my friend."

The Early Life of an Apache Scout

John Rope

---

*In the two decades following the Civil War, the United
States government attempted to gather the remaining hostile
Indians of Arizona and New Mexico onto reservations "to
promote peace and civilization among them." Pacification of the
Indians was necessary to facilitate the continued expansion of
white settlement and to open virgin sources of immense natural
wealth to the nation's burgeoning commercial enterprises.*

*The United States Army shrewdly employed Apache
scouts in their efforts to subdue the wild Apache bands that
roamed the rough terrain from the Tonto Basin southward into
the Chiricahuas. Bitter, internecine rivalries among the Apache
bands made it easy for the cavalry to recruit Indians to track the
hostiles to their sanctuaries. Army pay and the added privilege of
drawing blankets, cooking utensils, clothing, and foodstuffs from
military supplies gave many Apaches the incentives needed to
change sides in the conflict.*

*In the following selection, John Rope of the White
Mountain Apaches reminisces about his boyhood and his
experiences as an Indian scout in the 1870s. Rope was nearing
eighty and living among his people on the San Carlos Indian
Reservation when he related his adventures to Grenville Goodwin
through an interpreter. As Rope recounts the patient,
unrelenting, monotonous days of pursuit, the military's strategy of
wearing down the Indians becomes apparent. The constant
pressure and flight were more demoralizing than defeat in pitched
battle. In time, the presence of Apache scouts helped convince
many of the hostiles that continued resistance was futile. Sensing
that their independence was doomed, the majority of the Apaches
eventually surrendered to the enforced peace and degrading
boredom of confinement on the reservation.*

I was born at a place between old summit and Black River, but I don't remember much till we were living at Cedar Creek, west of Fort Apache. I can remember playing as a child there with the other children. At that time we had lots of corn planted, and our people were digging a ditch and making a dam in the creek to water the ground. The men and women worked together, digging with sharp pointed sticks. The women carried the loose dirt off in baskets. After the ditch was finished, they started to make a dam to turn the water into it. They first put up a series of sets of four poles, tripod-like, across the creek in a line. These poles were driven into the creek bed in a square of about three feet, and their tops brought together and tied. The tripods stood about three feet high when finished, and between them they put piles of rocks to hold them steady. The men did this work, and when it was done they tied bear grass and dry bark into the tripods at first in bundles. Then they laid bear grass lengthwise along the upper side of the tripods from one to another. Over the bear grass they packed the dry inner bark of cedar and cottonwood, the men and women both working. This inner bark was pounded up soft and wadded in. Now, on the upper side, right in front of where the bear grass had been put, they built a wall of flat red stones all along till it was as high as the posts. They took great care that this wall and dam were made straight. Between this wall and the bear grass was a space which they filled with gravel and dirt which the women dug out and brought in their baskets. This space was completely filled with earth. Now the dam was finished; it took about two weeks in all. After it was made, the people watched it carefully to see if it leaked anywhere. If a leak was found, it was plugged right away. When the

From John Rope, "Experiences of an Indian Scout: Excerpts from the Life of John Rope, an 'Old Timer' of the White Mountain Apaches as told to Grenville Goodwin," Part 1, *Arizona Historical Review* 7 (January 1936): 31–68.

dam was finished, the water was turned into the ditch, and finally they were ready to water their ground. The head man of a community was always the first to get the use of the water. After him came the others. When the ground had been watered and had started to dry out a little, they planted the corn. When planting his field, the owner hired some men to help him; he paid these workers with cooked corn and would tell them to bring baskets or pots so they might divide and take it home. They used a metal hoe with a handle to dig the ground. I guess they got these hoes from the Navajo and Zuni. When the people saw the corn begin to come up after it had been planted, it made them happy. If there were any grass or weeds in it, the workers pulled them out. When the corn was up about one and a half feet, it was watered again, and when it was about three and a half feet tall, it was watered once more. At this time it was beginning to form ears; when it had reached this stage our people used to go off south of Black River to gather acorns, and the corn was left to mature by itself.

We used to gather acorns all the way from Oak Springs on the west to Rocky Creek on the east. When the acorns were ripe, we climbed the oak trees and shook the acorns to the ground, where they were picked up and carried back to camp in baskets. After a while we always sent someone back to Cedar Creek to see how the corn was getting on. If the corn were ripe all our people would pack up the acorns we had gathered and move back to harvest the corn.

In the late fall we used to go to gather juniper berries. That fall we started out and made camp where the White River bridge is now. We didn't know it then, but we were to have bad luck. The next day we crossed over south and camped by Turkey Tanks in the pines. That evening it was very cloudy overhead. Our whole band was there, but among us we had only six or eight horses. My father had a spotted mule. My grandmother and my mother built a shelter for the night by laying pieces of dead wood up against the trunk of a pine tree and all around it. I was still a little child at that time. It rained and snowed all night, and the next morning the snow was about waist deep when we woke up. Some of the people had not built any shelter at all.

It was some eight miles from here to the place we were going to gather juniper berries. We dug the snow away down to the ground and made a fire with some pine wood while some of the people went to look for the horses; it was hard to find them in the

27

snow. After the horses were brought in and saddled some of our band started out with them to break trail. A mule went in front, and the horses followed; in this way they broke a trail to a ridge above us where there was not so much snow. Then they came back with the horses, and we packed up and started off for the ridge. The people had to carry a lot of the stuff in burden baskets on their backs as we didn't have enough horses to pack everything. The people on horses went in front, and the others followed. In those days we wore moccasins which came up to our knees; we tied the top close to our legs. We finally got to a place near Hill Crest and made camp there. There was not much snow here, and under the trees there was none. Here under the blue oaks and junipers we made our wickiups, just like those we use today, only they were covered with grass and no canvas. We made our beds out of grass, and managed to keep warm.

We boys used to hunt rats with bows and arrows. A lot of us used to start out in the morning and hunt till mid-afternoon. The way we got the rats was by one boy poking a long stick into the rat's nest, while the other boy would stand near the nest entrance on the opposite side. When the stick was poked in, the rat would come to the door and stick out his head; then the boy would shoot him. Sometimes the rats would come to the door and then go back. If they would not come out we would tear the house down and dig them out of their hole. We would poke our stick in the hole, and if there were hair on the end of it when we took it out, we knew the rat was there and we would dig him out. Some rats were easy to get, and others were not. If a rat got away from us the older boys with us would make fun of us. It was a rule that once we started to get a rat out of his nest, we could never stop till we got him. When we came home from a rat hunt, the rats would be divided evenly among us. We used to hunt cottontail rabbits too and shoot them where we saw them sitting under brush or in the grass. The rats to be eaten were put in the fire and all the hair burnt off. Then they were skinned and either roasted or boiled. It was the same way with rabbits.

One time a boy called Been went out hunting rats. He chased a rat into a hole in the trunk of a tree. He could see it in there, but when he got hold of its tail with his fingers to try to pull it out he just pulled the skin off its tail. Then he squeezed his hand into the hole and caught hold of its hind legs. When he came to pull his hand out he could not do so. The hole was too small. He

28

stayed there all that night, crying and hollering for someone to come. Next morning his people decided they better look for him as he had not come home. They finally found him with his hand caught in the tree. One of the men took his knife and cut the hole a little bigger so the boy could slip his hand out. This way he got loose and got the rat, too.

We had been camping by Turnbull Mountain that spring, gathering mescal, and now we started home. We moved our camp on to the Gila River. From here we journeyed back to Cedar Creek. It took us a long time. Those who had horses packed them and took a load to the next camp, then returned and took another load and so on till all the mescal was brought up from camp to camp. They always made us boys carry the water bottles and sometimes the cedar bark torches. When we got back, the mescal shoots were stored in the branches of juniper and oak trees around camp.

Our people were camped near the falls on Blue River when word came that there were some white men camped at Goodwin Springs. A group of people started out from our camp to see what these white people were doing. I was still a boy, but I went along with them. We made camp at the cave on the head of Salt Creek, and the next day moved on toward the Gila River. Near where Calva now stands, we came out on a hill on the north side of the river. From here we could see a large number of our own people talking with white men on the flat across the river. We were afraid to go down there, so one man was sent ahead to see what all these people were doing. It was agreed that if this man should stand apart from the crowd, it was safe for us to come down. If he did not do so, there was danger. He went down, and we could see him standing apart from the rest, but all the same we didn't go to him. Instead we went up the river a way and then came down to its edge. There our man met us and told us what he had seen. Somebody found some little sticks with red points, which had an odor. These were matches, but we had never seen them before and did not know what they were. They had been dropped there by the white men. Someone struck one against a basket; it caught fire, and that was when we first knew matches.

Our people kept on the old trail up the river where there was lots of white grass growing. This was the south side of the river. Just the other side of Black Point were camped some of our people, and we made camp there, too. I was with my aunt. She got hold of some flour from the white men, but she had never seen it before and did not know how to cook it. My other aunt who was there also knew how—she took it, made it into dough and put it in the coals to cook. When it was done, she took it out and washed it off to clean away the ashes. This was the first time I ever saw the white man's food. The women gathered wild hay and traded it to the white men for this new food.

The next day we boys started over to Goodwin Springs to see the white people; we had never seen them before. We went up on the side of a bank and watched them. There were lots of them, all dressed the same. They wore blue pants, black shirts, and black hats. Later on we learned that they were soldiers; at that time they had the old guns, percussion caps. While we were watching they brought over a big basket of beans and meat and bread to us. When we got back to camp with this food there were some bones in the meat which had been sawed off. We thought the white people must have some kind of sharp knife with which they could cut through a bone. The women kept on trading wild hay to the white men for grub. We didn't know what money was in those days.

In two days we boys went back to the white man's camp again. While we were there, the cook took a sack over to where he was cooking and filled it with bread, which he brought to us. There was a big ditch there which we could not cross, but he threw the bread over and the boys caught it. After he had thrown it all, everyone had some bread but me. The white man saw this. He went back to camp and returned with a cloth coat and some bread. He told the other boys to stay away, and then he gave me the coat and the bread. I put the coat on; it was long, yellow on the inside, blue on the outside, and with a cape over the shoulders. It had fine brass buttons on it. The boys didn't know this kind of coat and had never seen fine cloth like this. They gathered all around me to look.

From then on we boys went every day to the white camp to eat. One day my brother and I went to the camp and got there about noon. We met a white man riding. He was leading a white horse to where they butchered their cattle. We watched him to see where he went. When he got to the place, he killed the white horse and told us to come and butcher it. We ran up, each of us grabbed a leg, and we said this part is for me, and this part for you, but we had no knife. In a little while lots of our people were there. They butchered and skinned the horse and took most of the meat. That white man had killed the horse for my brother and me, but my brother only got a front leg, and I got the neck.

30

After a while, when my aunt had gotten a lot of beans and flour from the white men, we started back to Blue River. The head man of the whites at Goodwin Springs had said he wanted to see Hacke-Idasila, who was the main chief of the eastern White Mountain people then. So Hacke-Idasila started out to Goodwin Springs. As he traveled along with some other people, he kept burning the brush along the trail and making lots of smoke. As long as we could see this smoke, our people would know that things were going all right and that there was no danger. But if the smoke stopped, we would know that the party had got into trouble with the white men. Hacke-Idasila also carried a white flag in his hand. All his band was with him, and after arriving at Goodwin Springs they met the white officer. I don't know what his name was, but we called him Guc-hujn, which means "wrinkle neck." Since that time we have always had an interpreter with us. In the old days we used to have as interpreters Mexicans whom we captured in Mexico as children and raised among us. Some of them got away and went back to Mexico. The head officer at Goodwin Springs told Hacke-Idasila that he wanted him as a friend. He said, "We white people are far from home here, but you Indians know all this country, where the water is, and where the best lands are. Your people should settle down and live around here in the good places. If you keep on living your old way, you will never eat this new food like we have, but if we are friends, we will all eat it. I see your people eating the guts, legs, hoofs, and heads of horses. If we are friends we shall have lots and eat only the good meat parts." "All right," Hacke-Idasila said, and now he told where he lived, at a place where two streams came together. Then he and Guc-hujn embraced and were friends.

From that day on they were like brothers and had no more trouble. It has been like that with all of us since that time, and it was Hacke-Idasila who made it this way with the white people for us. All those people who were full grown then are now dead. We don't remember our grandparents' times, just as you white people don't. It was sometime later that Jimmie Stevens' father, who used to drive the mail from Goodwin Springs to Fort Bowie, and whom we called "Paper Carrier," married a White Mountain woman, at Goodwin Springs. Jimmie Stevens says he is sixty-two years old now.

After the council the white officer gave out rations to Hacke-Idasila, and then this chief and his band moved back near Fort Apache, where Calva now is, where they had lived for about a

31

year. This chief had told the white officer he should put another soldiers' camp at the place where Fort Apache now stands, and shortly after he and his band moved back from the Gila River, the white men started up to the Fort Apache location to make a camp there. They drove wagons drawn with oxen and made their road as they went. When the soldiers' camp at Fort Apache was established (1870), they issued rations to us regularly. We drew flour, sugar, coffee, and meat. There were lots of our people and it took all day for everyone to draw his rations. We drew rations every ten days. After a while they stopped issuing beef and gave out the cattle for us to butcher ourselves. They allowed ten to fifteen head for each band. If the band was very large they gave twenty head. One time they issued blankets to us, similar to Navajo blankets, but a different color and lighter and thinner. Later they gave out black, red, and blue blankets, three to each camp.

While we were all camped here at Fort Apache, some eastern White Mountain people and western White Mountain people went on the warpath. They went south to Graham Mountain and stayed there quite a while. Then they came back and tried to make friends again with the white people at Fort Apache. Most of the Cibecue people and Tca-tcidn (a clan) were camped at this fort also on the east side of the river near the soldiers. All the White Mountain people were camped on the other side of the river. My family was living near the soldiers then. The western White Mountain people had six chiefs, and the eastern White Mountain people four. I think the white man in charge of the fort told the Cibecue and Tca-tcidn people to kill those men who had been on the warpath. They started to do this. They would kill one man, and in a few days they would get another. This way it kept on. One day they killed a certain eastern White Mountain man, and all the White Mountain people got mad and shot back at them. They killed nine Cibecue and Tca-tcidn men that day, and three of their own men were killed. At that time Si-bi-ya-na, Wan-a-ha, and Tsis-kije were interpreters for the Cibecue and Tca-tcidn people.

There were lots of soldiers there at Fort Apache. The agent there was called Tc-a-da-iz-kane. The agent at San Carlos was John P. Clum. I guess Clum heard about the killing that was going on at Fort Apache, as he sent a letter up to the agent there. Whatever he requested in the letter, the agent at Fort Apache said "no" to him. He wrote again, and the Fort Apache agent still said "no." Then Clum came up himself to Fort Apache. When he rode up to the

32

fort, he was riding a gray horse and coming fast. Just before he got to where the people were standing, his hat blew off. One of the officers picked it up for him. Right there he held a talk with the agent at Fort Apache. He took the letter out of his pocket and showed it to the agent. Then he said that all of us were to come down and settle at San Carlos—the eastern White Mountain and western White Mountain people, Cibecue people, and the Tca-tcidn (1875). We all moved down to the Gila River after that, all except the Tca-tcidn, who never came at all. They made an agency there for us; Crooked Nose was the subagent. It was about this time that the Indian Scouts were organized. One officer and some scouts were sent down to Fort Bowie. These scouts and soldiers at Fort Bowie captured a lot of Chiricahua Apaches and brought them back in big army wagons with high sides to live at Goodwin Springs (1875). Some of the Chiricahuas were never caught. Our band lived near the Chiricahuas, by Black Point. They issued supplies and blankets to them and sent some scouts up to San Carlos to bring back some cattle for them to butcher. I was about eighteen years old then.

Soon they sent the scouts east to bring back the Warm Springs Apaches living there. Richard Bylas' uncle was a chief then, and he was first sergeant of the scouts that went over after the Warm Springs people. After they arrived at the Warm Springs settlement, near Silver City, all the scouts except Richard Bylas' uncle, who knew most of these Warm Springs people, went into a building and hid. When the Warm Springs people came in, they lined up, and the officer took their arms from them. Then all of the scouts stepped out of the building with their guns and surrounded them. They started to bring the Warm Springs People back to San Carlos, some on foot and some on horses. Their grub they carried in a wagon. On the way, smallpox broke out among them. Our band heard about this, so all our people went off in the mountains and lived scattered in different places. When the smallpox was over, the subagent sent us word, and we came in again. Just after this they issued us some sheep, one to each man, for us to raise. But we did not want them and butchered them right away to eat.

The subagency was moved to where Calva is now located, and Crooked Nose was still our agent there. That spring we moved to Fort Apache to plant our corn, but we came all the way down to get our rations at the subagency just the same and drove our allotted cattle back to Fort Apache. When the corn was ripe and harvested, our band moved back to the subagency. From there some of the men went to join the scouts. They sent them off to different places, and in six months they came back again to the subagency.

The next time they recruited the scouts, a whole bunch of us went from the subagency to San Carlos to try to enlist. My brother and I went along on one horse, riding double. At San Carlos there were lots of Indians gathered to enlist. Yavapais, Tontos, San Carlos, and White Mountain people were all there. We lined up to be chosen. My brother was the first one picked. My brother said if he was to be scout, then he wanted me to go as scout with him. He told this to the officers. They asked which one I was, and he took them to where I was standing. These officers looked me over to see if I was all right. They felt my arms and legs and pounded my chest to see if I would cough. That's the way they did with all the scouts they picked, and if you coughed they would not take you. I was all right so they took me. After they had picked about forty men, they said that was enough and that they needed no more scouts. I was twenty or twenty-five years old at that time.

Our officer said we scouts would move out for Fort Thomas the next day. We made it as far as the subagency and camped. Next day we got to Fort Thomas. Those scouts who had wives were followed by them to Fort Thomas, and there they were allowed to draw out five dollars' worth of supplies from the commissary for their families. Our next camp was at Cedar Springs, and from there we went on to Fort Grant. From Fort Grant we went to "Antelope's Water" and camped. The next camp was at some springs just north of Fort Bowie. The following day we got into Fort Bowie, where we stayed four days while they were shoeing the pack mules and we were fixing our moccasins. Then they packed up the leather pack bags for the mules and said we would move out tomorrow to be gone for one month. This was the first time I was ever a scout. The officer said at the end of one month we would come back to the Chiricahua Mountains and camp there.

We started out and went to a big mountain southeast of the Chiricahua Mountains. Then near Sierra Espuela, in Sonora, we continually looked for a sign of the Chiricahua people. We didn't cross into Mexico this time. There was a lot of food with us. The first three days I got very stiff and sore; then after that I felt as though I was getting light, and it was easier. We scouts carried a belt slung across the shoulder and chest with fifty cartridges in it. Besides this we carried our rifles and canteen of water. We used to

34

eat early in the morning and again late at night, only twice a day. This is the way we rounded up the Chiricahuas, and it was hard work, but we had to do as our officer said. I was the youngest, so the other scouts made me gather the wood and get water for them, even though I was very tired. We traveled every day, making our camps at springs. We always kept a guard in front and back when we traveled. After about a month we started for our new headquarters. We found the soldiers camped at the southeast corner of the Chiricahua Mountains. There were scouts there from San Carlos also. They knew we were coming and had grub cooked for us when we got there. The officer told us to make our camp about three miles below the place where the soldiers were. There were two creeks coming together here. The soldiers were camped on the right fork, below them was our camp on one side of the stream, and a saloon was on the left fork. The day after we got there the San Carlos scouts moved out.

• • •

While we were there they used to line us scouts up every day and count our rifles and cartridges and other equipment. In fifteen days the scout company below us got a new lieutenant and started out again to travel. . . . The next day after our new officer got in, we moved out to the southeast, going around the corner of the Chiricahua Mountains and approaching the Mexican border, camping at Guadalupe Canyon. From here we went straight east to Round Mountain (near the head of Ammas Valley, New Mexico), and made camp there for four days. There were springs there and lots of willows growing near. The officer sent us out from this camp to look around. He told us to be back in four days, but we found no sign of the Chiricahuas. We all moved out at the end of four days, passed through a canyon and over to some springs where we camped again. The next place we went was the east side of Sierra Espuela in Chihuahua. The sand in the wash at this place is sort of streaked with a green powder, and that is why it is called Chihuahua (Apache name). We stayed here three days and reconnoitered. Then we circled over the hill and back down into a canyon on the other side; this was still near the east of Sierra Espuela. To our next camp we moved through a little pass to the northeast end of the Sierra Espuela, then toward Fort Bowie, and camped at "Red Standing Rocks" at the foot of a canyon. On Turkey Creek we camped at the place where the Chiricahuas often camped. From here we finally returned to the place where the officers had been drowned. The other scouts and soldiers were still there. They had seen us coming and had our dinner already cooked. It was our relatives who had done this, and they called us over to eat. This time we camped close to the soldiers, as this was better for us. The day after we got in, the other scout company moved out again to travel for one month, looking for the Chiricahuas around to the southeast. Our officer told us not to bother to fix our moccasins, as we would soon be starting back for San Carlos.

While we were at Rucker Canyon we had drawn twenty-six dollars of our pay, two months' time; we still had four months' pay coming to us. We were anxious to get back to San Carlos. Some of us had bought horses with our money, and others had lost theirs gambling. When we started back we drove our horses and also those horses that the scouts had bought who were not due home yet. The first night we stayed at a place on the east side of the Chiricahua Mountains. The next day we got into Fort Bowie. There were lots of soldiers here. That night most of the scouts got drunk.

At this place my older cousin, who was a scout, said to me, "You have done lots of work for me, getting wood, water, building fires, and cooking. You have done the right way." He had a good new Mexican straw hat on his head, and this he took off and gave to me for what I had done. He was the only one who gave me anything. When we young men joined the scouts, our older man relatives would tell us to do whatever the older scouts wanted us to do. If we didn't work hard as we should, then that would be no good. This way we boys who were the youngest in the company used to take turns doing the camp work. But unlike the boys of long ago, we had no other duties or observances when we were on the warpath for the first time. We used to kill lots of deer while on these scouts and eat all the parts we wanted.

From Fort Bowie we went to some springs. The next camp was "Antelope's Water," just north of Willcox. Then we got to Fort Grant. They used to have a good time at Fort Grant, and the soldiers had a band there. From here we went to Cottonwood, where we put on all new, clean clothes—moccasins, white drawers, gee string, shirt, and vest. Around our arms we wore copper arm bands. Some of us painted our faces red. We packed up and started out, passing to the north, then to Fort Thomas. Here we stopped and drew the rest of our pay and also the money that was due us for not drawing our uniforms. In all, this came to forty-seven dollars. This money we divided among our relatives.

That is the way we used to do in those days, take care of our relatives by giving them clothes and grub. The Indians around here don't do that now. Down on the flat at Fort Thomas our relatives were waiting for us, as they knew we were due. There were some young girls there all dressed up and wearing their hair done up at the back on hair forms with brass on them, as they used to do in those days. The girls were waiting for their sweethearts to come. We camped here, the next day moving on to the subagency. From here they took the pack mules up to San Carlos. Any men who wanted to join the scouts again were to come up to San Carlos, they said, but we could do as we liked, as we didn't have to join. I did not join again right away but stayed home for a little over a year, during the time it took for two scout enlistments to be made and discharged.

A Day at an Arizona Ranch

Byron D. Halsted

The prospect of a visit to a ranch conjures up images of cowboys lassoing and branding bawling calves. The scene is further set with low, adobe buildings encircled by rambling verandas. To the side, ranch hands hunker on their heels outside the bunkhouse, swapping yarns and smoking hand-rolled cigarettes after supper. Such ranching establishments were common in Arizona Territory, where cattle raising reached a peak in the late 1880s. But not all ranching activities were devoted to beef production.

In the selection that follows, the author visited a dairy enterprise located at the foot of the Whetstone Mountains near Benson in southern Arizona. With about 100 head of livestock, year-round pasture, and little competition, the owner earned a handsome income selling fresh butter to the residents of Tombstone, Benson and other nearby towns.

Byron Halsted's concept of the American wilderness had been formed in the green glens and gentle mountains of New England so that the apparent harshness of the desert environment, the vast distances, and the monumental stillness seemed to trigger anew his powers of observation. His keen eye and facile pen detected the subtle hourly changes of light and shadow in a landscape that at first glance seemed solemn and monotonous. He noted the ironic juxtaposition of crepe-paper roses and steel revolvers on his host's living-room sofa. And he commented on the special affection and tenderness that often develops between men and animals in the solitude and isolation of rural life.

It was the middle of February and at a time when all through the Mississippi Valley a blizzard raged with fury, striking terror to the heart of everyone whose lot was cast within the sweep of its relentless bosom. A heavy rain detained us at Los Angeles, California, for in a few hours the broad, dry riverbed was covered by a flood more repulsive than the Missouri, and almost as rapid as the Niagara. It swept away the railroad and carried the homes of the dwellers in the lowlands upon its turbulent and cruel tide. We took the first train over the hastily repaired bridges, preferring to run all risks in travel rather than to remain in a city which was almost literally swimming in mud.

The Eastern-bound train left the "City of the Angels" several hours behind the schedule time and thereby brought us to Benson, Arizona, in the afternoon. Here we were to visit the ranch of some old friends. They were New York people. The husband once held a good position on Broadway, was careful of his dress, stylish from boots to silk hat, but went to Arizona for health and wealth. Two years had wrought some changes in him. Instead of the pale face, close-cut hair, gloved hands, slender cane, and measured gait, there approached a person in high cowhide boots and a broad, gray sombrero, the space between being clothed with brown woolen shirt, broad collared and braided in front, and coat and trousers. The slender cane had long ago given place to a large six-shooter, which in that land is considered the best of company for any man. The sun and dry air may tan the face and the throwing of lassos can harden the hands, but it requires more than two years to change the heart and disguise the voice. He was glad to see us in a place where congenial meetings are unusual, and we greeted him as protector as well as friend, for there was a feeling that here human life is both rare and cheap.

From Byron D. Halsted, *Chautauquan* 9 (March 1889): 354–356.

40

Benson is large only upon the railway map. In place of the wide and regular streets with long blocks of fine buildings, which fancy paints for unknown towns, there were a few low wooden buildings trying to keep in a short, much-broken line before a broad area of barren sand. Not a tree or shrub cast any shade in the desolate forsaken town of perhaps a hundred souls.

The ranch to be visited was nine miles away and the almost continuous ascent to nearly five thousand feet was made in an open two-seated wagon and over a trail which could have been followed only by an experienced guide. As we left the forbidding, sleepy village behind, the Whetstone Mountains were before us, dim with distance and the gray of the early twilight. The dry half-covered yellow earth on either hand bore scattered yucca plants with their short, stiff, stout, and graceless trunks, of man's length, while here and there the century plants had sent up their tall flower stalks during the last rainy season, long past, and had perished in the struggle to be fruitful. All forms of vegetation bore the evident marks of hardship and intensified the barrenness of the scenery. No trees greeted the eye until the ranch neared, and then the live oaks of fair size, although small as compared with those of Southern California, added an indescribable charm to the landscape.

Evening had set in when we reached the home of our driver — a neighborless ranch at the foot of the Whetstone Mountains. The housewife, once accustomed to the best advantages of the metropolis, a graduate of a New England seminary, had been making paper roses for a church fair to be held in Tombstone, twenty-seven miles away, and the completed flowers, with the remnants of bright paper, were scattered upon the sofa, and in the midst nestled a huge revolver, encompassed by a belt of cartridges.

The main house consists of a sitting room and bedroom, separated by a curtain of a modern sort with a pole and rings suited to the furniture of a stylish city home. Everything was suggestive of the taste and refinement of an Eastern dwelling. A Winchester repeating rifle stood in one corner of the room close below an engraving of the "Huguenot Lovers." On the little table was the last number of a popular magazine, and the latest improved revolver. Bible and bullets need not replace each other simply because the unwritten laws of this otherwise somewhat lawless land demands that lead and powder shall stand guard over the interests of individuals, as the forts and mighty cannon keep the peace between the most enlightened of nations.

41

In another building, nearby, the table was soon spread with hot, fragrant venison, delicious coffee with whipped cream, and the various accompaniments of an appetizing dinner, all of which inspired a still deeper feeling of satisfaction with the first taste of ranch life in Arizona. It was midnight before the conversation lagged and long since the light of the nearest neighbor, seven miles away, had gone out and only the stars kept watch through a cloudless sky, over a land where the war-whoop of the Indian and the roar of the mountain lion have for countless ages been as echoes to each other. Just as the word for retiring had been hesitatingly spoken, there was a shout from outside and the sound of advancing feet. As newcomers we did not know what to expect and instantly thought of some bloody deeds of Apache cowardice and cruelty enacted in that region within the year and related to us during the past hours by an eyewitness. During this brief period of suspense the host had gone to the rear door and obtained the necessary information. It was "Pete," the herdsman of the ranch, who at this late hour had returned from the mountains. At his feet lay a big stag, the fruit of his deer hunting. It is the delight of this almost giant man, when his work for the day is done, to take his favorite rifle, go up into the Whetstones, a few miles back of the ranch, and bring down "something for breakfast." The exploits of this mountain hunter would fill a thrilling volume. The skins of various wild animals ornamenting the floors of the house, and the great wings of birds upon the walls are a few of the trophies of his skill and daring.

Early the next morning we caught the first glimpse of the measureless view obtained from the ranch. The irregular shadow of the Whetstone Mountains extended far beyond the little cluster of buildings and gradually came up the slope from the west and in front of the ranch, like a retreating wave of darkness, leaving bare the shining shore of earth and desiccated herbage. If a person's ideas of nature in its primitive wildness have been gathered in the Adirondacks, White Mountains, at Niagara, or Lake George nestled in the arms of its many protecting hills, then a new experience is needed of a scene broad enough to include all these, and the ocean in its vastness and solemn grandeur besides.

From the mellow shade of a wide-spreading live oak, overhanging the doorsteps, a broad valley is seen stretching away to the eastward until abruptly stopped in its gentle ascent by the Dragoon Mountains, which stand with perpendicular sides and keen-angled pinnacles, a picture of the impenetrable abiding place of demons and giants. The somber thought is heightened as we listen to the tales of fiendish slaughter caused by the treacherous Apaches who from this mountain stronghold defied the nation's bravest soldiers and bathed the broad territory in innocent blood. As we gaze, Cochise and his tribe of dusky devils seem to come from the rocky chasms and stealthily creep out into the valley; but the ranchman assures us that the fantastic figures are great cactus trees which stand here and there like specters to remind one of the un-neighborly habits of nature in this land of magnificent distances.

Far away to the north are indistinct irregular banks of snow, the visible white, back of the San Bernardino Mountains, too far to seem above us and too distant to give a chill to the warm air of the valley. To the south the sun lights up the peaks of the Huachucas, and the great patches of snow lie like ingots of silver in a matrix of azure. From this pure perennial source the city of Tombstone pipes its icy water, yet leaves an abundance to feed the springs which flow as a perpetual benediction upon their fortunate owners. At once the eye may sweep over a grand variety of wonderful views, but they are all blended in a never ceasing, solemn, distant, awful harmony. Every hour of the day brings new lights and shadows. At midday the valley lies sleeping in a mellow haze through which the smoking locomotive draws its freight, slowly, lazily, and silently, because so far away. The field glass may shorten the distance by a half, but it only magnifies the stillness. The sweeping glass brings Contention and Tombstone into view, towns which in their names preserve something of their past, if not of their present character. Deeds of darkness, border cruelty, theft, bloodshed, and a long catalogue of unclassified and indescribable crimes are sadly com-mingled in the early history of these cosmopolitan towns. The white man here has often out-Apached the Apache.

The ranch at which the day was spent is located where it is because here on the western slope of the Whetstones has for long ages flowed a spring of water at which the early Indians quenched their thirst while on the trail from one mountain fastness to an-other. A spring of flowing water is so precious in this arid, half-desert country that when once possessed, it holds the surrounding land as securely as a patent from the government. A ranchman buys a "water right," and the territory it controls depends upon the proximity of another spring. There are vast areas in Arizona and New Mexico where the grasses grow but no stock feed upon them because water is too far away. The Whetstone ranch has three

43

springs, two near the house, and the third, the oldest and freest-flowing, about a mile away. These three together are worth several thousand dollars. From them as central points the livestock, a hundred head or so and rapidly increasing, can wander for ten miles or so into the valley or ascend the foothills in search of herbage. If a neighbor's cattle get within the same circle they need to return to their own spring for water. A passing Mexican woodchopper on his way to the mountains for fuel has no more right to water his team at one of these springs than to enter the house and take a loaf of bread. In fact we were told that as high as five dollars has been offered and refused for a single drink for a wood team. Once the right is granted, the key to the mountain forests is secured, and in time the ranch is doomed. Clear off the trees, and the snows which now feed the perennial springs would soon melt each spring, form transient surface streams, and the wild gramma grass would grow uncropped by the branded cattle.

Secondary to the water supply is the corral. This is made of medium-sized poles driven close together so as to form a stout fence, ten feet high, enclosing a space sufficient to quarter a herd by night. This stockade is rectangular or any shape suited to the pleasure or convenience of the owner. At one side is a wide heavy cattle gate and at another a narrow entrance for the herdsman. On horseback the herder in his picturesque garb goes into the recesses of the foothills and with shout and whip brings in the milk-laden kine. Twice each day the large bright buckets are taken to the corral and each cow, known by name and caressed by all, gives her portion which goes to make up the "setting" in the row of pans upon the long hanging shelves in the capacious milk-room. Butter making is the chief business in which the family is engaged, and the milk house is the main building of the ranch. It is a one-story, thick-walled structure, sixteen by twenty-four feet, built of bricks of adobe mud, molded and dried in the sun. A second smaller flat roof of boards stands two feet above the first to secure proper ventilation and coolness. Within are tables, water tanks, churns, and butter-workers of the latest and most approved patterns. In one corner ready for market are the yellow rolls of sweet fresh butter. Twice a week this golden product is taken down to Tombstone and delivered to anxious customers who are glad to pay a price that would be extreme for the finest gilt-edged half-pound prints on

Murray Hill in New York City. With no great competition and no cost for winter keeping, the profits are large from this dairy. A good income helps to dispel the thought of isolation.

To one side of the adobe milk house, and as a lean-to built of the same material, is the saddle room; and from this you can pass into the sleeping apartment of the herdsman. On all sides is the dry surface of the adobe bricks, except where some newspaper picture adorns the walls or square portholes, left through the two feet of clay, furnish places for the discharge of the Winchester rifle which stands guard close by when not out upon more active duty.

The other buildings of the ranch are the house proper, to which the reader was introduced upon the evening of our arrival, and the culinary department standing only a few feet away. Both of these buildings are about the same, twelve by twenty-four feet, and each divided into two nearly equal parts. They are made of boards and, as neither winter blizzards nor summer cyclones sweep that land, the construction is simple but not inexpensive, for the lumber in them, of only fair quality, costs seventy dollars per thousand feet.

The horses have a board stable and close by stands a stack of native hay. The wagon house is as broad as the plains and its roof reaches up to the cloudless sky. The big friendly dog has his kennel, and he may find some society in the companionship of the well-behaved hens and chickens.

To fully appreciate the place occupied by the most ordinary of pets in the life of the isolated family, one needs to go out upon the confines of civilization where the human face in its higher stamps is rare indeed, and of any sort uncommon. For some estranged souls there may be society in solitude, but most of us are molded after another type and, if we cannot do better, will cultivate the best that is in cats and dogs, and caress a calf or colt with all the tenderness and affection that a majority bestow upon their children.

Toward nightfall we strolled up to the mountains, soon leaving the ranch out of sight behind the live oak scattered everywhere—live oaks whose great vitality permitted them to grow where nearly all other forms of ligneous vegetation fail. Now and then a dwarfed "mesquite" was found struggling with arid adversity, while cactus, century plant, and yucca nestled close to the dry soil. All woody plants seemed to be armed with spines and thorns as if standing perpetually on guard, fearing that some half-starved steer might rob them of their tenderest parts.

While standing there, at sunset, upon the side of a vast amphitheater of mountains and plain, the herdsman came up from the ranch on horseback. The stag he had shot on the mountains that afternoon was too heavy for him to "back" homeward and he had hastily returned to get the aid of a horse before the night set in. He told me that his timid game was bounding rapidly forward as he shot and the first bullet only grazed the shoulder, but by improving his calculation the next shot instantly brought the crazed stag to the ground several hundred yards distant and in an almost inaccessible spot. The stag arrived in due season and was safely laid under the hind seat of the wagon which was to carry us to the station shortly after midnight.

A late retirement was soon followed by an early breakfast. The night was moonless, and clouds intercepted any light which might have stolen through the deep darkness from the cold, distant, twinkling stars. The sure-footed horses were soon in their places and with all aboard, including the stag, we started on a nine-mile drive down to the depot. A small lantern was held over the dashboard to light us on our way, but it only served to make the darkness visible. The horses were depended upon to strike and follow the trail, but they failed, and we wandered around for some time before the fact was spoken that we were lost. At this trying moment the little lantern light flickered in the cool wind and went out in the darkness. By driving in a circle, as nearly as could be guessed, a trail was shortly struck, down which the hopeful horses quickly started. Certain stones, knolls, and sidling places were soon recognized as features in a wood-road leading to Contention, and—we were on the wrong track. It, however, lead into the right one and we turned about and began our journey toward Benson.

At one point a piece of the harness broke and some of the party were almost breathless while the repairs were being made. But we were on the right track, had passed the worst portion of the road, soon drove into the sleeping hamlet, and greatly to our joy found that the train was an hour late, but would be due in a few minutes.

46

An Adobe House

Helen Baldock Craig

The first glimpse of an early Arizona town was unsettling to Eastern travelers, whose eyes were attuned to cities of masonry or clapboard buildings with a mix of architectural styles from Gothic to Georgian to Victorian. Low, mud-colored buildings clustered haphazardly on the desert floor in the midday heat had the curious look of ghost towns even as they bustled with life.

The modern visitor to Arizona frequently comments on the distinctiveness of southwestern architecture. A resident of Rochester, New York, who was thrilled to be back in her sleety, snowy habitat, described modern Tucson as a town where ". . . sand is the building material; houses hug the ground and have about them an impermanence that is shattering to one accustomed to the solidity of Eastern Cities."*

But the natives know that earthen buildings are well suited to the southwestern climate. Natural insulation properties make an adobe house a welcome respite from the searing summer heat and a snuggery in winter. Helen Baldock Craig's memoir of her life within adobe walls is a veritable hymn to the humble dwelling.

Growing up in a pre-Civil War farmhouse in Iowa, Helen Baldock moved to Arizona in 1928 in search of health, teaching job, and a husband. She taught at Globe High School before her marriage to Gerald Craig in 1932. For more than forty years the Craigs lived at historic old Pinal Ranch where Gerald's grandparents settled in 1878. What seemed to this new bride to be a dirty, grayish, disjointed group of ranch buildings became a well-loved home. A "careless symmetry" distinguished the earthen walls, and the floor levels varied, depending on the natural elevation of the land. Simple tasks like hanging doors and bookshelves or carrying dishes from one place to another were likely to require extra attention and care. Manmade as well as handmade, these houses of mud and mortar had character as well as personality.

---

*Dorothy Livadas of Rochester, New York, letter to the editor of the *Arizona Daily Star*, December 22, 1980.

The adobes used to build the homes on the ranch have been used by choice as well as economic necessity. But the older I have grown, the more I like the feeling of being a part of the earth around me. Originally, these houses were built by Mexicans, many of whom were artisans.

The clay earth was dug from the ground and mixed with water and old straw from the corral. About a half a dozen wooden frames, four by twelve by sixteen inches, were made and placed side by side on the ground in a sunny clearing. The mud was poured into these, and if it were the right consistency, the form could be removed in a few minutes and used again.

The bricks were left in the hot Arizona sun for a couple of days until a firm crust had baked on them. Then came the laborious task of turning each brick on its edge so the "cooking" would continue. Ofttimes they would be moved until each surface had had direct exposure to the sun. Inside of two weeks they were ready to be stacked for later use.

Fortunately, the soil on our ranch lends itself to making very strong adobes, which are a dirty grayish color. We know they will last through the years for the bricks used in the library of the Old House were placed there ninety-five years ago and have withstood rain, wind and snow from the north with never a crack showing. Of course, the heavy ivy that now mats the walls acts as a buffer as well as a beautifier.

All of this process is rudimentary until it comes to laying the walls. It is then that our ranch houses are unique and bear little relation to the modern burnt adobe structures built in nearby Phoenix or Scottsdale, for the actual laying of the walls was gener-

From Helen Baldock Craig, *Within Adobe Walls 1877–1973* (Phoenix: Art-Press Printers, 1975), 46–55, 68–70. Used with permission from the author.

ally left to the Mexicans. I can't explain to you what a challenge two taut strings put up to mark the line of the wall on its foundation can do to a true, old-time Mexican adobe layer. But I do know if you stood at one end of my house and looked along the walls, you'd begin to get dizzy. You'd swear there was a definite waviness, and you'd be right, for there is. No matter how many times the laborers were forced to tear these bricks out to bring the wall into a semblance of a straight line, it was only a matter of moments until their imagination veered it slightly to starboard. Try to put bookshelves or hang doors and you'd understand. Time was when I was quite embarrassed because one of our doors looked as if it were struggling under its own weight and would soon fall on its face, and my bookshelves were two inches narrower at one end than the other; but later I could ignore those things in my pride to live in an authentic adobe house.

Almost forgot to tell you that the bricks are held together by more mud and mortar. Really sounds sloppy, doesn't it? But wait until I tell you about the floors in our houses. Or maybe I shouldn't. For once while visiting in my native Iowa, I was telling about our homes and their dirt floors, when my father called me aside to caution me that people's imagination could go just so far, and please not push them for he had to live with these old friends.

Our rock foundation and adobe walls were laid directly on the ground, thus each floor level might be three to ten inches lower than the one above it. The land sloped that much where the houses were built and rather than filling it in, it was easier to have a sunken room. The men hauled in loads of dirt then and dumped this in the rooms. With their shoes and socks off and pant legs rolled above the knees, the men turned on water and proceeded literally to make mud pies by tramping back and forth in this mess until all of it was thoroughly mixed. The top was smoothed off and the whole mixture allowed to dry for several days. Finally, it was ready for a man skilled in adobe work to go onto and polish in much the same manner as concrete slabs are handled. The end product was a smooth, almost as hard as cement, floor into which had been placed two by fours at the edge of the walls so that floor coverings could be attached to them later. I found these floors most resilient to work on. Later, they must be covered wall-to-wall with carpeting or linoleum, and I will admit to a root or two that appeared unexpectedly years later.

49

Where else could one find floors as cheap and satisfactory? Too many heels dug in and left their impressions, but I can remember a very touching song about "little fingerprints upon the windowsill"—why not romance a bit about "little heel marks on my old dirt floors"?

All of the walls were sixteen to twenty inches thick, so there were deep windowsills. Naturally, when the partitions were of adobe, too, much insulation makes for extra coolness or warmth, depending on the season.

A 'dobe house was an integral part of our ranch life and it thrills me to hear our daughters tell someone that some day they'd like to build one just like these. I'm afraid I never was too nervous about the atomic bomb scares when I was behind these sturdy walls of our own good earth.

Though we had completed our home across the highway several months after we were married, we spent a great deal of time across the road as the ranch activities centered around the old place. To differentiate, we soon found ourselves calling the original home "The Big House," and this name stuck with the family and friends.

Because the Big House is so impressive-looking as it sprawls out when the fashion of its day dictated bungalow or two-story types, it was a unique structure for many years. But more important, one day it occurred to me that I had discovered the origin of the popular "ranch style" home. Now that whole tracts are dominated by this one-story type of architecture, I have to pinch myself to remember that forty-five years ago when I first became acquainted with the ranch, I was very impressed with the house for I had never seen one just like it.

There are fourteen rooms which seem to have been rather loosely thrown together, yet give the impression of careless symmetry through careful planning.

Originally, on this isolated ranch, separate units of adobe rooms had been erected—for cooking, eating, sleeping, housing the hired men, and just plain living. Building them apart from each other minimized the possibilities of loss from fire in a place where sufficient water was an ever-present problem. One found, too, that each was on a different floor level, dependent on the natural elevation of the land.

In the beginning the stockade kitchen was entirely separate from the rest of the rooms. There was still a great deal of influence of the Southern ways of life dominant in our early Southwest along with the Spanish. There was always a Chinese cook presiding over the kitchen at the ranch in the early 1880s and I am sure that he was much happier to work unobserved. Another small room was placed next to it for his sleeping quarters.

The dining room, living room and bedrooms were always joined under one roof as a matter of protection to the family. Each of these was heated with a fireplace where only one side of a person could be warm at the same time. It wasn't until we had been married many years that I was able to persuade my husband to put fireplaces in our own home. Finally, after being put off with the excuse of lack of funds, impracticability, etc., I found the real reason for his aversion. Simply enough it was his having to cut wood when a youngster to help feed those ever-empty, insatiable wood eaters. The day of the chainsaw changed the picture.

Originally when help was plentiful and cheap, the distances between kitchen, milkhouse, meat room and dining table made small difference in the housekeeping routine. However, as civilization encroached, the pattern of living at the ranch perforce was changed, too, and then it seemed desirable to get these many units under one roof. This proved to be an architectural challenge which through years of planning and some correspondence courses my mother-in-law, Geraldine, met superbly. The old kitchen had to be destroyed, but the other rooms were melded into a flowing continuity that was quite remarkable. Odd spots were filled in with additional rooms, and a long low porch along the highway side gave us a delightful patio. In 1922, the new transcontinental highway was being built right through our place, but it was going on the opposite side of the house from where the old wagon and pack trains had traveled for so long. This meant that there must be two front doors so that people entering from either side might have easy access.

Now wouldn't you like to take a quick trip through some of these rooms with me?

The milk or cooler room was quite a revelation to me for I had come from the North where the storage rooms were underground. This milk room on the ranch was made with extra thick adobe walls and a viga ceiling (beams hand-cut from trees on the place.) A dirt roof originally covered it so in case of an Indian attack the burning brands put on arrows, if shot into the roof, would not ignite. Thus, it could also serve as a small fort in case of

51

Indian trouble, though we are happy to say that never once was this necessary. At one end was a small casement window (originally a heavy door) opposite a heavy rip-sawed entrance door which could have been barricaded. A stone floor made the insulation complete. Because in desert country, at our altitude of forty-five hundred feet, the nights are always cool, it was the custom to open the window and door at sundown to "air condition" the room, then close both at daybreak. Screens gave protection against varmints prowling at night.

The milk that was poured in shallow pans and placed on cooling racks could be kept sweet for two or three days even when the temperature during the noon hours of a summer's day soared to the mid-nineties. The rounded pats of butter placed in order of use on more flat racks against the wall tempted one to forget diets and heap yellow gobs on the newly made hot bread fresh from the oven in the kitchen.

Next door was the meat room made identically. Here the freshly killed beef and cured hams and bacons were stored. Instead of the flat racks along one wall, in here were thick slabs of oak cut and fastened high near the ceiling. In these were implanted deeply great hooks which held the quarters of beef or pork and the cured hams. Under the window where the light was better stood a huge block which was really a cross-cut section taken from one of our jack oaks. Time and usage had given it a veneered and satiny patina.

When there was fresh beef hung in the room, it was necessary for the cook or one of the men to carry it outdoors every night and hang it in a tree so the night air would chill it and keep the meat sweet and tasty. As a result, a quarter of beef was left in one piece so that it would be easier to move, and it wasn't until the days of freezing and canning that we were ever given a choice of cuts for the next meal. In other words, we ate our way through meals of roasts, ribs, steaks and boiled sections. Funny as it now seems when I read this over, I can well remember at times I objected to that type of restriction in meal planning. In these later days, when we can ill-afford waste involved with butchering when prices are so high, I think with regret of those fine meals. And I marvel too at my husband's patience when I complained, for he knew of no other way of life.

The kitchen I worked in was huge. Homemade cabinets around the sink were high enough for all of us tall Craig women. A big old-fashioned wood range is still in its corner, and on this were prepared all of the meals for the family and men. Our modern stoves were never really adapted for easy cooking where three square meals a day must be served and a lunch or two in between thrown in. The bean pot could stay on the back of the range and simmer along, which made the beans much better as the days went by. (Beans were the main-stay of all meals, even breakfast.) Our big granite coffeepot was ready to serve its strong brew to drop-ins. The warming oven was a delight. Here the bread dough raised on a cold day, and here food could be kept for late arrivals.

I will admit that at first coping with the wood-eating monster was almost beyond me. I soon learned not to wander off into other rooms with no mind to its stoking for that kind of fire needs constant attention. Since there was no temperature gauge on the oven, I worked out quite a different method for baking my angel food cakes. By building a very hot fire first, I could put the cake into the oven with the door wide open for the first fifteen minutes. Then every ten minutes or so I would ease the door a few more inches until at the last it was completely shut. The cakes were beautiful, but I never submitted my recipe to a baking contest.

There were never curtains at the kitchen windows so we could look into the mountains and orchards while we worked. Several chairs were placed around the wall so that whenever there was no cook reigning in the kitchen, our menfolk would stop a few minutes on their way through. A thoroughly pleasant room, it was never used for a dining or real living room. Mother Craig was very sensitive of the fact that for so many years she had lived in a rather isolated spot. To counteract this, she and the family lived by some rigid rules that perhaps seemed silly to others. No meal—even after she was all alone—was ever served in the kitchen. During crop times we all ate with the men in the big back dining room; other times, help or no help in the kitchen, the table was set in the smaller dining room with good silver and linen. She felt that social standards must be met daily so that the family might not become careless. As a result, anyone coming for a meal could instantly feel a family solidarity as everyone gathered at the table where Father and Mother always took their places at the head and foot, and all were quiet for the blessing.

In the dining room there was a beautiful hand-carved English sideboard that also lent dignity. An old-fashioned china

53

cabinet displayed a complete set of ironstone china, including the immense turkey platter and soup tureen. All of this was used.

The living room, two steps down from the dining room, was a joyful place. In the days long before picture windows were widely used, Mother Craig had ordered six-foot by six-foot windows so the mountains, orchards and lovely yards could become part of this room, too, for the family used it daily. The furniture in here was old and invited one to sit awhile. Even the warm Oriental rug on the floor never discouraged any of us from coming in with our work clothing on to lounge for awhile and talk over current ranch problems.

In one corner, the organ sat where it had been placed at the time it came to the house first. How many times friends from nearby towns gathered for picnics and later a song fest led by the sweet strains from the reeds of the old instrument that accommodated itself so well to church hymns and "Home Sweet Home."

The library off the living room had originally been the dining room. The door and the floor were of rip-sawed planks as well as the casings and all of the woodwork. One wall had floor-to-ceiling shelves with well-read books and magazines on them. Close by these for years was a big highbacked leather upholstered chair with a drop leaf fastened on one arm (like a modern school desk chair). This was hinged so it could be pulled up and used to rest your book on. It had been in a saloon in Silver King where the owner had kept his accounts on the arm. Other stories said that these chairs were common in the old saloons for the benefit of the customer who was served free lunches with his beer.

All around the room on tables, in cabinets, and on other walls were the mementos gathered through the years right there. Musket loading guns; a bow and arrow; a water jug; the old vacuum cleaner; crude handmade tools used on the place; heavy leather chaps; a fine mineral collection; a wind-up Victrola; the first radio with earphones and horn speaker; a beautiful antique desk where Father Craig kept the copies of the weather report he had been submitting faithfully once a month since 1890—acclaimed once as the veteran of all U.S. volunteer weather observers; a cross-stitch sampler made by a nine-year-old in 1844; another one—"God Bless Our Home"—over the door; a charcoal-burning foot warmer used in the horse and buggy days for the four-hour trip to Globe; early wooden-shaft Spaulding golf clubs—all of these and many more priceless memorabilia. A veritable museum.

54

The three bedrooms in this part of the house (the cook's was at the back to insure privacy for him) each had storybook furniture. In one were the twin beds made long ago on the ranch and held together by square-headed nails and fashioned like the modern Hollywood type. The rooms had traditional marble-topped dressers and washstands that had been brought in over the trail. Colorful hanging lamps, hung in the center of all these rooms, cast shadows. With their original adobe floors and walls, each room emanated a feeling of comfort, quiet, seclusion, and security.

To live in a house like this that has compromised with time and progress without losing its originality is a real experience. I think it most fitting that our new homes have kept this unique Southwestern style, for it so aptly fits in with the feeling of space we cherish so much in this part of the country.

And I would like to leave you with this feeling of continuity and self-reliance that even a casual trip through the big old ranch house could give you as you rambled along from room to room, each of which was filled with treasures and working tools of four generations. It has made it easier for me to have faith in our future when we've been able to see and use these things spread around us and realize a bit at what odds our grandfathers won for us this good life we enjoy today. No wonder it had been named an Arizona Historical Site in 1972.

There was an old Estey organ in its walnut case that sat in the corner of the living room for ninety-three years. I had grown up with one in our Iowa home and can remember the time when my piano was moved in and the organ given to a cousin who had no instrument. She in turn had a lovely desk fashioned out of it and no one grieved, but neither did it have as romantic a background as the one at the ranch. This one is so well-traveled and has withstood so many hardships in its early days that it has earned a good retirement.

Grandmother Irion had taken many music lessons in her school days and loved them. But, for years after she left the Young Ladies Academy and lived in Colorado, she had had no instrument of her own.

One evening in 1880 a salesman who was traveling through the country stayed after supper to visit with the family. During the conversation evidently her musical talent was mentioned, whereupon he asked her if she were really interested in having an organ, providing he could get one sent out when he went East again. They must have discussed it in great detail before he left, but I'm sure that Grandmother dismissed it from her mind once he had gone.

About a year later word came that an Estey organ was being shipped from Boston to Pinal Ranch. Imagine the trust people had in one another in those days. No papers to sign for time payments. No cash changing hands. Simply that an organ was on its way. Those were surely the days when a man's worth was judged by the evidences of culture and good breeding that showed in his home and appearance.

The little organ was loaded on a ship in Boston, taken around the Horn to San Francisco, thence by train to Casa Grande, and then by freight teams to Silver King. Finally, someone coming over the trail brought word that it had arrived in Silver King and could be picked up there. Now the question was just how it could be brought across the tortuous trail when there were several places that were hardly wide enough for a horse and rider.

Evidently Grandmother Irion had appealing ways for it was no time at all until her beloved Bob and one of his men decided they could manage it somehow. With their trusty pack mule they started out with the organ tied securely to its back. Negotiating corners was one of the most difficult tasks and it is said that Grandfather Irion and his man walked the entire ten miles to balance the load.

How gratifying to Grandmother and her family for her to be able to spend extra stolen moments playing the old tunes with the tremulo stop out to add plaintiveness to the song. How proud she must have been to show passing travelers her organ. Certainly it and long shelves filled with heavy tomes—both in content and size—were in direct contrast to the loaded guns found on the tables or in the corner of every room.

One felt certain these people had chosen their way of life and stood ready to defend it.

A Joyless Arizona Christmas

Joseph Neal Heywood

Arizona has always offered a variety of ways to celebrate the Christmas holidays. The northern pine forests with their snowy slopes suggest traditional scenes of sleigh rides, carols, and family gatherings at grandmother's. In the southern deserts amid barren, rocky mountains, the clear air magnifies the beauty of the star-encrusted heavens, inspiring thoughts of that first Christmas night in the desert of the Holy Land.

Throughout the state, various groups mark the season with special practices and observances. Indian communities conduct ancient and symbolic tribal rites and dances. Hispanic peoples reenact Mary and Joseph's search for lodging in the song and responses of the traditional "las posadas." And residents from the northern states quickly adapt to their new homeland by mingling red pepper wreaths and native cactus with the traditional poinsettia and holly.

The Christmases that live in memory are usually the happiest ones, yet in daily life tragedy often intervenes regardless of the season. John Neal Heywood's account of his Christmas as a young boy in Alpine, Arizona, is a memoir of bedbugs, sickness, blizzards, lack of medical care, and death. He depicts the harsh and uncertain conditions that confronted all pioneers. He recalls their ability to accept death in a season that celebrates birth. The bleak hope that future Christmases will be better is little consolation, but it is this hope alone which sustained the pioneer.

I think it was fifty years ago. That's a long time ago, so long that I cannot be certain as to exact dates, but December was the month, and the twenty-fifth the unforgettable day. It usually is—Christmas Day—but this was different.

We lived in an old log house in Alpine. This old house had been built some years before down on the farm. At that time nearly all the settlers lived on their farms. Gradually they moved to town. Father was Bishop and it seemed necessary for him to live in town. Since he had this log room built he decided to move it rather than to rebuild. He chose winter to make the move because of the snow. It could be put on runners and drawn like a sled. The structure was about sixteen by twenty feet and very heavy. It was pried up (they didn't have jacks to jack things up in those days) and two logs for runners were slipped underneath. When let down on these it was braced and anchored. Every team in the valley was requisitioned. You see, Father was Bishop. The owners of the teams came with them, bringing axes, chains, double-trees and anything else that might be needed.

This move was unique. It was different from any I have ever heard of or read about. None of the men, some of them old-timers, had ever seen anything like it. I don't think anyone ever will. It was routed through the bottomlands to avoid rocks, stumps and hills and the snow was uniform instead of there being drifts and bare places. The distance was about two miles. That was long enough, and then some. The trip took several days. I don't remember just how many, but I do remember that a Sunday intervened. This was fortunate. We all needed our faith renewed so we could endure to the end and Sunday helped us over this hump.

From the Joseph Neal Heywood Collection, "Christmas Fifty Years Ago," unpublished manuscript from the last quarter of the nineteenth century, Arizona Historical Society Library, Tucson, Arizona. Used with permission of the Arizona Historical Society.

Log chains were attached to the ends of the runners and several teams hitched to each runner. There were big teams and little teams and some of them balky, and just about as united as the people in a small town. Some would pull and others would fly back. Sometimes one runner would be some distance in advance of the other and it would seem that the building would be twisted completely out of shape, and at times it seemed certain to collapse. Had it collapsed, I know it would have been in answer to prayer. But I hadn't lived faithful enough. Undoubtedly I swore too much, though no one knew anything about it except myself and, I guess, the Lord. The snow was a foot or more deep. Delays were frequent. A chain, a single-tree or double-tree would break and then most of us would have to stand in the wet and cold and wait. How the men kept their patience as well as they did was surprising. When night came we were all wet, tired, hungry, and chilled.

When relocated, the building was blocked up about two feet above the ground. That gave room beneath for the dogs and cats. Then, too, going up and down the steps several times daily provided exercise for an expectant mother.

We moved in. I think there were seven of us in the family at the time. Here we were living in one room about sixteen by twenty feet. As soon as we were able a lean-to was built on the east side of the house and later a similar one on the west side. These were each divided into two rooms for kitchen, dining room and bedrooms. Any of the common comforts of today were unknown. The logs in the walls were roughly hewn and uneven. The building was not square. Cracks between the logs permitted the winter winds to howl through. Cheesecloth was used to line the walls and stretched overhead for ceiling. Accumulated dust made the ceiling sag between the strips that nailed it to the beams above. Floors were of rough boards. Straw or wild hay was spread over the floor and homemade rag carpets stretched over it and tacked along the walls. Before long, the powdered straw or hay beneath and the dirt tracked in and tramped into the carpet collected great quantities of fine dust to be stirred up each time the carpet was swept. Crevices in the walls and the wooden bedsteads were infested with bedbugs. Periodically the bedsteads were taken apart and scalded.

Bedbugs are nocturnal—they come out at night. Sometimes the legs of the bedstead were set in cans of water so the bugs could not crawl up, but this did not help where they were hidden in the crevices of the framework of the bedstead, nor when they

59

would crawl out of the ceiling and drop down on the beds. The bug when empty flattens out and can squeeze into a small crack, but when filled with blood sucked from the sleeper the body acquires surprising dimensions. Often pillowcases were speckled with blood where the sleeper had mashed them. One way to identify a bedbug is to mash one between the fingers and smell. Like the skunk, it takes only one smell—it is never forgotten.

As indicated, bedsteads of fifty years ago were of wood and usually homemade. Springs and mattresses were to us unknown. Slats were laid across the frame and a straw-filled tick placed on these. Usually these were opened, emptied, washed and refilled with fresh clean straw each autumn after threshing time. By the end of the year the straw was pulverized and dusty. When winter-time came those who were fortunate had feather ticks to place upon the straw ticks. These were a luxury and added greatly to warmth. The thrifty housewife saved the best feathers whenever a chicken was picked and the breast feathers of the ducks and geese were plucked several times during the summer from the live birds. In the bitter winter weather to settle down in feather beds soon gave us delightful warmth. Feather beds are now in the discard, but in those days when one went into a cold chilly room in subzero weather, perhaps already chilled, to sink down into their feathery warmth was gratifying.

Fifty years ago this December! It was a cold month and a cold winter. I can almost live it over again. My sister, Mattie, was eleven or twelve. I was fifteen or sixteen. I was the oldest boy, she the oldest girl. About the eighteenth we both acquired colds, severe colds. I had had many colds, but this was different. It seemed to go deeper, not "a cold on the lungs," but a cold in the lungs, deep and penetrating. I was apprehensive. Mattie's cold was also deep-seated but apparently not so severe as mine. I well remember that one night. She slept in the "front room" where there was a fire. My brother, Spence, and I slept in the northeast room which had no stove or fireplace. It was cold and stormy. As I went to bed (It would seem hardly right to say "retired"; I went to bed), the thought occurred to me, "This may take one of us. I wonder which one." I wasn't afraid, but apprehensive. I thought of asking to sleep in a warmer place, but didn't. It would have been awkward.

I must have had a little temperature, because when I undressed in the chilled room my teeth chattered and I shook with a chill until the feather bed beneath and heavy quilts above warmed

60

me through. I was quite miserable and coughed considerable most of the night. Toward morning a change took place and I rapidly improved. During the night the wind howled and whistled as the snow fell. In the morning our bed was covered with a layer of snow that had drifted through the cracks.

During the night Mattie made a change for the worse. Mother was worried and fearful. I realized that she was real ill, and felt a sort of guilt. It seemed that I was selfish in getting better and letting her get worse. Mattie breathed more rapidly and with each breath a grunt—pneumonia. There were no doctors to call—only the practical nurse and the kindly neighbors. Steadily she grew worse.

Sometimes I wonder if family ties in those days were not a little closer than now, whether the affections were not a little deeper. I believe the family members were more intimately associated and worked more together. They were together all day, every day, week after week, year after year. I wonder whether the death of a loved one did not hurt more deeply, whether grief was not more prolonged. It seems so to me.

In cases of illnesses, misfortune or calamity there was a proneness to wonder if these were not sent as punishment for sin—doing something wrong or neglecting to do something right, the sin of commission or of omission. Was Mattie's illness due to some sin on the part of parents, other members of the family or herself? Perhaps had we done differently she may have been spared. Such questions were frequently discussed. It was easy to feel a sense of guilt and self-censure. It was the times.

We were religious. We believed in prayer, in anointing with oil that had been consecrated and set apart for "healing the sick in the household of faith" and sealing of that anointing with the laying on of hands by the elders of the church. This was done repeatedly. We had family prayers each night and morning and Mattie was remembered in these. Then we had special prayers where we all knelt about the sickbed and earnestly pleaded with the Lord to heal Mattie. We were taught that the prayers of faith should heal the sick, but if they died they "died unto the Lord and if they lived they lived unto the Lord." Mattie seemed too ill to recover, but when the elders came, hope was renewed. Instances were related where doctors had said it was impossible for a patient to live and through administration miraculous healing resulted. This would naturally give some hope, for a time at least. Mattie was remembered in church services on Sunday. Still she grew worse and the time came when the Lord was asked to not prolong her sufferings, that, if she must go, to let her be taken without further suffering.

It was a gloomy time. Everywhere several inches of snow covered the ground. We had to shovel paths to the corral, the barn and the woodpile. It was cold, bitter cold, zero weather. Logs of pine were pulled out of the snow, cut or sawed in lengths for the fireplace, carried and stacked in the house and a fire kept blazing all night.

The privy, or outhouse, was some little distance from the house. It had to serve for all except the patient, whether day or night. It need only be suggested that this was often awkward, unpleasant and, during zero weather, distressing. The extreme modesty of those days not infrequently occasioned embarrassing meetings along the line of march, and the path shoveled through the deep snow was not a two-way thoroughfare. In such a chance meeting along the route one, sometimes both, would go suddenly in reverse. For safety, the females, where possible, would go in twos.

Many details for the duration of the illness might be related. There were the chores. Wood had to be cut and carried in. Cattle, horses and chickens had to be fed and watered. Often holes had to be cut through the ice so the stock could drink. The cows were to be milked and the eggs gathered. Often the eggs would be frozen and burst. Details of each kind of chore might be interesting but hardly needful. During the illness everything was off schedule.

Christmas Eve Mattie was very low, and passed into unconsciousness. If she was not to recover, why the prolonged suffering? I wondered why. I still wonder. Christmas her breathing became irregular and weaker until it ceased. The worst had come, and yet after the long days of suffering and uncertainty there came a sort of relief, a relief from the tension. And since we all must die sometime we were reconciled—all but Mother. She would not be comforted. Weeks, months and years passed before she was herself again, and then through grief and hard work her health was impaired never to be fully regained though she lived more than forty years.

Funerals were different from those of the present day, quite different. Coffins (we heard of no such thing as caskets in those days) were made by local carpenters of native lumber. The thought of how soon the boards would rot under the ground and let the earth cave in on the corpse was far from comforting. Coffins were lined with white cloth. I believe there were some edged with black, and the letters and envelopes announcing a death were sometimes edged with black. It was customary for one or two to sit up all night with the deceased, lest it be disturbed. Especially were those sitting up watchful lest a cat get to the corpse and mutilate it. Stories were told of the excessive fondness of cats for a meal from a corpse, and how they had been known to steal in and eat a hole in some part of the body. Stories were also told of bodies prepared for burial and placed in the coffin and then come to life unexpectedly to the surprise, embarrassment and gratification of relatives and friends. Because of this every possible precaution was taken to avoid such a mistake. I recall the corpse was carefully examined to see if mortification had set in. That is, to see whether the body or parts of it were discolored or turned black, an indication if death had certainly occurred. As soon as possible after death the body was "laid out" on boards covered with a sheet, after being washed, the arms folded in the desired position, the eyelids closed and held in place by coins and the lower jaw held closed by a bandage or handkerchief tied around it and the head. A sheet was then placed over the body. It was placed in the coldest place possible so it would keep. Cloths soaked in saltpeter or carbolic water were placed over the face and changed frequently to prevent discoloration. The Relief Society made the burial clothes. When dressed the corpse was placed in the coffin, either then or shortly before conveying the remains to the "meetinghouse" for funeral services. There were no buggies or carriages so the casket was placed in a wagon and taken to the meetinghouse. Here it was placed on a bench.

The building was a log structure, the logs having been hewn with the broadaxe. Cracks between the logs were filled with chalk obtained from a chalk ledge on the mountainside about two miles away. The floors were of rough lumber: a raised platform was built across the north end of the room to serve for church leaders on Sunday and for the teacher on weekdays. It also served as a stage for the infrequent plays with local people as actors. A large fireplace was in the north end, its inside face flush with the wall and the chimney built outside the wall. This furnished the heat. The blazing pitch fires sucked the cold air from the imperfectly fitting entrance doors at the south end and the windows in the wide walls. This roasted from the north and froze from the south. Colds were frequent.

63

Not many people attended the services—there were not many to attend, just a few families scattered in the small valley.

There were no seats except those made at home from the native lumber. We used to call them benches. Some had backs and some not. A long board about a foot wide was nailed across some legs. They were far from comfortable. (This reminds me of the large, fat brother who came to church and sat down on one of these which was split in the middle. The crack spread as he sat and widened as others sat on the same bench. As services closed others, less heavy, got up a little ahead of him. As he rose the split closed in on him. The bench was attached to his anatomy. The other brethren had to sit down again so he could get out.)

The Bishop, who presided, with his counsellors and two or three speakers sat on the platform. The choir sat just below on the east side. There were only a few voices and none who could sing from note. I believe there was a small reed organ. A hymn was sung, perhaps "Come, Come Ye Saints!" The hymns were old hymns that had been sung during drivings and persecutions. They were associated with trials and sufferings and hardships and were an outlet for the pent-up feelings. Any discordant voice was unnoticed in the earnestness and pathos of the singers. They were songs of the soul and rang from the soul. One voice, the voice of Sister Noble, a soprano, rang out clear and full above the rest. It filled the room and touched the heart. It seemed wonderful. We were fortunate to have such a voice in so small a place.

Following the song a prayer was offered, simple and direct, just as if talking to a Heavenly Father. Another song and then the chosen speakers. They were not orators; they were uneducated; they knew nothing of grammar. But they were ones among us and for us and with us. As best they could they portrayed the future full of hope and certainty of a future life and resurrection when loved ones would meet and know and love again those who loved us here. Another song and then the closing prayer, a prayer that beseeched Providence to bless the bereaved and give them strength to meet bravely the temporary separation. The casket lid was removed and those who desired viewed the remains. As the lid was replaced Mother's grief was pitiful. She had risked her life for Mattie; she had nursed her through infancy and through illnesses; she had pictured her future; she had passionately loved her; she had sacrificed for her. What had she done to merit this cruel blow?

64

The wagon conveying the casket was followed by two or three others, a dismal procession. They moved slowly. The ground was rough and frozen and the wheels crunched in the snow. It was Mattie's last ride.

The cemetery (we always called it the graveyard) was about two miles down the valley. Snow had to be cleared away and the frozen ground picked through to dig the grave. The few people gathered for the funeral. Snow lay like a shroud over the entire valley and cold cut to the marrow. After services a few wagons followed to the cemetery where the homemade casket was lowered. The little group sang one of the hymns, and the grave and its contents [were] dedicated to the Lord. The profound depth of agony, I believe, was reached when the first frozen earth was dropped with a thud on the casket below. It seemed the last act in an eternal separation, and a cold, cruel last resting place. Only those who have lost can know the emptiness upon return to the home and the sadness, gloom and heartache.

My Early Life in Florence

Sue H. Summers

In the fall of 1879 Sue Summers left the comforts of San Francisco to join her attorney husband in making a new home for their family in Florence, Arizona. Living conditions in small Arizona towns were still primitive, with few municipal services and "innumerable saloons and drinking stations." Despite constant rumors of impending Indian attacks, Mrs. Summers never experienced a hairbreadth rescue from flaming Apache arrows, yet Florence provided her with a variety of excitements in other, tamer forms.

In Florence "sociability reigned." Impromptu dances at nearby ranches and picnic parties with delicate strawberries and other fresh fruits delighted residents. There were musicales and literary evenings at the Sanhara Club, card parties, and Sunday night suppers. And when the residents wearied of socializing, they turned their energies to civic improvements, education reforms, and the offerings of the lecture circuit to improve their minds.

Mrs. Summers's memoir, written in her ninetieth year, recalls an era when life in a small town was stimulating and festive and remarkably free from care. Life, even on the wildest of Arizona frontiers, aspired to a level of civility and hospitality which has not since been excelled.

I left San Francisco by Southern Pacific Railroad to join my husband in Arizona about the third of October 1879. Mr. Summers
had been in the Territory since 1869. The mineral wealth of Arizona was attracting considerable attention at that time, and he
hoped to secure a goodly share of the hidden treasure. He found it,
though, more than hazardous to attempt to penetrate into the
mountains prospecting for minerals, as the warlike Indians were
continually on the alert, to capture or kill all parties they found
during their murderous raids. But he secured by courtesy of General Stoneman of the U.S. Army an escort of soldiers and made
some promising locations in the vicinity of Globe near to where the
Old Dominion Mine has unearthed its riches—but such was the
condition of the country that any attempt to hold them proved un-
successful. He met with hairbreadth escapes from the poisoned
arrows of the Apaches—his mount at one time was shot so badly
that he afterwards expired—so, after spending all his available
means, he returned to Tucson, where he was engaged in the practice of law; afterward he moved to Florence, and to this place myself and daughter were on our way to cement the family circle. We
had a very pleasant trip till we were crossing the California Desert,
when we encountered a washout of such proportions that it was
dangerous to proceed. A dispatch was sent by special messenger to
the nearest telegraphic station and the passengers made as comfortable as possible, all sharing their lunches with each other so
that no one was really hungry. The next morning a wrecking train
arrived bringing relief by way of provisions, but after an investigation was made of the condition of the damaged road, it was thought
best to return us to Colton, where we were housed till it was considered safe for us to proceed. On this train was Judge Porter of

From the Sue H. Summers Collection, unpublished manuscript, Arizona Historical Society
Library, Tucson, Arizona. Used with permission from the Arizona Historical Society.

Phoenix, who was a host in himself to the passengers, allaying the fears of many of the ladies on the train. Mrs. Carl Hayden, Sr., was also a passenger, with her baby, Carl, then about fifteen months old. He was a fine-looking little chap, and his mother was intensely proud of him, prophesizing he was to be a future President of the United States. We started again on our journey, and met with no further trouble arriving at Casa Grande, where we expected to meet Mr. Summers, but were obliged to remain there overnight, as he had telegraphed on account of court business, he could not be with us till the morning. The station was not very inviting, but we were hospitably cared for by the proprietors, Mr. Fryer, afterwards Sheriff of Pinal County, and Mrs. Fryer, the former famous Pauline Cushman of the Civil War.

The next morning my husband arrived in a private conveyance, and we were soon en route to Florence about thirty miles distant. I had heard so much of the raging Gila River, which I now understood we would have to cross before reaching our destination, that I must confess I had a feeling of fear at the prospect of fording it—imagine my astonishment when we came to a halt within a short distance of Florence, and my husband, with an amusing smile, announced that the huge valley of sand on which we were resting was the bed of the Gila River—but I have seen it since and know it well deserves the name of "raging" as its waters inundated the land on its south bank, bringing the flood to the boundaries of Florence. After the barren appearance of the desert, Florence presented an inviting sight with the green trees bordering its avenues and the acequias or irrigation ditches flowing with water, and so we reached Florence on the seventh of October 1879. In a few days, we had a copious fall of rain. Going uptown the next day to attend to some shopping, I met several parties who inquired with apparent interest, "How is your roof?" It seemed a silly question to me, but I responded, "All right." Going into the store, the salesman propounded the same question, "How is your roof?" So then I asked an explanation, and found that most of the residence property had dirt roofs. I had not known we were so supplied with nature's gift, and did not feel very comfortable about it. It seems in early times lumber was at a premium. I learned to appreciate the despised dirt roof as a great protection from the summer heat.

At the time of our reaching Arizona, the present Gila County was a part of Pinal County and when court was in session there was a lively time in the little town. Sociability reigned—

everyone kept open house, showing all hospitality to the comfort and pleasure of the visitors. I found dancing was the greatest pleasure of the community—impromptu affairs would be gotten up with but little notice—the music always on hand and lively messengers soon brought the little community together and the slogan would be, "On with the dance. Let joy be unconfined." There was a beautiful ranch a short distance from the heart of Florence owned by Mr. Reemy, a Frenchman—he served the town with milk, and raised delicious strawberries and other fruits. He had a beautiful little home, and kept a court in nice condition for dancing in the open—[at] this ranch, impromptu dances were arranged, and old and young participated in the sport. Picnic parties were a source of great pleasure—there were many beautiful spots on the different ranches under the foliage of the oak trees, and hardly a week passed but some such festivity was arranged.

I can look back on those early days, and note how free from care everyone seemed to be—pleasure seemed to be the first essential of life. Florence was free from the aggressions of the Indian (Apache) though there were often startling reports of their being in the vicinity. The Pima Indians with their friendly attitude to the whites were surely a safeguard to them. I well remember . . . a report that the Apaches had been committing depredations at Pickett Post, afterwards called Pinal City, and would soon be en route to Florence. There was some consternation in the town, and it was hurriedly decided to send out scouts to investigate the situation, and in the meantime if necessary the women and children were to seek refuge in the old Court House and now County Hospital. I was sick at the time, confined to my bed with lumbago, but I was badly frightened—such was my willpower, that I deliberately rose from my bed and dressed preparatory to seeking the proposed refuge. Pima Indian scouts assembled on the grounds surrounding our house, which was the first in the road leading into town—all looked warlike, but the messengers of investigation returned, saying there were no grounds for danger, and we were all made happy with the satisfaction of safety, but I found myself a standing joke in the community on my sudden recovery to health. I enjoyed the joke myself, but the willpower I displayed on this occasion proved a good lesson to me in after years in overcoming many obstacles in life.

Among the earliest social affairs that I can recall was the formation of the Sanhara Club, by Colonel and Mrs. Daly—Mr. D. was the Register or Receiver, I forget which, of the Land Office which was then located in Florence. The club was devoted to literature and music—it included many of the early talent of the town—Mrs. Daly was a fine instrumental musician, and her husband a first-class baritone singer. The well-known Arizonian Mr. Thomas F. Weedin [had] a pleasing tenor and was a fine performer on the guitar. Mr. Taylor, the publisher of the weekly paper, was first in elocutionary talent, while his wife possessed a dramatic soprano voice. *I* helped out on the contralto. As our home then was the only one holding a fine piano, the meetings were held with us, and they certainly were a source of great pleasure, but unfortunately of short duration, for Mr. Taylor disposed of his paper and sought another locality, and the Land Office being removed to Tucson caused our losing Colonel Daly and his wife and the club lost its chief attractions.

When I first went to Arizona, I found in Florence there was a separate public school for girls and boys—a private school for girls, also a thriving department conducted by the Sisters of the Catholic Church, who also taught music, painting, and other branches of advantage—so the feminines of the town were well looked after, but the boys were crowded into an old building which was supposed to answer for the demands of our seventy pupils. An effort on hand to build a large schoolhouse for the benefit of both sexes was objected to by the Mexican population who were averse to co-education. After the schools had closed for the summer vacation, one early morning a deafening report aroused many from their slumber—the air was full of dust, debris scattered in all directions; the morning's sun revealed the boys' school in ruin—the large posts and beams supporting the massive dirt roof had decayed and the building collapsed with its adobe walls shattering the furniture of the school. There was but one thought and that was that the catastrophe had not occurred during the school session. In one way it was a messenger of good, for it led to a new school building, accommodating both sexes. About this time a new School District was formed north of the Gila—the schoolhouse was built of stone (excavated on its surroundings) for the accommodation of fifty pupils—it was well furnished and I had the pleasure of having charge of the students as their teacher for at least seven school years. Besides the educational advantages, I had many social gatherings on holidays during the year, entertaining both the children and parents, and I can never regret the time and work spent for the pleasure of all—it was truly missionary work.

71

What troubled me in my early life in Arizona was the universal use of intoxicating liquors—saloon and drinking stations were innumerable—located on the chief streets of Florence where women and children were obliged to pass—the situation attracted the attention of many of the ladies, and a few gentlemen, mostly newcomers, and it was resolved to form a Lodge of Good Templars, which soon was organized. Many joined with temperance motives—others from curiosity, but became so pleased with the attractive meetings of the society that they became devoted, efficient members using their influence in the temperance cause—many had been the prophecies of failure, but on the contrary, the number of drinking resorts were materially reduced, producing a good effect on the morals of the town. Mr. Abbot Colter was very active in the work.

The ladies of Florence had a great influence for good—they formed a society for civic improvement—they conducted a system of sanitation, having the streets and habitations that were repulsive, thoroughly cleansed—erected signs for marking the streets—and a Public Library successfully started—also were influential in efforts being made for incorporating the town. For some time there was but one church in Florence—the Roman Catholic Church, where preaching was only given in the Spanish language—from time to time there were preachers of the Protestant faith among us, but no regular services were held—and the ladies of the town proposed holding regular meetings for religious service. We secured the use of the Court House and invited the public to attend on Sunday afternoons. We used the prayers found in the Common Prayer Book of the Episcopal Church. I had a number of Henry Ward Beecher's sermons—other ladies had selections, which were read by all, cooperating. A small melodeon belonging to one of the rural schools furnished the music—we continued these meetings till the warm weather caused a recess, to meet later on—and more for the *result* of their meetings.

It happened about this time that Rev. I. T. Whittemore from one of the Middle Western States (I think Kansas) was looking over the field of southern Arizona preparatory to location. He heard of this project the ladies had been assuming and became much interested, and decided to recommend Florence as a suitable mission for the Christian efforts of the Presbyterian Church. A result was the building of a beautiful brick church of sufficient size to accommodate the parish, to be used as a church for all denominations, with Rev. Isaac T. Whittemore as minister. He afterwards secured by his personal influence with a Christian lady friend in the East, a bell for the belfry, calling the hour of church services. This building was of great importance to Florence, being used for holding lectures, and in every way open at the call of good. The mission was at first supported entirely by its founders, and the community owes a great deal to the faithful work of Mr. Whittemore and his family. The Ladies' Auxiliary organized by Mrs. Whittemore brought closer relations with many of the people, harmonizing differences and assisting in the work of the mission. After Mrs. Whittemore's sudden death from heart disease, Mr. Whittemore removed to Pasadena, California, where on an errand of mercy he was killed, his bicycle on which he was riding colliding with a trolley car.

I cannot close this reminiscence without speaking of the unique musical club, organized by Mrs. Nora Kibbey, the wife of Judge Joseph Kibbey, afterwards Governor of Arizona. It was composed entirely of ladies, with music adapted to female voice. Mrs. Kibbey was one of Arizona's finest musicians, incomparable as a leader. The club responded to her efforts in making a musical success by attention and practice, and our recitals were red-letter days in Florence when a certain number of tickets of invitation were issued for the occasion, and all felt proud of the success of a program which would have done honor to the rendering in musical circles of the present day. On these occasions we always insisted on the Judge and Mrs. Kibbey playing their duet on the piano which they learned in their early married life. This club had a lasting influence on the musical circles of Florence long after Judge and Mrs. Kibbey removed to Phoenix.

I found a number of bearing fruit trees even in my earliest residence in the valley—we had on our grounds peaches, apricots, figs, and some of the most luscious Bartlett pears I ever tasted, besides several kinds of grapes. The yard surrounding the home of Colonel Ruggles was a veritable garden spot, with its blooming flowers, especially roses.

My husband was called from earth in January 1895, and since that time I taught in the Public Schools of Florence till 1910 and had a pleasant experience during that time. I have tried to show, as far as I can remember, the chief practical memories of about the first ten years of my Arizona experiences, noting the circumstances which the light of the present day may deem of

73

minor character but at that time led to the improvement of the community and showed the influence of women's work even in that early day. The time since then has brought many changes as the new life of modern thought and invention has entered in, and brought a more active condition of life. Memory's trail recalls many of the old-timers, as they were called, now passed from their old, earthly scenes, and I am left, at the age of *ninety* years, to say for them, after the past banished hopes and dreary waitings handicapping the prosperity of the valley, "May the time be hastened for the building of the long-looked-for San Carlos Dam, that the present generation may embrace the advantages of irrigation that only lead to successful farming." Arizona is grand in its valleys, deserts, mountains, and scenic effects, and I am proud that so many years of my life have been passed in its domain.

Arrested for Polygamy

Roberta Flake Clayton

Lucy Hanna White Flake was one of thousands of Arizona pioneers whose lives paralleled the early history of Mormonism in the West. Her earliest memory as a young child in Knox County, Illinois, was of seeing the Prophet Joseph Smith during his martyrdom at the Carthage Jail. In 1850, with her parents and other members of the faith, she walked from the Missouri line to the Valley of the Great Salt Lake in search of the new Zion.

In Utah Lucy married William Jordan Flake, the son of a wealthy Southern Mormon who had migrated from Mississippi. As a part of his dream to extend Mormon settlements as far south as Northern Mexico, Brigham Young had asked William Flake to explore Arizona for possible suitable locations for settlements. The harsh environment and physical isolation caused Flake and his companions to abandon the search, but in 1876 they obeyed Brigham Young's order to return and colonize Arizona.

Despite the extremes of climate and the rugged terrain, most Arizona Mormon settlements prospered. Their population grew steadily. Mormon colonists from Utah suffering under extreme persecution sought relative isolation and anonymity in Arizona. Although the national press portrayed polygamy as a universal Mormon practice, it was common among a minority only—usually the most devout and those most able to afford plural families. In addition, the general practice was for the husband to seek his first wife's permission to another marriage. Many wives flatly refused, while others consented with reservations and reluctance.

After ten happy years of marriage, Lucy Hanna Flake heard from her beloved William that question that all Mormon wives must have dreaded. Her initial response was disbelief, then anger, then tears. But after several days of prayer and reflection she asked, "Will, who is the young lady we are going to marry?"

With the stoicism of her faith Lucy accepted the Church's position on polygamy. And she even learned to love her rival, Prudence. But her world was disrupted again when William was imprisoned on the charge of illegal cohabitation. As the public outcry against polygamists increased in the late nineteenth century, entire families fled to new Mormon sanctuaries in Sonora and Chihuahua while other men sought only temporary refuge south of the border. These were difficult times for divided families, and the bishop's storehouse and communal assistance programs responded generously.

Despite the pleadings of his two families and the advice of a sympathetic lawman that he flee to Mexico, William Flake accepted imprisonment. Heartache accompanied Lucy Hanna Flake's acceptance of polygamy, but her belief in marriage and the family within the framework of Mormon theology was more compelling than her desire for the exclusive claim on her husband's affections. During these dispirited times Lucy continued her habit of writing in her journal and from those recollections her daughter fashioned her mother's "autobiography."

Since the organization of the Church of Jesus Christ in these latter days, its adversaries had not been content to leave us alone.

Now it was the persecution of the men who had honorably married more than one wife and were raising respectful families.

The motto of our Church is "Mind your own Business." If our enemies had been as considerate, much suffering could have been avoided. I shall not try to place the blame where I know it belongs. Suffice it to say that the passing of the Edmunds-Tucker Act was an aim at the heart-core of Mormonism. The brutal actions of some of those who were placed in official positions, in the states where polygamy was practiced, were barbarous in the extreme.

Men were hounded and thrown into filthy prison to serve sentences imposed by judges of the lowest moral calibre.

The persecution spread to our little town. Many of our men fled to Mexico for protection, while the polygamous wives went to visit their people or hid out to avoid humiliation. One incident happened that afterward often furnished us with a hearty laugh. Every stranger was looked upon with suspicion. We were holding conference when a stranger came to the door. The men with more than one wife who still remained, made a break for the back door.

The man in charge of the meeting had a heart of gold but never had much education and was entirely unaccustomed to presiding. He got up and went down to meet the well-dressed stranger who introduced himself as Seymore B. Young, whom we all knew by reputation as one of our leaders from Salt Lake City. In his excitement, Brother Mann wildly waved and shouted, "Sit down, brethren, it is only Elder Seamless B. Young."

From Roberta Flake Clayton, *To the Last Frontier, Autobiography of Lucy Hanna White Flake* (n.p., reprinted 1976).

Homes were broken up, children left fatherless and wives made to bear the duties of providing for themselves and their children.

William declared he had done nothing to run from, but he helped others to go to Mexico, where they were given refuge.

One of our neighbors came one night and asked for help to go to Mexico. He only had one team and his boys would need that to harvest their crop and haul wood for the family. He had no money to buy another outfit so could William lend him one. Well, a wagon, cover, water barrels and a span of our best horses were rigged up for him. The horses were harnessed up, hitched to the wagon and driven up to his door after nightfall. He and his plural wives slipped away. In about a year he returned the outfit, with thanks. That was all that was necessary. If he had never brought them back, it would have been the same.

Not long after that another neighbor came to the house at midnight, said he had just gotten word that the Marshall would be there after him in the morning and he wanted the best horse we had. Our husband was not at home, but the boys knew what he would have done if he had been, so they saddled old Babe and told him not to worry as there was not a horse in Arizona that could overtake him. When our friend got to the Mexican border he sent the horse and saddle back by some people we knew who were coming our way.

It was always the same, if anyone needed anything and we had it, they knew it was theirs.

Rumors reached us almost daily that William was wanted for polygamy, that the Marshall had a warrant for his arrest. Our friends, both inside and out of the Church, begged him to leave until the storm was over, but his colors were not the kind that run no matter how severe the tempest, and he stayed.

The United States Marshall sent word to us, himself, about the first of September, 1884, that he would be after him about the fifteenth of the month.

When they met, Mr. Donevan took some money from his pocket, and said, "Mr. Flake, take this money, buy your ticket and get what you want. No one needs know you are traveling with me." "No," answered William, "treat me as you would any other prisoner. Let them know it. I have done nothing of which I am ashamed, I am merely a victim of persecution."

The train pulled in and the two men got aboard. This was William's first train ride and he did not like it. The close, hot, stuffy air, filled with tobacco smoke, gave him a headache and made him sick to his stomach. He said to himself, "Anyone can ride on the cars that want to, but for me give me Old Sport and wide open spaces."

When they got to Prescott, William was put under a two-thousand-dollar bond to appear at the November term of court. He brought the bond home to get it signed and returned.

Everyone in our part of the country knew William had two wives. When anyone came to our home who did not know us he would introduce us as "My wife, Lucy" and "My wife, Prudence." All of the other polygamous men had been run out of the country, but no one would sign the complaint against him.

Mr. Shone, for whom William had bought a bunch of cattle in Utah, was at our home very often. He was asked to testify against us, but refused time and time again. One day, however, when he was drunk he signed the complaint.

After William's return from Prescott, Mr. Shone came to him and acknowledged what he had done. Accused himself of being a Judas, who betrayed his best friend, cried like a baby and begged William to leave the country and he would pay the bond. William put his arm around Mr. Shone and told him that was all right. If he had not signed it someone else would, that our enemies were bound to wipe out Mormonism if possible and would resort to any means to try to accomplish their purpose.

William found four other of our men from St. Johns when he got there for his trial. It was a long drawn-out affair. Nothing but mockery.

The men had never met. The officer knew him only by reputation, that he was an honorable, law-abiding citizen, and he did not want to make the arrest.

At the appointed time he drove up from Holbrook, reaching our place about noon. William was there to meet and welcome him. Marshall Donevan introduced himself and told his errand. "Well," said William, "I am the man you are after." The papers placing our husband under arrest were served.

"Unhitch your team, put them in the stable and feed them, my wife will get us some dinner while I go get ready to go with you," William said as he sent one of the children to tell me we had company for dinner.

Of course I knew the arrival of the Marshall and the purpose of his visit. The children knew, also, and as they followed me around from stove, cupboard to table we were all crying like our hearts would break. Four-year-old Joel was going to "kill that bad man so he can't take Pa to Prison." I didn't have the time nor inclination, just then, to tell him how wrong that would be and that "two wrongs never make one right."

The Marshall was very ill at ease and told us that he wanted to return to Holbrook at once, that the train did not leave until two p.m. the next day and that William could stay at home another night and be there to meet the train.

After dinner Officer Donevan left. "See you tomorrow," said William. "All right," answered the Marshall.

Never in our lives had things looked so dark to us. The persecution against the Church was so bitter, we felt there was no chance of us escaping the full punishment of the man-imposed law. As usual our husband tried to cheer us, even made light of the situation. Asked us how we thought he would look in stripes and with his head and beard shaved. Wouldn't we be proud of our jailbird? All of which made us feel even worse.

Poor Prudence said if it hadn't been for her we would not have had to suffer this humiliation, or if William had not introduced her to strangers as his wife. That brought reproof from him. "You are my wife before God, and I am proud to own you before men," he said hotly.

It was about an eight-hour ride on horseback to Holbrook. We got up early the next morning so that William could get a good start and not cause the Marshall any uneasiness.

A series of humiliations . . . brought all the good American fighting blood that William had, up in arms. Ammon Tenny of St. Johns was tried first, and declared guilty. He was taken at once and thrown in jail—a dirty, filthy hole filled with criminals of the worst kind. William was indignant, begged for his friend to have the liberty of the grounds, and offered his head as a guarantee that Mr. Tenney would be there when wanted to be taken to the penitentiary in Yuma. His pleadings did no good. Ammon was seized and forced in where the prisoners were cursing and shouting. The jailer remarked that "he would be all right, we are all humane men." "Yes, Hell is full of just such," shouted William, who went out and

80

did not stop until he found some of his friends and had Brother Tenney out of that dungeon.

Two more of our men were convicted without evidence. Our Gentile friends were doing all they could to keep William out of the penitentiary. They wanted him to plead guilty. He said he would if the complaint was changed from "unlawful cohabitation" to Plural Marriage. The indictment was so changed and he and dear old Brother Jens Skousen pled guilty.

As soon as Mr. Stinson heard of William's arrest he came from Phoenix to Prescott to help him. By this time Mr. Stinson had identified himself with public affairs, had plenty of friends, money and influence. With some of his friends he determined to free William and told him not to say a word and they would. [He said] the full extent of the law was to be given—was eight years in the House of Correction in Detroit, together with a fine of one thousand dollars each.

William said, "I am as guilty as they are. I won't go free and see them go to jail without trying to help them. If Judge Howard sentences innocent men to that fate, it will be his damnation and I am going to warn him."

We had known Judge Howard in Utah where he had done all he could against our people.

Shortly before they were to be sentenced, William walked into the Judge's office; there he made a strong plea for our friends. "You know they are not criminals," said William, "so why treat them as though they were?" The Judge was silent so William continued pleading for these men who were honest, honorable citizens. Especially did he recommend leniency for Brother Skousen, who was an old man.

When it was time for them to return to the courtroom, the Judge said, "Flake, this visit will cost you six months in Yuma and five hundred dollars more, but I will cut off three years from the prison terms of the others and reduce their fines one half."

"Give me another six months and five hundred dollars more, and reduce their sentences again," pleaded William. They were now at the door. As he went ahead the Judge shook his head. The sentences were given as he told William they would be, only that Brother Skousen's was the same as his. Thus, on the fifth day of December 1884, our husband was sentenced to serve a prison term

81

for marrying two wives and providing for us and our children, while his persecutors patronized houses of ill-fame.

Just as William was getting in the waiting stage to be taken to Yuma, one of his acquaintances came up and begged him to go his bond. "I am a convict, I cannot go your bond," William answered. "You have friends who would if you would ask them to," he begged. "I haven't a friend here, and will have to lay in jail six months waiting for my trial if you don't help me." William turned to Mr. Stinson and asked him to go the bond. "It will require two bondsmen," answered Mr. Stinson.

Another of William's friends came up just then to bid him good-bye. William asked him to sign with Mr. Stinson. "I will," he answered, "if you will insure against loss." "I'll do that." William's word was as good as his bond. He afterward had to make it good as the fellow jumped his bond and skipped out to Mexico.

When the prisoners reached Phoenix the Marshall asked them if they had any friends in Mesa who they would like to visit, as it would be twenty-four hours before their train would leave. The "jailbirds" took advantage of it and were back in time.

"That which we persist in doing, becomes easy, not that the nature of the thing changes but our power to do increases." Because of the accident he sustained in his youth, when he dove from a bank and kinked his neck, William claimed he could not hold his head down long enough to write a letter, and yet we got at least one a week. He wrote often to Charley, who was still in the South, and wrote many letters to our friends. In fact he kept a diary, from it I glean many of the things contained in this chapter.

To begin with our own tribulations. Prudence's affliction was our chief concern. She now had the son that had been promised her in the Temple, by a servant of the Lord. When her first child came, ten years after her marriage, and less than a year after she had been promised a son, she was just a little disappointed that it was not a boy. We comforted her by telling her that she would have both. There was another daughter before the son came. Of course she was thankful for her children, but her lack of health prevented her from caring for them as she wanted to. Every little change of weather or exposure would give her fresh cold and then she would have another severe attack of asthma. She would have to sit propped up in bed for days to get her breath and her wheezing could be heard out to the gate.

82

My children were as thoughtful and kind to her as though they were her own. I would cook the meals and either take them up or send them to her. We did all we could to make life less hard for her.

I had three children in school, Charley on a mission, and two little boys at home with me. Jimmie lived on the same block. He and Nancy were great help and comfort to their "Auntie" and me.

We waited with what patience we could for his letters. They were always full of concern for us, but never a word of rebellion or complaint. If there was a funny side, he always found it and wrote it to us.

First thing, instead of having his head shaved, the considerate barber only clipped his hair and beard a very little.

William was surprised when the warden handed him his first letter, to find that it had been opened. "I am to read all letters you write and receive," he announced. "All right, go ahead," said William. "Read them, they will either save or condemn you, for you will hear the gospel of Jesus Christ, and be left without an excuse." When the next letter came, the warden brought it in, tore the end of the envelope off and handing it to him said, "You see how much I read your letters."

One of the first things William objected to was the quality of meat being served. All of the prisoners felt the same, but dared not say a word. He told them if any more spoiled meat was put on their plates to let him know. "What will you do?" asked one of the men who had been there longer. "I'll tell the warden about it." "Lots of good that will do! You'll be sent to the snake den," warned one of the men. "All right, but let me know if any of you get any more rotten meat." He didn't have long to wait. In a day or two the plates were brought in. The one who was served first smelled his meat and, looking at William, made a sign. When William's plate was brought in he took a sniff, turned to the guard and told him he wanted to talk to the warden. He was brought in. Not a man had started to eat, all waited anxiously. William said, "Captain, this meat is not fit to eat."

"Eat what is set before you," commanded the officer in a stern voice. Disregarding the warning looks of the other inmates William continued—"Captain Ingalls, that meat is rotten. I wouldn't feed it to my hogs. I am a citizen of this state and a heavy taxpayer. I am in your power, now, but you cannot keep me here very long. I have plenty of friends and when I get out of here we will turn this place upside down. We pay for decent food for our prisoners and they are going to have it or we will find out the reason why."

The warden ordered the tainted meat taken from the table and other food supplied for the meal. "If you ever find any more bad meat, let me know," said the officer as he left the dining room. Only once after that were they served "spoiled" meat, and when the warden was notified, it was taken from the table and other food substituted.

The meat was not the only unpalatable food served, as the wheelbarrows full that were dumped into the river after each meal proved.

No one who had gone hungry, as the pioneers had, could see that terrible waste of food, without making a protest. William mentioned this to the warden and asked him to give Brother Robson a chance in the kitchen. He did, and in a month the food bill was cut in half. Pigs were bought to eat the potato peelings, corn husks and what little there was left from the table. These helped supply the prisoners with fresh pork.

When our men first went there the prison was in constant turmoil. The snake den, a dark, damp, filthy hole, was the horror of all the inmates. The least offense brought the punishment of being thrown in there and fed on bread and water.

William hadn't been there long when he noticed a sullen-looking man, hauling dirt in a wheelbarrow. With a big heavy ball chained to his ankle he trudged back and forth. He would shovel the dirt in, then pull the ball in the wheelbarrow and wheel them to where it was to be dumped.

One day when he was passing, the warden happened to come up to where William was. William asked why this man was being so persecuted. "Because," answered the warden, "he is a desperate man, the worst one we have in here. We either have to keep him in the snake den or in chains to keep him from trying to escape. He had tried to kill me and the guards as well as himself, and cannot be trusted." Then sneeringly, "He is one of your Mormons."

"Let me have a talk with him, then," requested my husband. "Gladly, go ahead," answered Captain Ingalls. William went over to where the poor fellow was and began talking to him in a

84

friendly manner. He would not say a word, just sat there on his load of dirt, with his head down and a scowl on his face.

Finally he cried out, "Go away, and let me alone. I am going to get out of here or die in the attempt."

William tried in every way to appeal to him. He found that he had been married, had two little girls, his wife had died, he had gotten reckless, was accused of robbery and falsely imprisoned. In desperation he had gained and merited the reputation the warden had given him.

"Wouldn't you like to see your little motherless babies?" asked William. A convulsive sob shook the poor emaciated figure, tears came at last to those fiercely blazing eyes, and William knew the battle had been won.

At the end of two hours William went to the warden and said, "Captain, cut off the ball and chain. He will give you no more trouble." And he never did. Soon he was given the position of head baker, and held it as long as he remained in prison. Shortly after William's sentence was terminated he got a pardon for the other 'Mormon', who from that time lived a model life. All that poor man needed was a friend, and he found a true one in my husband, as did countless others. Every courtesy that could be, was shown to William and Brother Skousen. William was given an easy chair at one of the gates to check the other prisoners as they went in and out for work.

Captain Ingalls had two young lads who were very fond of fishing but he didn't want them to go alone. William suggested that Brother Skousen be allowed to go with them, as he was very fond of children and would take good care of them, so he was allowed to pass in and out as the boys wanted him.

That which was intended to be a punishment to my beloved was an opportunity. The men who had doggedly got out three carloads of dirt a day from an excavation were allowed to have a certain amount to do and then have the remainder of the time to do as they pleased. Now they got out four cars in two hours. Thus he quietly went about turning what had been a seething inferno into a place of well-fed, cheerful men, as was attested by the warden who said, as William's time was up, "Mr. Flake, I do not want to keep you from your family, but I hate to see you go. You have done more good than you realize. This is a better prison and the inmates better men because of you and their association with you."

85

The most wonderful thing that happened to William during that six months was one day he was called into the warden's office. He wondered what was wanted. He entered and was taken into the arms of his foster brother and lifelong friend, Francis Marion Lyman.

Captain Ingalls gave them the best room in the building and left them. After a couple of hours spent alone together, William asked that the other Mormons be allowed to come in. They were given the remainder of the day to themselves. They were served in the room a delicious dinner especially prepared.

Every courtesy was shown the visiting Apostle by the warden and the guards. It was truly a day of thanksgiving for those incarcerated Mormons. William asked for a slice of bread and a glass of water, and within those prison walls the sacrament of the commemorating death and resurrection as instituted by their beloved Savior at the Last Supper was partaken of by His lowly followers, in His name.

Because of the delay in the mails, the money to pay William's fine had not arrived when his sentence was up. Some of the prisoners found this out. They had money of varying amounts deposited with the warden. They drew it out and presented it to him. He only accepted it as a loan and returned it as soon as he got to Mesa.

Besides the money, his fellow convicts gave him many presents they had made. Among these were a horse-hair bridle, an elaborately carved cane and a workbox with two thousand four hundred pieces of native wood inlaid in it.

To prove William's loyalty to his family, he told the Judge who sentenced him, that he had married two pure, beautiful women, that they were his wives in the sight of God, they were the mothers of his children. He went on to say that his second wife was now an invalid, and that the only way they could keep him from living with her, loving, protecting, and providing for her was to keep him in prison the rest of his life.

Judges have a reputation for keeping out of trouble. He suggested that our husband "Give Prudence the money and let her pay her own bills." This solution to the problem did not suit William, and after his return, life went on just the same for us.

The day of his homecoming was June 11, 1885. He had ridden from Mesa on horseback. He came riding up to the gate, like a General. I always knew he was handsome, but on a horse he

86

was at his best. We were overjoyed to see him, and for days we did nothing but entertain our friends and visit.

Prison life had proven more of a blessing than a punishment. It had given him a much-needed rest, a chance to do good to poor discouraged social outcasts, and an opportunity to do much reading, which his busy outdoor life had prevented. His hair, beard and skin were soft and free from the effects of harsh winds and sun. For the first time in the forty-six years of his pioneer life he had time to take care of himself.

There were the stern realities of life to be faced when he came home. We had managed the best we could, but there were the lawyer fees, court costs, and fines to the amount of fifteen hundred dollars to be paid. Money was scarce and hard to get. Things looked pretty blue. On top of that a letter came from Prescott, stating that the man whose bond he had secured, had failed to appear at the summer term of court for his trial.

His name did not appear on the bond, but that made no difference to William. His friends who had gone the bond at his request should not lose a cent. He went immediately to Prescott and asked to be allowed to deliver the man. He was told that the man was in Mexico and they could not get him. "We don't want the man, we want the money," said the Judge. He did grant us a little time to raise the money. Money was scarce and interest high. We got it, however, and sent it. It took us seven years to square that two thousand dollars and the fifteen hundred dollars we had to raise for William's bond, etc.

On the third day of July, after William's return, his friends from all over the country made it an occasion to show their love and respect to him by giving him a surprise party. The Stake House was decorated with flags, bunting and flowers until it looked like fairyland. It was filled to capacity to welcome and honor him.

I had given a birthday dinner at our home to which a few of our most intimate friends were invited. After it was over, one of his friends suggested that they go for a little walk; this was about two o'clock. Everything had been arranged to the minutest detail.

I have heard many church bells, but never one with the clear, sweet tones of the one we had in the belfry of our Meeting House. It was only supposed to be rung on special occasions like New Year's Eve, when it rang out the Old Year and ushered in the New, to call the townspeople to worship or some other gatherings, unless sometimes when a mischievous boy got hold of the end of the rope. Three or four times while we were eating our birthday dinner the bell rang.

The after-dinner walk was purposely conducted through the Public Square, past the building. The bell sent forth another set of chimes. Bishop Hunt said to William, "There must be some rowdies in there ringing the bell; let's go in there and stop them." Suspecting nothing, William walked ahead, and as he put his foot on the threshold the band struck up "Dixie," the audience arose and remained standing while he was escorted to the stand and a big easy chair by several of his friends. A program of songs, music, readings and sentiments, all written for the occasion, took up the afternoon. Everyone was anxious to show honor to a man who had spent his life and means helping others. There was a pass around. All the folks had brought their picnics and all ate while they praised their beloved townsman.

The King of Arizona Mine

William Keiser

Gold and silver were the first metals mined extensively in
Arizona, and the search for them was a major influence in the
territory's development. Initially the lone prospector with his
burro trudged the rocky wilderness panning the streams or
locating a vein embedded in a mountainside. Few individual
prospectors had either the inclination or the capital to mine gold
trapped in the rocks, so Arizona mining quickly became the
province of wealthy speculators and wildcat promoters. Soon the
engineers and the technicians followed, but there was always a
demand for the brute labor of the ordinary miner.

William Keiser's memoir of his experience mining gold at
the King of Arizona Mine in 1898 is a matter-of-fact account of
one of the most harrowing of jobs. Hardrock mining was
hazardous; underground the heat could rise suddenly to 120
degrees, and the air was often so foul that a man suffered
constant nausea. Each shift meant new perils. A man might be
blown away because of improperly placed dynamite or he might
fall victim to poisonous gases. Fires, underground flooding,
scalding thermal springs and cave-ins menaced the miners. Given
the greed for profit and the surplus of human labor, equipment
was scarce, heavily used, and often in poor repair. But "men
were cheaper than timber" and when one miner fell there were
usually two or more eager to earn his three dollars a day.

Leaving his home in Lykon, Pennsylvania, in 1896 where
his "domestic affairs . . . had taken a turn for the worse," Keiser
traveled first to California. There he worked as a laborer on the
Otay Dam near San Diego. When the foreman learned that he
was a miner experienced with the steam drill, he quickly
promoted Keiser to breaking rocks instead of hauling them.

When the dam was completed, Keiser and the foreman
Rogers set off for the King of Arizona gold mine in Yuma County.
In the following selection, Keiser recounts day-to-day life as a

89

miner. He describes the dominance and clannishness of the
Cornish miners, the brutality of the work, the exhaustion, and the
squalor of camp life.

All the stereotypes of mining lore were present at the King
of Arizona in flesh and blood: the shrewish wife who beat her
drunken husband, the garish camp followers, the mysterious
loner, the garrulous bully, the venal boss, the ill-tempered
Oriental cook, and Keiser, the drifter. The memoir shimmers with
life and vitality as he recalls the ultimate single-male existence.
His is an engaging and thoroughly human record of that fleeting
era when gold reigned before copper was king.

Rogers and I took the train to Yuma where we stopped over a day to make enquiries and found that Yuma was a division point on the railroad; that an extra engine, and sometimes two, helped trains the eighty miles upgrade to Mohawk Summit where they had to stop to let off the engines. From there it was fifty-five miles to the KOFA Mine, but only eleven to the Mohawk post office on the Gila River which George Norton, a civil engineer, ran as well as a small hotel on his ranch.

We decided that Rogers would take my suitcase to the King and I would beat my way "Blind Baggage"; for I had sent money home and did not have much left. Although we had a good supper, Rogers insisted that we eat again before train time. I noticed that he ate little, but he remarked that I did not know when I would eat again. How thoughtful and how prophetic!

At that time there was nothing along the tracks but sand dunes and a tank. I selected a spot about where an engine hauling a long train would stop. I had made a good guess, and as the bell kept ringing I knew it would soon be on its way, so decided to board the blind baggage next to the engine the minute it started.

All at once something grabbed me and an old Indian squaw, drunk as a fool, held onto me and said "Wine. You ketchum wine." I tore her loose, pushed her back on the sand and jumped for the baggage. She let out a yell and ran after me and then the brakeman looked and saw me get on.

So did someone else, for I had no sooner made myself comfortable, congratulating myself that I would get a ride as far as Mohawk Summit, than I felt something poking me in the ribs. The train slackened speed at Blaisdell, ten miles out, and a Wells Fargo

From the William Keiser Collection, undated manuscript, 22-45, Century House Museum, Arizona Historical Society, Yuma, Arizona. Used with permission of the Arizona Historical Society.

agent poking a double-barreled sawed-off shotgun into my ribs said, "Get off! Get off!

I "got" and as the train picked up speed, at every opening between the coaches was either a brakey or a porter all giving me the horse laugh. I still had seventy miles to go and it looked like a long, long hike; so I started counting the ties.

About three in the morning I was beginning to get pretty weary. I ran across two other fellows at a water tank. "You fellows counting the ties, too?" They said they were headed for the mines—ten-day miners, broke. A freight came along and I was all for jumping it, but was cautioned not to. "Some of these brakeys are awful tough." They told me that brakeys' bodies as well as hobos' have been found along the tracks. They all carried clubs to brake with. The old-style brake meant running along the tops of the cars and braking the wheel that governed the brakes with the help of a stout club.

So we plodded along. By eight a.m. we still had about forty miles to go. The sun came up warm and we only made about three miles an hour. We would rest under a culvert. Got water from another railroad tank and were thankful when the sun went down. After dark we could see a light ahead, but it never seemed to get any closer. We made guesses, and at about ten o'clock caught up with it; a lantern hanging on a switch.

These fellows said they were broke, and no doubt they were. I sent one of them to the section boss with a dollar to buy something to eat. He returned with one big potato, a half-pound can of corned beef and six crackers. Not much for a dollar, but we roasted the spud and ate heartily and separated. I headed for the Norton ranch—about eleven miles. My feet, I knew must be one solid blister, but I reached there about two a.m. A Mexican woman gave me a bed. The breakfast bell woke me about six and I decided to get up and eat. I was hungry and how I enjoyed that breakfast! Real hotcakes fresh off the griddle and fresh eggs.

Norton said he couldn't offer me any encouragement about getting a job at the King as it was a "Cousin Jack" (Cornish) camp and they were very clannish. "Secum, the foreman, is rabid regarding employing American miners." He advised me to wait a few days until Mike Nugent returned—that is if Secum turned me down, and it was a foregone conclusion that he would. Nugent and Alexander ran the store and boardinghouse and Nugent was an owner

92

of the mine and he might have Secum change his mind (although at first chance he would fire me.)

It is hard to believe but some of these "cousins" have a job before they leave Cornwall, while Americans in their own country can't get a job. Some of these Cornishmen never become citizens and return home after making some money.

I found Norton quite a character. He said he had a telephone line to the King of Arizona mine. About thirty-five miles up the line was a relay station for his stage and freight lines where there was a well and they changed horses. A man looked after the stock and served meals. I asked if he was a Cousin Jack and he said no. Then I might be able to get a bite from him. I told him I didn't have much money. I decided to walk up there if my feet would allow it, for Norton said he did not think MacBeth would take me on the stage unless I had the dough.

Norton had received sixty thousand dollars from the government to build a road from Yuma to Ehrenberg. He said the department would not give a contract to boats to carry the U.S. mails as they were too uncertain. This was to be a stage road to deliver mail all along the line, Picacho on the California side, Norton's Landing for the Castle Dome district, Castle Dome Landing, Silver District and Ehrenberg, thence to Quartzsite. . . . soon the mail to Quartzsite would come through his office and a stage would ply between the King and Quartzsite, also to Ehrenberg, for the sixty-thousand-dollar road was in bad shape and he intended freighting to Quartzsite (Fort Tyson). He would extend his telephone to Quartzsite also.

At seven p.m. the stage left for the King mine. It drove up with a flourish—four horses. Alex MacBeth, the driver, looked down at me, and upon my request to ride to the King and pay him later said, "No. I can't take you. It's a Cousin Jack camp and you won't get on." He was very pompous; great leather gauntlets, high-heeled flashy boots, a bright blue silk shirt with a bright red bandana handkerchief knotted about his throat and a big Stetson hat. He had only two passengers and I felt that he could have taken me, but he drove off in a cloud of dust.

I started walking the thirty-five miles to the well, taking a quart bottle of water which soon became warm; but thirst didn't bother me so much as my blistered feet. It took me till about ten to reach the station about ready to drop. A heavyset man came out and looked me over and then laughed. He said, "I know you. I met you on the train going to San Diego. What did you do there? What are you doing hiking? Are you broke?"

"Now, isn't that a hell of a question? Me with blisters on my feet after walking 116 miles? Don't you think I'd have ridden on the stage if I had any money? But what in the world are you doing here?"

He said, "I don't know, Billy, whether you can get on at the King, but with those blisters and worn out, too, just forget a job for a while. I have a cot and you'd better come in and eat a cold snack before you go to bed."

The man's name was Burch. Later I was to have many dealings with him. How lucky I felt. I went into his board shack dining room and the cold meat and biscuits tasted so good! And beans. We had a lot to talk about. I told him about Rogers. He said he must have gotten on. Went through several days ago and had not returned. "Funny though, unless he's a 'Cousin.'"

Burch said he was doing pretty well but thought he would go to the new camp at Ft. Tyson (Quartzsite) about fifty miles north of the King. I made myself useful; stayed at the well about four days. The phone rang and MacBeth said to expect about six besides himself for lunch—four men and two women. Burch said, "I bet they are fresh from the Old Country."

Lunch was about ready when the stage drove up. Burch already had the harnesses on the fresh team. He unhooked the others and drove them into a separate corral until they cooled off before watering them. In the meantime I had set the table; nice tablecloth consisting of a lot of clean newspapers, then put a pile of potatoes with jackets on at each end of the table, two dishes of beans, a large platter of sliced roast beef and two bowls of gravy.

Burch came in and told the guests to take their places at the table, went to the oven and took out a pan of biscuits beautifully browned. Burch could make good biscuits, but Oh! the service! He came in right from the corral without washing his hands, still smelling of the corral. (Everybody those days smelled of the corral.) I saw the women look. The men took it more philosophically; they began to help themselves, but the women hesitated. Urged on by the men, they finally took a few dainty helpings. Alex sat at the head of the table.

Burch came around with a big black coffeepot and asked, "What will you have, tea or coffee?" Of course, these Englishmen said, "I would like tea, please." "You will have to take coffee—we haven't got any tea," Burch would say. This was his little joke. He poured everyone a cup of coffee, and it was good coffee, freshly made (I made it), but it was scarcely touched except by MacBeth, partly because they did not like coffee and partly because the big black coffeepot did not look inviting, but the inside was clean.

MacBeth asked if I knew Burch before and I told him, "Yes." He said, "Well, if I had known, I might have made an exception and given you a ride, but you don't know how many want to ride and never pay me."

An eight-horse freight team drove up one day—one of George Norton's. They stayed overnight and the next day I went with them to the mine. It was only fifteen miles. I went over to the store and met Alexander. He told me Rogers was working and had given him my suitcase, saying I would be along in a few days. As it was about quitting time I waited to see Rogers and also the boss, Secum.

Usually at these small mining camps so far from the railroad it was customary for a miner, if hard up, to stand at the boarding-house door as the men filed in for a meal and be invited in by someone, someone you had never seen before, having the meal charged to him. I stood at the door and not one invited me in. These "Cousins" were not only too selfish, but were ignorant of this custom.

Finally Rogers came along walking beside the boss. When he separated from him to go to the bunkhouse to wash up, he saw me and all he said was, "Hello, I see you made it." I thought, "That's funny"—he was chilly. I soon learned that most of these men were afraid of losing their jobs if being seen intimate with some American. Meeting Rogers as I did was quite a shock. I was dumbfounded, for he knew better than anyone else my circumstances. I saw Secum a moment and was informed that he had nothing at present.

I went over to the store and had a talk with Alexander. He told me that when Rogers left the suitcase with him he thought it was funny. Guess he was afraid to be too friendly with me. I told him about the Otay dam and how we started out for Yuma—never met a finer man. He made it as easy as possible for me at the dam and no matter how he acted, there would always be a warm spot in my heart for Rogers. Alexander said, "Don't you know he is a 'Cousin'?" and I said "No, I thought he was of Scotch descent."

95

"Well," he said, "he is not. He talks just like a Cornishman from the Old Country." "Why," I said, "he can talk just as good as you and I. Never so much as an accent to indicate just where he hailed from." "Well," he said, "you should hear him talk now!"

He told me I could sleep on a cot with the watchman at the back of the store until I got on. He gave me a note to the Chinaman and I went over and ate, and we waited for Mike Nugent to get back and persuade Secum to change his mind. He came in next day and we had a talk with him. Within an hour Mike told me I could go to work for Mr. Barker at the cyanide plant in the morning. So I got a blanket and a quilt and a pillow from Alex on credit and went up to the bunkhouse.

I did not get into the same room as Rogers, but I could hear him talking. To hear him one would think he had just come across. I could hardly believe my ears. I thought "Is that Rogers? The polished Rogers that I worked for at the dam? The man who was so nice and so considerate of me before we parted at Yuma and who now dropped me like a hot potato?"

At lunchtime Rogers did address a few remarks in my direction; seemed to want to be friendly now that I had got on. He worked in a tunnel blasting chutes. I could tell that he wanted a shift boss job.

The vein seemingly ran southwest to northeast and dipped to the south, the ore occurring in a rhyolite porphyry with quite a lot of manganese which did not retard cyanidation. The hanging wall had eroded away for about a thousand feet up the mountain, exposing a large vein which was in some places thirty feet thick; very convenient to keep the fifty-ton mill running steadily. This was called "The Glory Hole." (Some of this ore went for a dollar a pound in gold.)

Here Secum had thirty Cornish friends working at $3 per day. Two men with eight-pound hammers on one drill. They usually put down one three-foot hole in a half day; plenty of resting and conversation. These thirty men cost the company about twenty-seven thousand dollars a year for four years. But the expense was not noticed because the King was making money and the high-grade ore had not yet paid out.

Later Secum was fired and an air drill on a tripod was placed in the Glory Hole with two men ($3.50 for the machine and man and $3 for the chuck tender). This broke as much ore as the thirty men had. Secum had been working in the interests of his

Cornish friends and not in the interest of the company [owners,] who, by the way, were all Americans.

The King of Arizona mine had been discovered the year previous, 1897, by Charlie Eichelberger, a prospector. I later met him in Quartzsite in 1907 and he told me about it. He had packed some burros up from Mohawk and decided to go into the canyon that headed at the King vein to try and locate a water tank for his animals in order to be able to prospect that section. He found a tank that would last a month or so. (These are natural tanks in the rock that hold rainwater.) He proceeded to prospect.

An old Indian trail went over the mountain and going up this trail he discovered a small cave, an overhanging rock where the evidence showed that the Indians cooked there. He sat down under the shade as it was fairly warm. Where the smoke covered the wall he noticed some bright yellow spots—gold—and found he was right on the best portion, as proved later, of the whole vein. He located a group of claims and he and his partner, a Yuma businessman who had grubstaked him, sold for $250,000.

Eps (Epes ?) Randolph, division superintendent on the Southern Pacific Railroad, immediately headed a list of buyers. His partner took cash but Charlie took part cash and part stock. The latter he sold afterwards but lost most of his money in the awful San Francisco earthquake fire, April 1906. He had a laundry that burned to the ground and he did not have it insured. In 1907 Eichelberger moved his family to Quartzsite to try and recoup his fortune. He did find another mine which he called "The Success." This he sold to Dick Wick Hall who rechristened it "The Apache" and made several shipments, but Charlie did not make anything out of the discovery.

I went to work for Mr. Barker and moved into the bunkhouse, a long adobe building now disintegrated. It had six rooms and took care of about thirty men. It had a corrugated iron roof and the partition only went up as far as the adobe walls, so of course one could hear all that was going on in the room adjoining. The company furnished cots and pads. In the room I was to occupy I found an Irishman, the blacksmith, McGraw; a Cornishman named Billy Horan; and three other Cornishmen. These latter had just come from Cornwall and were a fine bunch of boys; all clean, never left the bunkhouse at night, did not drink, swear or tell smutty stories. In the evening they would gather in front of the bunkhouse with others and sing for the benefit of men and their wives living about the boardinghouse. Perhaps eight women. Sometimes they insisted that I sing with them, which I did several times. They sang as well as the Welsh in my hometown in Pennsylvania. I began to feel like a "Cousin Jack."

I became acquainted with Billy Horan at once. He asked me what kind of a job Secum had given me and I told him I was to help at the cyanide tubs, presumably a shovel job unloading them. He said, "Why, that's no job for a miner!" I said, "Beggars cannot choose and I will work a while and then quit. This is the best Nugent can get for me." Billy said that Nugent was a fine man. "Just take it easy. I will have a talk with Secum." I learned that he and Secum were raised in the same town in Cornwall, and as most of the Cornishmen could not run a machine, Billy had it his own way with Secum. The next morning I reported to Mr. Barker, a Cousin but well-educated, no doubt having lived in this country many years. He looked at me as though he could tear me to pieces, told me to get a shovel and get in one of the tanks and help the Mexicans unload the tailings. At that time all one had to do was shovel them over the sides. In time elevators became necessary. I worked hard nine hours a day for three dollars per. One dollar a day for board and two dollars a month for the doctor. If I worked as a miner I would have to join the Western Federation of Miners and pay two dollars per month more.

Nearing noon of the fifth day I was working real steady when Barker came over and looked at me fit to kill and said, "Hurry up!" This was so uncalled-for that it flashed through my mind that he was trying to fire me. (Burch and others had said that I would last about a month.) I never was so mad in my life. I looked at him and thought if I hit him with the shovel and the edge turned I might cut him nasty, might kill him, and I decided in a flash it wasn't worth it. But I threw that shovel as far as I could and looked him square in the face and said, "Mr. Barker, you can go to Hell!" Then I went back to the bunkhouse and got ready to move. "Just hang around a few days, Billy, something may turn up," said Horan.

Horan had a talk with Secum, who was all for letting me go—said I was too smart, told Mr. Barker to go to hell. Billy said, "You know he was goaded into saying that, and anyway I want to try him out as chuck tender on my machine." So he told me to come out tomorrow to go to work with him in the tunnel.

I went to the store and purchased a candlestick—which I still have. All the mining at that time was done with candles. In the morning the shift boss would be at the shaft or tunnel and hand each man two candles. After lunch he would hand out two more. It was not a square deal, for if one worked in a windy place, a candle would not last long, and especially on machine work, so we had to conserve our candles by using only one at a time. Seemed to me that the company could at least have given a kerosene lamp to each room, but no! We had to get along at night with what stubs we saved during the day—stab the candlestick into the wall at the head of the bed and read by the stub we had so carefully hoarded. But it burned down—only too soon; nothing else to do but turn over and go to sleep. Giving out only two candles to a machine man, the same as a single-jack man, seemed so unreasonable. Many times I noticed that these single-jack men would have nearly a whole candle to use in the bunkhouse at night. Oh, well, if they did not have any we would all have to go to bed with the chickens. As it was we had at least one candle to light up our room.

The fellows seemed to want to count me as one of them since I had been promoted (so to speak) by telling Mr. Barker to go to hell. They were a pleasant bunch and McGraw, the blacksmith, was a card. He had been in China for eight years. One evening he stood out on the dump and began a Chinese sort of sing-song. All I remember was "*Muca Hi!*" The Chinaman he was singing for outside the cook house looked up and yelled, "Go to Helly." I asked what he was singing, or did he know? He said it was about that Chinaman's ancestors and what a rotten cook he was. *Muca Hi* was a cuss word and he kept on beating time with his foot.

One night coming off shift about two a.m. an awful scream like a woman's scream came from across the wash. We all rushed to the bunkhouse to wake the fellows up; someone was murdering his wife. We were all outside when the scream came again. McGraw said, "You fellows better come in; that's no woman. That's a panther. No woman can scream that loud." Evidently he had disturbed him while he was eating swill that the Chinaman had dumped over the hill. Next morning while going up the trail I saw him. He was about six feet long, tawny in color and was hugging the ground and sneaking up the mountain.

Another night I found a new man in our room and he was snoring. My! How he did snore! Seemed everybody was awake in our room, for someone yelled from one of the other rooms, "For God's sake wake that fellow up! Nobody can sleep around him." Several threw shoes at him and all at once he ran up against a knot, for everything was quiet and you could hear a pin drop. Someone raised up in bed and said very earnestly, "Thank God. He's dead!" We all had a laugh and did not hear him again that night, but due to complaints, Secum let him go.

In my new-found prosperity I was all for asking Mike Nugent for oil lamps, but these Cousin Jacks were funny. Even Billy Horan was afraid to make anyone higher up sore, and the new respect they had for me was not enough. They were all afraid of losing their jobs. Rogers came over with several of the boys in the evening and tried earnestly to get into conversation with me. He said one evening, looking straight at me, one should not hold a grudge; life was too short for that. I could never hold a grudge against him after all he'd done for me.

I was lying on a cot one evening reading a book Rogers gave me. His wife sent him reading matter. While I was settled with my candlestick jammed into the wall, I heard a commotion—some woman cussing to beat the band. This was strange up in our part of town. Then I heard, "I know you are in there. Come out of there you so-and-so!"

Just then a big rock was hurled through the window of an adjoining room. The house was built against a hill. I got up and blew out the light as I did not want a rock to come hurtling into my room and I wanted to learn what it was all about.

It seemed a man named Chappel and his buddy occupied the room next to ours. She was crazy about him, but he was not crazy about her. When she saw him with another woman she followed him home—drunk as a hoot owl. Everybody was out as she was raising Cain; and the language she used! McGraw wanted to go out and knock her senseless, but none of us wanted to take a hand. It was up to the constable, who was a Mexican and no doubt down on the other end of town drunk himself.

Finally she came around in front and I heard her opening the door. The boys had unlocked it. I thought at first they had stolen out, but I heard her say, "Now I've got you- - - - - - -!" Then a bang and some groans. We all went out with candles and found Ollie on the ground bleeding like a stuck pig from a gash on her head. Doc Fraser came over, as he, like everyone else, was out listening to her rant and cuss. He had some of the boys carry her on a stretcher to his office where he patched her up and some of her friends from the Red Light came up and took charge. I went into the room.

100

The boys had taken to tall timber and I could hardly believe my eyes. I found a two-inch plank about twelve inches wide and two feet long split in half where Chappel came down on her head with it. I wonder it didn't cave in her skull. Later Secum sent a couple boys down the road to tell the others to come back, that no charges would be made and that they had not killed her. She left town as soon as her head healed up. They all said she deserved everything she got, but I'll bet it sobered her.

Well, I got started as a miner with Billy Horan. The ground was all in ore and this rhyolitic porphyry was hard. We had to drill twelve holes about four feet deep: three cut holes, three uppers, three breast holes and three lifters. This usually broke ahead about four feet. Billy and I got along fine. He was getting $7 a foot. After paying my wages, explosives, etc., he did pretty well. Of course he had to allow a certain amount for drill sharpening and for hauling water. He had a Mexican, the "powder monkey," to bring us water, that is, fill up the pressure tank about fifty feet from the face of the tunnel, and to take out our dull steel and bring in fresh. Later he had to cut the fuses, connect the primers and bring in the dynamite, Billy telling him how long to make the fuses and how much powder.

The shortest fuses, about three feet, were for the cut holes, three feet, two inches for the breast holes, three feet, four inches for the uppers (back) and three feet, six inches for the lifters, to make sure they would go last. They were then lighted, or spit in that order. Billy was a careful miner. He always, Cousin Jack style, lit his fuses with a candle stub in each hand. If one went out he re-lit it with the other. If both went out I was there with mine. Once he started, there could be no delay, for those fuses, if fresh, burned a foot a minute.

After I had been with Billy a few days, he said he would see Secum and try to arrange to take me in as a partner on a fifty-fifty basis if I would take the night shift. I did not think Secum would stand for my sharing in this contract, but his friends could not run a machine and I could. He called me up on the carpet and quizzed me. After a little he reluctantly agreed. But he got square with us. He would only allow the Mexican mucking after us to take so many cars each morning, so we had to do some of our own mucking before being able to set up another round.

The next thing was a chuck tender. Secum solved that problem, too. He gave me a young Cornishman and Billy, a

Mexican. Both chuck tenders were good, but I felt sure I would do something to enable Secum to fire me. I did.

As Secum would not give the Mexican enough cars to take out all the ore we broke, mucking became quite a problem. I told Billy that if we had a piece of sheet iron, we could lay it down before we blasted and put a few sticks of powder under it with a long fuse so that it would go off last after the muck from the round was on it; the muck pile would be far enough back and the tunnel clear so that we could get set up again. Billy tried to get one, but I guess Secum was peeved that we tried to beat his game and would not give us any sheet iron. I have always thought it gave him the idea with which he was able to finish me. In the meantime we went along, Billy and I making good money and hoping for another contract for two hundred feet that was coming up.

Finally when I was on night shift I found a piece of sheet iron—as I thought—at the mouth of the tunnel and decided that finally the night boss had dug one up for us. I felt very elated and instructed the "powder monkey" to bring it in. I put twelve sticks of powder under it and a long fuse and after I shot the round I went in and found that I had loaded a little too heavy. The face was as clean as if someone had swept it with a broom. Muck scattered on both sides of the track for fifty feet. I went home feeling fine. I thought next time I would only put half as much powder under the iron sheet. I did not know there would not be a next time.

At noon as I was coming out of the dining room I met Billy. He said, "I told you to be on your toes, and now you're fired." "Why?" "Well, you blasted a thirty-five dollar turn sheet."

The sheet had been intended for the one-hundred-foot level and the shift boss made a mistake and put it at the mouth of the tunnel. I did not examine it or I would have recognized a turn sheet, but it was rusty. A turn sheet is a piece of steel three or four feet square, the center being raised and oval shaped. It is used where a drift takes off at right angles. The loaded car can be swung about due to the center being raised. I learned later from a Mexican who worked on the one-hundred-foot level that they did not need a turn sheet down there. I will always think it was a put-up job. Anyhow I fell for it. I had been doing very well. I had $125 coming and Billy was reduced to one shift with the Cornish boy as chuck tender.

102

Before I left, Felix Mayhew, who had a saloon in the lower part of town, had quite a fight. (Later on, 1905, Felix discovered the North Star mine, received ten thousand dollars as his share and was broke in eighteen months.) A big Cornishman would go down to the saloon and persisted in fighting Felix. Every night the fight was declared a draw. I think the Cornishman was influenced by his friends who could not understand why, with his great size and strength, he could not whip Felix, who was slim but wiry, nimble and all muscle. Felix said he understood the man was coming down again that night and suggested that I stick around and enjoy the fun. I stuck; and presently the big fellow and his friends came in, sidled up to the bar and asked for a drink. Felix had said to me that he would like to bash his brains in with something but that he wanted to show those Cousin Jacks that he could whip him. Anyway he said, "You know you came down here for a fight, so let's get it over with," and he came out from behind the bar and slapped the fellow on the mouth. The Cousin let out a roar and went to it. Several friends of Felix got some clubs and told those others not to interfere and give them plenty of room. We did. They had the whole barroom floor to fall around on.

Felix was too quick for him. He would strike and fall all over himself. If any of those blows had landed, it would have finished Felix, but he was never there and landed on him as he was going by. Finally they clinched and rolled all over the floor. Both were pretty bloody and I could see the big fellow was winded. He panted and Felix pinioned his arms on his sides and prepared to make jelly out of his face; but one of his friends said, "Felix, make him say he's had enough. No sense in beating him up anymore." The fellow said he'd had enough and Felix made him promise to stay away from his place. Doc Fraser fixed him up with a few stitches. His face was black and blue. He took the next stage out. Felix was all battered up, too, but he stayed away from the post office and any remarks. The victor wasn't hurt.

All the Cousins were not as clean and sober as the boys I roomed with. One fellow, a buddy of the one who fought Felix, generally went on a drunk every two weeks. Secum told him if it happened again he was out of a job; that that was final. But he went on his drunk, so no more work, and he came to breakfast awful blue. This, coupled with his hang-over, made him pretty grouchy— a fact that most of the boys noticed, so that when the

Chinaman brought him his eggs that he had ordered straight up, he took a look at them and said, "I can't eat these." (Straight up was awful hard to do after they had been hauled on a freight wagon fifty-five miles, and warm, too.)

The cook could not be blamed for the way the eggs looked, and, believe me, the yolks did not look fit to eat. Someone suggested, "Send them back." He said, "I'll do just that." I was sitting beside him. The Chinaman took the plate and soon returned with two eggs. He gave one look and said they were as bad as the others. "Blimy, I believe they are the same bloomin' eggs." Another Cousin said, "Why, they are the same!" Another said, "Don't you know any better than to send anything back with a Chink? They just go behind the door and spit on it and bring it back again." Another said, "So, that's why he went behind the door!" By that time they had him all riled up and when the Chinaman came by with a dish in either hand with that peculiar dancing gait that they have, he turned and slapped the plate of eggs squarely in his face. The man let out a yell, dropped the dishes and beat it back to the kitchen with eggs all over his face. There was some jabbering in the kitchen and then the big, fat head cook came to the door with a butcher knife in his hand and said sternly, "What's a malla you?" About that time someone hit him on the mouth with a cup.

This was a signal for everyone to throw something and so there was a lot of broken china about the floor and in the kitchen. Mike Nugent, who sat eating in the officials' dining room, came in. He looked about and said, "Some of you fellows will have to pay for this damage. What is wrong?" The Cousin yelled, "They are feeding us rotten eggs. That is what is wrong." Mike said, "Well, boys, the Chinamen are not to blame. Guess I will just have to stop feeding you eggs until the weather cools and I bring them up on the stage."

He went on to work, and later when he came for lunch, which we felt might not be served, we found the Chinamen on the job again. Mike had sent a team down the road about five miles and induced them to return. We were served lunch, but Mike Nugent was right there the whole time. They were afraid of the bunch and demanded that he stay. After they found that it was all over and that most of it had been in a spirit of devilment, they got back to normal and could laugh a little.

Alex MacBeth, the stage driver, had his idea of a joke. Alexander at the store told me that some men and women from the

Old Country were on the stage and MacBeth would be sure to give them a thrill. Before reaching the post office there were two arroyos and two hills, both fairly deep and sidling. We could not see the stage until it came around one of the toes of the horse-shoe-shaped mountain behind the mine. Alexander said, "If he walks the team he is conserving energy to put on a show the last few hundred yards, but if he comes up the canyon on a small trot, no show." This time he walked his team so we looked for a show.

When about to approach the first hill, he rose up and waved his big hat and yelled. The horses jumped and went down the first hill with a lean, but as the stage body was strapped on and the wheels set out quite a distance, it did not turn over. We heard some screams and then he took the second hill on a jump. As he was opposite the post office he yelled, "Whoa!", slammed on the brakes and pulled the horses back on their haunches.

What a lot of screaming! Pretty soon the men and women crawled out all mussed up. They were in a heap at the front of the stage, the women scared to death. They thought the team had run away. MacBeth got a big kick out of it. So did everybody for that matter. It was a dirty trick, but MacBeth was full of them.

Alexander told me that the stage was never held up, that the company shipped bullion every week, so that in case they were held up they would not lose too much. Sometimes Nugent would take it out and sometimes he would go as a blind and the bullion would go on a slow freight while he waited at Mohawk for it. From there Norton took care of it.

I attended a meeting of the Western Federation of Miners, a very strong organization, and had a big surprise. The rules and regulations provided that shift bosses, bosses, superintendents—in fact any officials of the company could continue as members if they came from the ranks of the organization; and many of them had. They could not hold office or attend meetings.

To my surprise I found Joe Julif, shift boss, the chairman. This organization could cause the discharge of miners refusing to join, and mining companies usually discharged men when asked to do so by the Union. These Cousin Jacks did not understand the principles underlying this organization. Mr. Gilbert and Mr. Secum really ran the Union. What a farce!—just like the Welsh in my hometown in Pennsylvania, but at least when I left I would have a card that would be accepted at the next camp.

105

The Welsh talked of Pontepool, the Cornishman of Penzance and the Irish boy who was not going to America but to Butte; so I guess the only ones who are not clannish are Americans and the ordinary run of Englishmen.

Before I left I saw Rogers and he said he did not think he would stay long, as he had to return to his family and he thought he could do better elsewhere. He sympathized with me, but I was really glad to quit that tunnel. I thought of what use is the money if I ruin my health and I felt sure Billy Horan was killing himself going back of the muck pile and breathing that powder gas. I know it affected me, for I often had headaches, and Doc Frazer's pills did me no good. "If Billy doesn't watch out he will be buried here." I was a better prophet than I knew, for he died after I was at Quartzsite and was buried at the King.

I was told he actually had turned yellow before he died. His lungs were burned out, I guess.

I saw Felix Mayhew, too, and told him I was fired. "Never mind," he said, "Secum won't last much longer and you can come back later."

I was persuaded to stay over for the Cinco de Mayo activities. I did not dance but enjoyed watching. My parents were very strict—no cards or liquor of any kind in the house. If I went to a party we were told to be home at a certain hour. None were allowed to learn to dance and I know I missed a lot of pleasure by not being able to. Due to my raising I was too self-conscious to get out on a dance floor and try, not having the least idea how to begin.

When supper was over on the fifth of May, the Chinamen moved the tables outside and put benches along the wall and three chairs for the orchestra, an accordion from Mohawk, a mandolin and a guitar. The Mexican women began to congregate with their daughters, some real nice looking. One thing about these mothers—they never allowed their daughters to come alone or with a boy, but when they were on the floor, the mothers very patiently sat on a bench and waited until the dance was over, never once demanding that they give up and go home. If the dance lasted all night, they would just sit there and allow their daughters to have a good time.

Riding for the Old C O Bar in 1904

Earle R. Forrest

The Arizona cowboy has become a permanent part of
America's national mythology. In the popular mind, the cowboy is
a colorful and splendid creature who flourished in that brief
period in the American West between the disappearance of
nomadic Indian civilization and the arrival of modern white
settlement.

In this Middle Ages of the American frontier, a curious
feudalism sprang up. Wealthy ranchers became "cattle barons" in
the penny press. Brands were the frontier's heraldry while rodeos
and roping contests replaced the jousts and tournaments of old.
Life on the open range with a canopy of stars overhead by night
and boisterous masculine companions by day represented the
epitome of independence and individuality. Yet, in reality, the
daily life of the Arizona cowboy was neither as carefree nor as
glamorous as it has been portrayed.

Earle R. Forrest's memoir is a realistic account of a
cowboy's job on a big ranch near Flagstaff. The era of the long
trail drive with stampeding herds, rampaging rivers, and
marauding Indians was past when this college boy from New
Jersey went west to join the Babbitt family's C O Bar outfit in the
spring of 1904. But the cowboy's seasonal work of corralling and
branding and moving cattle to summer pastures remained
unchanged.

A cowboy worked and lived, ate and slept out of doors in
all kinds of weather. Managing cattle was as dirty, unpredictable,
and physically exhausting as it had always been. But the men who
chose this occupation were, on the whole, a society of grand
fellows. Educated in the moods of the seasons and the contours of
the land, they were wise about weather, animals, and human
nature. Accustomed to long stretches of isolation and hard work,
most cowboys were comfortable with solitude. As a group they
seemed more at ease with nature than with organized society. One
life-long observer of the Arizona cowboy summed it up when he
wrote, "He was what he was, nothing more."

My introduction to Flagstaff, the home of Babbitt Brothers and their C O Bar outfit, was about three o'clock one cold morning in early March of 1904, when I climbed out of the eastbound Santa Fe train, and was greeted by a chilling blast of cold air right off the ice-capped San Francisco Peaks; but it felt more like it came from the North Pole. What a reception committee, I thought. I had been near Oracle in the Santa Catalina Mountains all winter, where we only had two snows, and ran around most of the time in our shirt-sleeves. I had thought that all Arizona was like that. I had not learned then as I did later, what a difference a few feet in altitude up or down can make.

• • •

In addition to being greeted by that cold blast from the Frisco peaks, a Negro porter asked me if he could take me to a hotel. "Any place to get out of this cold," I told him, and he took my grip and guided me to John Weatherford's hotel. . . .

After I was somewhat thawed out I went to bed, and the next morning I went to Babbitt's store. I had had some experience in cowpunching in the mountains of Southwestern Colorado during the summer of 1902. When I arrived in Tucson in the fall of 1903 I got a job from Charley Bayless, who was a prince if ever there was one. First he sent me to the sheep ranch at Oracle, and then to the cattle ranch at Redington, where I had charge of a field a mile square, in which were a large number of hogs. It was surrounded by a barbed wire fence with barbed strands laid under the ground for about a foot to discourage hogs from digging their way out and

From the Earle R. Forrest Collection, a paper prepared for the 4th Annual Arizona Historical Convention at Tucson, 35 p., March 1963, Arizona Historical Society Library, Tucson, Arizona. Used with permission from the Arizona Historical Society.

coyotes from digging their way in after some pork chops; and in a way each succeeded. It was a job patrolling that fence, and I was glad when the roundup wagon appeared.

The foreman of the roundup crew was a half-Mexican named Clark, and a darned nice fellow he was. He detailed an American cowboy to help me with the hogs for a few days, then they left to comb the mountains. I stuck it out for a month, and then sent word to Mr. Bayless to get someone else for a hog-puncher. He took me back to Oracle and placed the American cowboy I just mentioned in charge. I heard later that he stuck it out for a week. Then he quit cold and high-tailed it for Tucson and a big drunk.

• • •

The Babbitt store was really several stores, for each department occupied a separate room. I went into the grocery, and when I asked a rather large man with a neatly trimmed Van Dyke beard for "Mr. Babbitt," he told me that he was one of them. When I explained why I was there he introduced himself as George Babbitt. About that time two more of the brothers came strolling in, and all three looked enough alike to be triplets; but they weren't. It was just those Van Dykes. George introduced me to his brothers, Charles and David. Charles, who was manager of the outfit during the absence of his brother, William, told me that Jack Hennessey, the range foreman, would be in from Cedar Ranch in about a week, and I could go back with him, as he would bring the wagon in for supplies.

I kept pretty close tab, and it was just a week when Hennessey came in. The next day he loaded the wagon with all kinds of supplies at the stock room in the rear of the store. I threw my saddle and bedroll on the load and we started. Our first stopping place was The Fort, about nine miles from Flagstaff and in the Fort Valley. The valley was as beautiful a spot as I ever saw. It was a big open park in those days, right under the shadow of the San Francisco Peaks, which are as beautiful as any mountains in all the West.

• • •

It was back about 1886 that those four Babbitts—Charles, David, George and William—arrived in Flagstaff from Cincinnati,

Ohio, to go into the cattle business. I once heard Bill Rhodan, an old man at that time, say that he was their first cowboy. Well, I'll say that they made a good selection, for Bill knew cattle from their horns to the ends of their tails. Older cattlemen smiled at those young eastern tenderfeet, who had the nerve to invade the Arizona cattle range, and said knowingly that they wouldn't last until "the snow flies." A good many snows have come and gone since then; the original five brothers have long been dead (Ed, the fifth brother, remained in Cincinnati to conduct a successful law practice), but long before their passing they built a multi-million-dollar empire in the Babbitt Brothers Trading Company, which their sons and grandsons carry on with the cattle ranch as only a part of one of the big commercial enterprises of the West.

From the very beginning the C O Bar prospered. Even if the brothers did come as green tenderfeet they were quick to learn, and good sound business methods were born in them. When I joined the C O Bar in the spring of 1904 it was the largest cow outfit in all Arizona, with the possible exception of Henry C. Hooker's Sierra Bonita Ranch and his Crooked H brand.

• • •

Massy, the first cook at the Bucklar Ranch on Hart Prairie, was a Southerner who came to Arizona with TB or the "bugs" as we called the disease in those days. Massy needed the work, so Babbitts gave him the job, and we didn't give a darn if he was lousy with TB bugs. Nobody ever gave a thought to the disease being contagious. That was before doctors began to tell you that TB was as contagious as smallpox. As camp cooks go he was good, and I don't know of any of those boys who ate his cooking that died of consumption. Babbitts got him a better job teaching the Navajos at Tuba City to farm. He knew farming all right, for he had been raised on a Southern plantation. Years later Bill Babbitt told me that he went to California.

Al Murray followed Massy as cook. He was a pretty rugged type, and while we had left Massy alone we took special delight in deviling Murray. Finally, he decided that those C O Bar cowboys were too much to take, so he went to town, got on a big drunk and quit. Later we heard that he went to Goldfield and made a big strike.

110

Rosendo Levario was a good rider and he knew how to handle horses. After he had taken a few kinks out of their backs he was
good at training them to rope, herd and cut. He was a Mexican as
you have probably judged from his name. He worked for the outfit
until the snow began to fly, and he drifted south. Many years later I
heard of his death at the Spurlock Ranch in Bloody Basin, where he
had been foreman.

• • •

The C O Bar Ranch on Hart Prairie and the chuck wagon
were pretty much like a boardinghouse for neighbors and drifting
cowboys. But they were all welcome to come as often as they
wished and stay as long as they wanted to. That was the way of life
on the Arizona cattle range in those days. Many of the little fellows
who were neighbors got most of their meals at the C O Bar. On the
other hand if the outfit needed extra help in a hurry it was always
forthcoming from those cowboys for as long as they were needed,
and no wages were ever asked or expected. Some of the big outfits
like Babbitts' always made it a point to help the little fellows. That
was life on the old-time Arizona cattle range.

Now I'll get back to my story. When Jack Hennessey and I
arrived at The Fort, several cowboys were waiting for him to come
with the wagon so that they could get something to eat. Cowboys
are always hungry, but when necessary they can go longer without
food than any other animal. . . . It didn't take long to whip up a
meal, for practically all cowboys were pretty good cooks in those
days. They had to be or go hungry. . . . No stove was left in the
house, but that made no difference. A good fire was soon blazing,
the coffeepot was simmering, and the Dutch ovens were full of
baking powder biscuits. The smell of the sizzling bacon was enough
to drive a hungry man crazy. The bacon in those days was cut with a
butcher knife by the cook from a nice big slab, and it was not paper
thin like it is today. There was enough meat and grease left in it to
stick to your ribs.

The meal was quickly disposed of and we were soon on our
way to Cedar Ranch, about twenty miles to the north. The cowboys
took a short cut, but Hennessey and I with the wagon had to follow
the road, which took much longer; and it was dark long before we
reached the ranch. It had not been uncomfortable during the day;

111

but the instant the sun disappeared that same cold wind came down from the snow on the peaks, and we were soon chilled to the very marrow of our bones. . . . One of the most welcome sights I ever remember was a big blazing fire in the cabin at Cedar Ranch. The door was open and we could see that fire long before we got there. Even the very sight of it seemed to make us feel a little warmer.

When we reached the cabin a cowboy came out to take care of the horses while we went inside to thaw out and get something to eat. The boys who had gone over the trail had been there a long time, and they had a hot meal waiting for us in the Dutch ovens at the big stone fireplace. This time we had fresh beef instead of bacon, the ever present pinto beans or "Arizona strawberries," baking powder biscuits, stewed dried apples, canned corn, and plenty of "lick" or sorghum molasses for the biscuits. Babbitts always fed their cowboys well. There was always plenty of what we called "Java," but the package was labeled "Arbuckle," and canned milk. Some of the other dishes we enjoyed were oatmeal, rice with raisins, canned tomatoes, and sometimes canned peaches; but they never lasted long, for we ate them pretty fast. We always had fresh beef unless some of the boys went out with a pack outfit. Then they took bacon and shot a deer or an antelope now and then. Yes, there were game laws, but no officer trailed along to enforce them, and nobody cared.

Whenever we ran out of fresh beef we just hunted up a yearling and butchered it. There's an old saying, and it's pretty true with most cow outfits, that no cattleman ever ate his own beef. But as far as the C O Bar was concerned that was never true. Babbitts just wouldn't stand for it. They had enough C O Bar beef to feed their own punchers, and they made it very plain that we were to let other brands alone when we ran out of fresh beef.

When we butchered a yearling we always had a big beef stew for supper. My mouth waters even today when I think of them. Into that stew everything went except the hide, horns and hooves. We used the liver, the kidneys, the heart, brains, marrow-gut, and I'm not sure but that the lights (lungs) went in, too, and sweetbreads when we could find them. I remember once that Bill Babbitt said that was just a fancy name, that they were really tonsils; but that made no difference to us. We liked them and we ate them, tonsils or sweetbreads, it was all right with us.

There was a wonderful spring back of the cabin at Cedar Ranch, which the A Ones had piped down to a big pole corral below the house, and built a big barn across the road from the corral. I have been told that the barn is still there. This was the main winter camp of the A Ones.

Hennessey told me the next morning after our arrival that we would remain at the ranch a few days. Then he would leave Eli Lucero and me there, and take the wagon and the rest of the boys back to town, where we would turn the outfit over to Bob Gleason, who was to be the wagon boss. When Bob returned there would be other cowboys as reps for other outfits. We would then hold a big roundup, and move the C O Bar cattle to the mountains for the summer.

Hennessey pulled out several days later, leaving Eli and me together. That was the beginning of a friendship that lasted down through the years until his tragic death forty years later. Just before leaving, Hennessey had killed a yearling. He took part of the meat, but left enough to last us until the wagon should return. Eli claimed the head, and that night showed me how the Mexicans cooked this delicacy. First he rolled the head in a section of the hide. Then he wrapped the bundle in a wet gunny sack, and buried it about fifteen or eighteen inches in the ground. The next step was to build a big fire over it, which he kept going until quite late. When we awoke the next morning the fire had died down, but the ground was still very warm. With a long handled shovel Eli unearthed the head, and when he removed the gunny sack the hide came with it. Well, it was good—meat, brains and tongue all well cooked. Eli set it up on the table in the cabin, and we enjoyed it in spite of those big calf eyes staring at us, sort of reproachful like as if we had played a dirty trick on a promising young steer.

The wagon returned several days later in charge of Bob Gleason, who was to be boss of the roundup, and we went to work combing the cedars and the whole country for miles around. Cattle belonging to other outfits were turned over to their reps and the C O Bars were driven to their summer range on the mountains. . . .

That was the old-time cattle range. There wasn't a fence except around a horse pasture, for many miles. In fact, I don't think there were any fences except at pastures. We rode from daylight until dark, only taking time out to change horses when we brought some cattle into the herd, and scarcely took enough time

113

to eat at noon. There was no place to hold the herd at night, and so we had to night herd, each man taking his turn of two hours.

After the country was pretty well combed we started branding calves. This was hard, rough dirty work. The branding fires were some distance from the cattle, and even then it was a bit dangerous at times when some mama cow came out on the prod because we were maltreating her baby; but a cowboy was always standing by with his loop ready to drop over her head if she ventured a little too close. After the branding and cutting, we started with the C O Bar cattle for the mountains, and the other outfits drove their cattle to their own summer range. The home ranch of the C O Bar for the summer had been changed to the old Buckler place on Hart Prairie; and The Fort that for twenty years had been one of the big cattle ranches of Arizona was abandoned. Never again was it occupied except during an occasional roundup. . . .

The Buckler Ranch was in a beautiful location, high up on the western slope of the San Francisco Peaks, where you could see for miles, to Bill Williams Mountain. Miles and miles of pine woods lay before us on all sides. Back of us towered the rugged, rockbound Humphrey's Peak, the highest point in Arizona, 12,670 feet above sea level, and covered with snow. A big horse pasture was back of the house, and a short distance below was an old frame bunkhouse that the A Ones had built; but it had not been used since the company folded up. Near the bunkhouse was a spring, the water from which was impounded in a tank built by Babbitts that summer. A big prairie-dog town was below the ranch with several eagles always hovering near, ready to pounce down for a toothsome morsel. We never bothered those eagles. In fact, we hoped that more would come and clean out those prairie dogs. How we did hate them because they made riding in that section rather dangerous.

The house wasn't much to speak of, it was made of small logs with a pole and dirt roof. The main room was the kitchen, dining room and parlor. The other room was used for storage. We rolled our beds on the outside with only the sky and stars for a roof, unless the night was very stormy, and then we slept on the kitchen floor.

Bob Gleason told us that as soon as Bill Babbitt came from their ranch south of Dodge City, Kansas, work would be started on scooping out a tank to hold the water from that spring. Any of us who wanted to work on the grading at extra wages could do so; but there were no volunteers. Digging and manhandling a scraper was not work for cowboys. Anything we could do on a horse, no matter how hard, was all in the line of range work, and we would have plenty of hard work when the roundup wagon started out again. In the meantime we would take things easy; just ride around over the mountain and see that the cattle did not stray back to their winter range. When nobody seemed to hanker for a job on the grading outfit, Bob said that when Bill arrived he would bring a crew of laborers from Flag.

Several days after we were settled I rode to the ranch one afternoon, and went into the house for something, I've forgotten what. When I came out a man rode up to the cabin and dismounted. He was rather slender, about average height, and his upper lip was adorned with a heavy mustache. He wore a suit of store clothes and a slouch hat. The only things to indicate that he might have anything to do with the cattle business were his high-heeled boots and stock saddle. I liked him the instant I saw him. He looked to be about forty years of age; his face was pleasant.

He walked up to me with a smile and held out his hand; "You're Forrest, aren't you? I'm Bill Babbitt." That was the beginning of a long friendship. You couldn't help but like Bill Babbitt, and he was one of the best friends I ever had except my father. I want to say right here that Arizona never produced a better cattleman, and for that matter no other territory or state did either, not even excepting Texas. He had no superior in the business, and he was one of the finest gentlemen I ever knew. I think that just about describes Bill Babbitt. He has been dead these thirty years, but my opinion of him has never changed.

In a few days he had ten or a dozen laborers, drifters he had picked up in Flagstaff; wagons came up with scrapers, picks and shovels, and all the necessary tools for gouging out a water tank in the bosom of mother earth. It was then that Massy came as cook; and in a very short time Babbitt had the work under way. One of the men who had done some construction work was put in charge. The grading crew was not composed of bums as you might think. They were drifters going from one section of the country to another; but they were good workers, and they were a pretty good crowd. I remember that two or three had been in the Alaska Gold Rush in '98, and whenever Forest Ranger George Campbell was at the ranch, which was pretty often, especially at supper time, he and those men had a great time swapping experiences, for George was a sourdough of ninety-eight, too.

They were paid by the day, and I heard Bill Babbitt tell them that they did not have to work on Sundays, but if they wanted to it was all right; or they could take the day off to rest, do their washing or anything else. Generally they worked. In fact, I only recall one Sunday that any of them took time off, and that was when four climbed Humphrey's Peak with me. I had climbed up a few days before, and when I described it those four wanted to go up. There was a monument on the summit, built of rough stones just piled up high. We could see it from the ranch, and it may still be there. It wasn't a dangerous climb from timberline to the summit, but it was really hard work in that high altitude. I rode my horse to near timberline on both occasions and went the rest of the way on foot. I had been on high mountain peaks in Colorado, and I have climbed high mountains since then; but I believe that view from the summit of Humphrey's Peak is one of the most magnificent in the entire country. It seemed to me that we could see the greater part of Arizona. The rim of the Grand Canyon and farther north the dim outline of Navajo Mountain could be seen. The great Painted Desert stretched out to the horizon, and far to the south the smoke from the smelter at Jerome could be seen, and to the west Kendrick Peak, and Bill Williams Mountain seemed only a few miles away.

How well I remember those nights at the ranch when the cowboys were not out with the wagon. Massy, the cook, always cleaned up the breakfast and dinner dishes or to be exact I should say tin plates and tin cups, for there wasn't a dish on the ranch. But after supper it was the job for two men to wash and dry the dishes, and we were supposed to take turns. We paired off, gathered at the big table, and played seven-up to decide who would wash and dry the dishes. When the decision settled on one pair, they always suggested that we play another game, and so it would continue until it became quite late. Then everybody would pitch in and clean up the dirt in no time flat.

After the weather settled a little we were out with the wagon, combing the country around Cedar Ranch, down towards

116

the Little Colorado, and west almost to the Grand Canyon Railroad. Bill Babbitt was always with us. He did not have to be there, but he liked the life. In fact, I never knew a man who enjoyed outdoor life as much as he did and he could rough it with any man in the outfit. I've seen him standing by the campfire holding his tin plate in his hands and covered with a slicker when it was raining so hard that he would have got soaked if he had sat on the ground. And I've seen him kick the snow off the ground as much as possible so that he could roll his bed out. A stranger would never have dreamed that he was one of Arizona's biggest cattlemen.

When we were out with the wagon we had no tent or any place to keep dry when it rained or snowed. We just stood around the fire, which was pretty smoky with wet wood, and took it or else went to bed and tried to imagine we were dry. Each man had his own bedroll, consisting of a canvas tarp about fourteen feet long and six or eight feet wide, six I believe to be exact. A sooghan (comfort), sometimes two if we wanted to be a little fancy, was laid down on half of the tarp. Then double blankets were made up on top of that; and when you pulled the other half of the tarp up over the blankets and tucked them all in at the sides you were ready to go to bed. Snow didn't make much difference, for you could sleep good with a blanket of it over you; but rain was a different matter after the ground got soaked. You could lay nice and comfortable with the tarp over your head listening to the rain patter on the canvas, and think how nice and comfortable the life of a cowboy was on a stormy night. What would you do with a tent anyhow? Then, just as you were drifting off into a nice snooze, you would suddenly come to with a start and declare that the campfire must be under your bed. But it wasn't. It was just rainwater that had finally run under you and soaked up through the tarp and sooghans. You could swear that it was hot; but it wasn't, it just felt that way. You soon got used to those things, though, and you learned to sleep in a water-soaked bed as sound as under a dry roof.

But in spite of all the hardships; in spite of all the hard, rough work; in spite of all the danger, it was a great life, and we had a lot of fun. We were young and healthy, and full of the love of life.

Those laborers at the tank on the mountain were a pretty good bunch. I remember one young fellow who was rather quiet, and a great reader. He read everything that he could get his hands on. When I was at the ranch Babbitt always sent me to Flag with

117

the wagon to bring back a load of supplies. Occasionally this youth would go in with me and spent the day until I was ready to return. He never drank, at least I never smelled liquor on him.

Owen Wister's *The Virginian* was a best seller at that time, and Dustin Farnum as the Virginian and Frank Campeau as the character Trampas were touring the big cities in the stage play. On one of my trips to town this young fellow came back with a copy of the book, and every time we got a chance when the owner wasn't reading that book some of us were.

Bill Babbitt had read it, and one night when we were talking about it he remarked, "Owen Wister sure knows cowboys." I thought then and I still think that that was the greatest praise I ever heard given to any book, coming as it did from a cowman who sure knew cowboys himself.

One of the principal commodities with which we stocked the ranch and the wagon was Arbuckle coffee. We drank it by the gallon, strong enough to curl your hair, but it was good. I'll bet that in those days there was more Arbuckle's sold west of the Mississippi than all other brands combined. Printed on the side of each package was "Arbuckle's Ariosa," or something like that. Just what the "Ariosa" meant or stood for nobody knew and cared less; and I doubt if "Old Man" Arbuckle himself knew. One of the boys once said that it was intended for "Arizona," but that "Old" Arbuckle did not know how to spell it.

Just about all of us carried Colt's six-shooters in those days. But make no mistake. We didn't use them to shoot each other or to shoot the town up. In fact, the so-called gunfighters never had any place with a cow outfit. We carried those guns to shoot snakes, coyotes, and other wild animals; and then if you happened to get caught afoot with some steer or mama cow with blood in their eyes, snuffing at your heels, a gun came in handy to fire into the ground just ahead of the brute. That always turned an animal. When we went to town our guns were hung up in the saddle shed in Babbitt's corral. If we failed to leave them in the shed, Ike Wheeler, the town marshal, would take charge of them and deposit them in the saloon of our choice where we could get them when we were ready to leave town or go back to the corral and to bed. . . .

And another thing; whisky was never permitted at the ranch or with the wagon. When a cowboy went to town he could get "as many sheets in the wind" as he wanted. Babbitt brothers one and all were opposed to liquor, but that wasn't the reason it was not allowed with the outfit. None of the outfits, big or little, would permit it. It was too dangerous. Whisky and cow work just did not mix in those days, like liquor and gasoline will not mix today.

• • •

In the latter part of June, 1904, we were back at Cedar Ranch with the roundup wagon, looking for strays and branding calves. One night Bill Babbitt said to me: "Forrest, you've been wanting to see the Grand Canyon. This is the nearest we'll be. Take that big workhorse we caught here, and pack your bedroll on one of your string. Ride the big horse, but watch him for he's been locoed, and you can't tell what he might do. You can leave in the morning and make it through by night. Spend the next day at the canyon. We'll go on to Moritz Lake tomorrow, and you can join us there."

It sounded like a good idea, and early the next morning I was off. I selected a sorrel horse, "Red" I called him, to pack. Cutting across the plain below the ranch I hit the old stage road that ran between Flagstaff and Grand View, over which tourists were hauled by coaches to the canyon in the days before the railroad was built from Williams. At Mesa Butte I came to the road. I made pretty good time without pushing the horses, and shortly after I passed the ruins of Moqui Station, where horses had been changed on the stages, I dismounted to tighten the ropes on the pack.

I dropped the reins of the saddle horse over his head, which we called "hitching to the ground." All saddle horses were trained to stand when this was done. I was busy at the pack, and did not watch the other horse. All at once I heard him let out a snort and away he went through the cedars. There I was left afoot, and I did the only thing possible. I pulled the pack off "Red," concealed it as best I could by a cedar, tied a hackamore with the lead rope on "Red," and started for Cedar Ranch, riding bareback. I had to make the ranch that night, for the outfit was going on to Moritz Lake the next morning, and I did not want to ride the entire distance bareback. It was bad enough going as far as Cedar Ranch, and I'm telling you I did not do any fast riding. I've been told that the plains Indians rode bareback when they hunted buffalo, and when they went into battle. I certainly pitied them. If they were ever as sore as I was long before I reached Cedar Ranch they were

119

indeed to be pitied. The outline of Mesa Butte in the darkness sure did look good to me, and when I saw the campfire at the ranch I could have shouted for joy.

The loss of the big horse wasn't anything to speak of, and Bill Babbitt told me that I should have shot him; but he had my saddle and bridle and my camera was strapped to the horn. Babbitt detailed Eli Lucero the next morning to stay at the ranch and wait for the fugitive to come in to water. There was a line of troughs in the corral, fed by a big spring on the hillside, the water from which was piped to the troughs. This was a watering place for horses and cattle, and that horse would come sooner or later for a drink.

I went on to Moritz Lake, riding with the cook on the wagon; and two days later Eli came with the horse. The reins were gone, broken off near the bit, but everything else was in place. The camera was a four by five glass plate of the folding cycle type that I carried in a case strapped to the side of the saddle horn. The only casualty was a broken ground glass which I later replaced at Flagstaff. A limb had probably hit the side of the case.

The next morning I started again for the canyon, but I took no chances with that horse. I rode him with an inch rope that the cook loaned me, tied around his neck; and every time I dismounted I tied him to a tree. I did not reach the canyon that night, for it was a long ride from Moritz Lake, and I made a dry camp. I hobbled "Red," but held the rope on the big horse while he grazed for a while. Then I tied him up for the night to a big tree that I felt certain he could not pull over, and I knew that he could not break the rope. I spent the next day at the canyon, and joined the outfit two days later at Moritz Lake.

• • •

When Bill Babbitt returned from the Kansas ranch in the spring of 1904, he brought old Bill Townsend with him. "Old Bill," I call him old because he seemed like it to us young punchers, had driven trail herds from Texas to Kansas before any of us were born, so it was natural that we should call him "Old Bill," although his mother was still living somewhere in Oklahoma. He had worked for Babbitt at the ranch south of Dodge City. He did not go out with the wagon, but spent his time riding the mountain.

I have already mentioned the big corral where we camped in Flagstaff when in town with the wagon. I have forgotten the date

120

now, but it was some time in the summer of 1904. We came into town and went to the corral as usual. We had been out with the wagon for several weeks, and we were sure a dirty, smelly crowd with whiskers all over our faces. Bill Babbitt came into the corral shortly after we arrived, and as soon as we laid eyes on him we knew that something was wrong. The habitual smile wasn't there, and a sad look was in his eyes.

"Boys, 'Old Bill' died yesterday. He got sick at the ranch, and when I got him to the hospital the doctors said he had typhoid pneumonia, and he did not last long. He's over at the undertaker's if you want to see him."

Of course we did, and so we followed Babbitt to the undertaker's "shop," for that was exactly what it was. A "funeral home" and "mortuary" were years in the future. Flagstaff was still the frontier, and men who prepared the dead for burial were not morticians; they were just plain undertakers. The "shop" was in a little one-story frame building with two small rooms. The building had been built of sheeting boards or barn siding, as it was sometimes called, with the cracks stripped.

When we entered, the undertaker was sitting at an old table that had seen much wear and probably many a poker game. His chair was of the type seen in barrooms, and he was tipped back with his feet on the table. A big sombrero adorned his head, and he wore a blue flannel shirt in spite of the hot weather. His black cloth pants were stuffed into the tops of high-heeled boots.

"We've come to see Bill Townsend," Babbitt announced, whereupon he unwound his legs from the table, got up and put on a Prince Albert coat, which I suppose he thought was the proper attire when in the presence of the dead, and led the way into the rear room.

"Old Bill" was laid out on some boards supported by two carpenter horses. He was covered with a sheet, which the undertaker laid back from his head. Then when he saw us all standing with out hats in our hands, he removed his sombrero.

I have often thought what a picture that would have made for some artist. Bill Babbitt was the only man wearing a coat. We were just as we had come in off the range; unshaven and dirty, and I remember one or two had not unbuckled their six-shooters. Most of us still had our chaps on. It was one of those pictures that live in memory as long as life lasts, and I can still see it as plain as on that day in old Flagstaff almost sixty years ago. . . .

121

No one said a word as we stood before "Old Bill" on his funeral bier. We remained there for several minutes, each busy with his own thoughts. Then someone moved; a spur jangled, and we all walked out to the requiem of jingling spurs. The next day Babbitt took Bill back to his old mother in Oklahoma.

Much to my regret I left Flagstaff in the fall of 1904, and returned to my home town of Washington, Pennsylvania. I had promised my father that I would go back some day and enter Washington and Jefferson College. Well, I kept that promise, and managed to graduate four years later; but to this day it has been a mystery how I managed it. The only explanation is that the college faculty got tired of me, for I was not what you might call a model student. Each year, by the time my last exam was over, I was on my way back to the open range.

• • •

1907 found me back with the old C O Bar. I just could not keep away. The old outfit had changed very little. "Wild Bill" Miller was the bronco twister. He was one of those picturesque cowboys who always dressed for the occasion, especially if ladies were present. He wore fringed chaps with nickled conchas down each leg, and silk shirts. His long black hair hung down to his shoulders like a great bushy mop. He was a perfect showoff, and you might think that he wasn't much of a cowhand. But make no mistake. He could ride anything with hair on or without, and he was an excellent roper. Only Eli Lucero was his superior with a lariat. We didn't know anything about his past for he never talked; but it was generally believed that he had left Montana just ahead of some sheriff.

During the bucking contest at the Fourth of July celebration in Flagstaff, Joe Isabel carried off first money when his horse tried to unseat him against a post in front of the grandstand; but "Wild Bill" came in for second place. I have often wondered when watching some of the rodeos in recent years how the riders would stack up against those horses of long ago when the only rules were: "Don't pull leather, don't ride on your spurs, and don't let daylight show between you and your saddle." You had to saddle your horse out in the open; but you were allowed a blind and a mounted helper until you climbed aboard the "hurricane deck."

Then you were on your own. The referee never blew his whistle for you to jump off. You stuck to that saddle until you either went skyward or the horse admitted that you were his master and quit. And those horses that were brought in by the different outfits were real "man killers."

Right after the Fourth celebration we started out with the wagon, scouring the country in all directions until the last of July when we held a big roundup one Sunday in the Fort Valley. Some of the Babbitts had visitors out from the East, Cincinnati I suppose, and Bill offered to show them some real Wild West right on the home grounds. They drove out to the Fort Valley that morning, and we really put on a wild west show; and I am sure that one young lady remembered it for many a day.

It was terrifically hot; and working around the branding fires and flanking big calves didn't make things any cooler. We were all hot, dirty and some rather bloody from the work of making beef steers out of those poor little defenseless calves. In flanking a big calf that was dancing around on the end of Frank Beale's rope, one hoof caught me on the side of the face as we both went down. The hoof took a patch of skin off, and blood oozed out of my hide; but I paid no attention, and continued work.

Shortly afterwards the cook yelled: "Come and get it or I'll throw it out."

Bill Babbitt thought it would be a real treat for those eastern guests to eat cowboy chuck at a real roundup wagon. Everybody got their eatin' tools from the box on the wagon, filled up our tin plates and coffee tins, and squatted around on the ground. The guests were most happy to do "as Romans do." After I got all my fixin's I "filed a claim" on the ground next to a very attractive young lady. That was why I took it up. As luck would have it I sat down with the bloody side of my face next to her. No, I didn't do that on purpose. Someone else had preempted the land on the other side of this young lady.

I don't believe that girl ate two bites. Maybe she did because I was busy with my own plate, and she may have got a few bites into her mouth that I didn't see. At any rate when she looked at me and saw that bloody, dirty, bewhiskered face she lost her appetite. That poor girl just couldn't take her eyes off my face. I wondered at first what she was looking at. Then I suddenly realized what must have happened and, dirty barbarian that I was, I delighted in the situation.

123

• • •

That was a great roundup, and we sure did put on a good show for those Easterners; Buffalo Bill never did any better. The roping was fine, the cutting excellent, and after the herd was turned loose, Eli Lucero gave an excellent exhibition of riding a pitching horse; and Eli sure could ride. The smell was typical of a roundup—branding—burned hair, sizzling flesh all mixed in with a few other odors found around a herd of cattle, all bad enough to send a skunk scurrying for the tall timber.

• • •

The Old Arizona that I knew was a wonderful land, a land where you could ride for days without being turned aside by barbed or Page woven wire. It was all open range, and what that meant only the cowboys of over a half century ago can understand. You could ride to the top of a hill and survey a land in which you were king. We were just a short distance as time goes, from the days of Indian warfare. Geronimo had surrendered only twenty years before. Several warriors who had escaped from his band still raided occasionally across the border from Mexico, and the Apache Kid was still a menace with a price on his head. The bloody Pleasant Valley War was a vivid memory to many of the older cowboys I knew. Up in the C O Bar country the Navajos occasionally got a little ugly over a clash with cowboys about a water hole; and northeast Arizona was then Indian country. The Arizona of those long-ago years was a wonderful land in which to have been young, and we who are left love the memories of it today.

Arizona's First Forest Ranger

Joseph Garrison Pearce

Arizona is famous for her beautiful deserts, the haven of winter visitors. The glowing red rocks of Sedona are unforgettable in the twilight; the formations in Monument Valley bespeak a brooding grandeur that makes human actions seem insignificant and transitory in comparison.

But there is another Arizona beyond the deserts that many casual travelers often fail to see—the forests. Arizona's vast forest lands are a rich natural asset. Greater in area than the woodlands of Wisconsin or Maine, these forests provide lumber for building, protection for watersheds, homes for wildlife, and areas for man's rest and recreation. Eight national forests contain almost three-fourths of the state's timber. And the largest stand of ponderosa pine in the nation grows in Arizona's high country.

In these vast wooded lands seemingly so serene, danger lurks in the threat of fire. A careless sportsman neglecting to drown a campfire or grind out a cigarette can leave the slumbering ember that ignites a holocaust for both man and animal. In the driest seasons, when the forest becomes natural tinder, the risk is greatest. But a summer shower that erupts into an electrical storm can trigger scattered fires sparked by lightning. Against these perils there is little protection except the watchful eyes of the forest ranger.

Joseph Garrison Pearce, whose memoir is reprinted here, was the first forest ranger in Arizona, supervising the Black Mesa Forest reserve. Born in St. George, Utah, in 1874, Pearce moved with his parents to Apache County when he was four years old. He grew up in the Mogollon Rim country and developed an intimate knowledge of the land and the people. In 1903 Pearce joined the Arizona Rangers, a small body of dedicated peace officers who helped keep order in the turbulent years before statehood. Pearce died in March 1958 at eighty-four, having seen the forest service grow into an organized and sophisticated modern force. And yet, the danger has not changed. Despite modern electronics and mechanization, the service is still dependent in modern times, as it was in pioneer Arizona, upon the special qualities of brave and astute forest rangers.

My most important duty as the first forest ranger in Arizona, then the same as now, was fighting fires. But in April 1899, when I was appointed, the chief cause of fires wasn't the stub of a cigarette or a careless campfire, but the intent and purpose of the Apache Indians, whose reservation bordered on the Black Mesa Forest. They set the fires deliberately for the smoke. They had a sincere belief or superstition that smoke would bring rain. And in the driest seasons, when the forest was all ready to burn like tinder, up would pop a big fire near the boundary of the reservation. And you couldn't catch them at it.

Before Teddy Roosevelt took a hand in his conservation program, had dams built and set aside national forests, the Black Mesa forest had no attention at all. The only folks interested in checking fires were the cowmen and sheepmen of the region, and they got interested only if their ranges were threatened.

That was a great stretch of timber I patrolled, alone at first, and then with several rangers under me and a title as chief ranger. It was the largest stretch of untouched virgin timber in the United States, and so reported to President Roosevelt by Gifford Pinchot of Pennsylvania, who was then chief United States forester under the original Roosevelt and who inspected the forest with me while I was a ranger. My territory included land from Flagstaff east to the New Mexico line, and from Springerville south to Clifton, a stretch larger than a couple of those New England states.

The Black Mesa Forest Reservation included the White and the Blue mountains, country almost unknown to the white man, range on range and ridge on ridge of thick close-standing pine and blue spruce and wide groves of white aspen, interrupted by

From the Joseph Garrison Pearce Collection, unpublished manuscript, 65–81, Arizona Historical Society Library, Tucson, Arizona. Used with permission from the Arizona Historical Society.

clearings in the valleys where no trees grew. There were very few trails. Some of the timber was thicker than a jungle to get through.

The forest was alive with game. . . . The streams ran full of trout, with not enough fishermen to keep them caught out. When I was a boy, the turkey came down within a mile of our ranch at Taylor, and we could hear them gobbling in the spring. But as the country settled up, they moved back into the mountains. The forest was thick with deer, every kind, black-tail, mule, white-tail. And I couldn't ride a day in the forest without seeing a flock of antelope streak over the hills and into the canyons, their white rumps bouncing. Mountain lions had their hide-outs deep in the forest, and from their caves sneaked out into civilized country to prey on sheep and newborn calves. Sometimes I spotted mountain sheep high on the ridges.

This was the kind of forest that was to be my home for three years, and I liked it. I liked my job. I knew much of the country from boyhood except for the deep parts of the forest. And I was able to take care of myself in the toughest spots—handy with an axe, handy with a horse, and even handier with a gun. My wages [were] sixty a month, and I had to mount myself with horse and pack horse, and feed the stock myself. . . . Later as chief ranger I was paid more money.

The toughest fire I had to fight was the one at Pinedale, and how I handled it makes an interesting story, I think. A cowboy came racking along at top speed to my headquarters at Nutrioso to tell me that a fire was blazing away at Baker's Butte and Long Valley, and the cattlemen were unable to check it. That was in the spring of '99.

My horse and pack horse were grain fed and in fine condition, and I had them packed and saddled and ready to go in fifteen minutes. In two and a half days I was in Long Valley, almost two hundred miles away, and much of the trip over mountain trails. I pushed those horses. When I arrived I summoned more help, cattlemen and sheepmen anywhere I could get hold of them, putting them on government pay. It took three days for forty men to get that fire under control. Smoke-blackened and tired, but satisfied, those stockmen returned to their ranches, with an order for two dollars a day wages from the Government in their pockets.

On my return along the Tonto Rim I bumped into the Pinedale fire mentioned above. It had no doubt been started by the Apaches, for it had nothing to do with the Long Valley fire. It was boiling along south of Pinedale, a settlement of twenty families in log houses. A south wind fed it and whipped it, and Pinedale was direct in the path of the fire. What made it worse, the folks at Pinedale, having need of logs for one thing and another, had cut down a great many of the trees surrounding the settlement and had left the dead branches scattered everywhere on the ground. If the fire got to those dead branches nothing could stop it. I didn't have much hope of saving the town.

But I rousted out every available man, promising them two dollars a day from the Government. I arranged for supplies at the Pinedale store, corralled axes and shovels and picks from everywhere, hired a cook to keep the men fed and have hot coffee available every minute.

Mounted and on foot we rushed south three miles through the pines to the fighting line. There was a fire! The smoke had piled up into a thick gray-black mist that made the sun the color of blood. With smoke stinging our eyes, we could see the red flames crawl up a hundred-foot pine tree in half a minute, and then like as not the pine tree would go down with a shivering crash. We saw the fire leap twenty, thirty, forty yards from one tree to the next. The fire was so hot we could only face it a minute or two and then had to turn our backs or move away.

I set the men to beating out the flames with green pine branches where the fire ate through the dry grass. This had been successful with other fires but now did no good at all. When we had the grass smudging and the fire almost out on the ground, the wind would make it jump clear over us to a pine tree behind us, and there it would crackle and snap through the green branches.

Stronger remedies had to be used. I ordered the men back some distance, and here we began to cut down a fire barrier two rods wide, chopping down the trees, cutting them up and rolling them out of the way, slashing out the bushes or pulling them up by the roots, raking dead pine needles and brush to one side. When the barrier was ready, we tried a back fire along the distance I thought we could control.

For awhile it looked like we had licked the fire. The back fire slowed it down, and we had great hopes it would burn itself out behind the barrier. But then the southwest wind blew up stronger, and one place or another it began to jump over our barrier.

The men were tired, back-weary, some of them slightly burned and most of them singed in their beards and hair, faces

129

black from smoke. They shrugged when the fire leaped over, spat on their hands, chawed a little harder on their tobacco. They was willing, but they couldn't do it. I needed more men. We had to build new barriers, fight harder. They couldn't do it. Yet I had called out every available man I could find. More than ever it looked like Pinedale would burn up.

I was about ready to butt my head against a tree trying to think where I could get more men. Then I had it. Why not? I grinned at the idea. It was worth a try, anyhow, I decided, and leaving instructions to the men how to continue fighting the fire, I saddled up and rode to the Cooley ranch, some twenty miles away and twenty miles north of Fort Apache. At Cooley ranch was the nearest telegram, and from there I sent the following message:

> Commanding Officer, Fort Apache:
> Forest fire, originating inside reservation, burning north to top of mountain, now moving fast toward Pinedale. Unable to check it. Send all available scouts and Indian police to Pinedale with three days' rations.
> Joe Pearce, U. S. F. R.

That was my idea. The Apaches had likely started the fire. Why shouldn't they help to stop it?

Thirty mounted Apaches, riding plumb wore-out ponies, reached Pinedale at dusk of that same day and went immediately south to the fire line, where I put them to work extending the fire barrier, cutting a new barrier where the fire had crossed beyond control on the other side. Some I kept busy beating out with green pine branches the spots where the fire crossed but could be controlled. I had some sixty or seventy men in all now, and worked them in relays. From behind the line drinking water was brought up on mule back and in camp the cook kept steaming hot coffee ready all the time.

We held back that fire until the direction of the wind changed, and the fire died out on its own accord. The Apaches had saved Pinedale. I sent back the following note by the scout Skippinjoe to the commanding officer at Fort Apache.

130

Your scouts and police saved the day. Pinedale was saved from going up in smoke. Good fire fighters and not afraid to fight. Many thanks.

Joe Pearce, U. S. F. R.

The tame animals in the Black Mesa Forest, the stock, caused me more trouble than the wild ones did. Just one example or two of dozens will show what I mean. It was part of my work to estimate the number of sheep and cattle using the forest and collect the government fee for grazing privileges. But the hard-bitten sheep- and cattlemen couldn't get this new idea into their heads and regarded the land as theirs. They weren't even willing to secure the proper permit for grazing privileges.

Many times I've come on close-packed flocks using forest land and have ordered them off, and more often than not they refused to go, the owners claiming the land had been theirs for forty years and they'd be damned if they'd give it up now, government or no government. When this happened it was my duty to report them to my head, W. H. Buntain, forest superintendent at Santa Fe, New Mexico, and secure warrants for their arrest. A few arrests and trials, with stiff fines, began to make the stockmen change their minds.

There was a bearded old-timer, a sheepman and a nester in a little shack on government lands. I went up to his shack peaceable enough for the third time.

"Come in," he says to my knock. He was cooking breakfast when I went in, looked me over scowling, went back to his cooking. "It's you again! What's on your mind this time, young feller?"

I told him, "Just wanted to make a little collection for the Government on your sheep. I'll need to make a little round-up to count 'em."

He turned around then, eyes on fire, and braced heavy on the flats of both feet. "You see the door there?"

"Sure I see it."

"Know what it's for?"

"Reckon so."

"Listen here, young feller. I pay the Territory and the County taxes on my sheep and goats. I'd like to see the color of a man's hair that'll make me pay my taxes twice in Arizona. You see that door?"

131

"I seen it already," I said. "I judge you want me to use it." I walked outside and he followed me and stood in the doorway. "I'm coming back," I told him, "and when I come there'll be ten rangers with me, and we'll round you up."

"Like hell you will!" He slammed the door shut.

But I returned with two other rangers and a warrant for his arrest, and in the end he paid the fee—about eighty cents a year per sheep—and in addition a stiff fine. There wasn't any more trouble collecting from him after that.

The wild horses in the Black Mesa Forest and other reservations caused trouble, but this didn't come until after my time as a ranger. I'm glad of that because I've always been a lover of horses, and I'd have hated to carry out the government order to clean out the mavericks.

There was reason enough for such an order. Wild horses were a bother and a nuisance because they used forage that might just as well be used by sheep and cattle that were of some use to man. The order specified in addition that any branded stock should be killed also, after the owner had been duly notified and had failed to remove his property from the forest land. A little sense in carrying out this order would have saved a mess of trouble.

But the rangers went to killing cowponies as well as mavericks, fine saddle stock worth a hundred dollars and up per head. One ranger named Fears shot several head belonging to a rancher named Trammel, and Trammel filed a criminal complaint against Fears, charging him with wantonly and maliciously destroying his animals. A stockman jury convicted him, but on appeal his case was thrown out of court on the grounds that he was merely carrying out orders.

In another case the stockmen warned a ranger who had been killing saddle horses that this was a very unhealthy climate for a man that would shoot down horses on an open range. The ranger replied that he represented the U. S. Government and intended to keep on carrying out his orders just the way he had been doing. A few days later he vanished, and no trace of him was ever found.

• • •

Besides fighting fires and collecting range fees and helping settle disputes, I had other jobs as a forest ranger, everyday jobs. Blazing trails, posting fire notices, marking timber to be cut.

132

After Pinchot's report about the value of the timber in the Black Mesa Forest, the McNary Lumber Company was organized in the East and got a contract from the government to cut standing timber. In the national forests, though, the Government doesn't permit a company to go through a section cutting down all timber. Where timber is thickest I had to mark trees for cutting, while a good healthy pine standing alone I left as seed pine.

Each tree to be cut had to have two notches, one above the cut and one that would remain on the stump. In the mill each log had to have a U.S. cut into it, and I had to estimate the number of board feet in each log and make a report of how many board feet had been cut. For this I used a Scribner and Doyle snap rule, getting the diameter of the smaller end of a log and then doing a little figuring.

I trail blazed on horseback, scalping the bark of the tree about six feet above the ground, which was safe above the snow line, usually about four feet. I made trails to possible fire areas and trails that could be used crossing the mountain and trails to springs that stock and humans might use. I cleaned out and deepened the springs.

Generally in trail blazing over rough country I would follow the backbone of a ridge, as this was usually the safest and best way down off a high place. One could stay away from the ups and downs of gorges and canyons.

I got well acquainted with those mountains, living there for three years alone and during the fire season on the move all the time. I've often been lost in a storm. There are two kinds of lost: being turned around and being stranded. For being turned around there's one way to safety that I've never known to fail. A good horse—not a bronc, mind you—but a good saddle horse will always remember the last place where he has had feed and water, and he will know the way there, give him his head. In a storm if I've thought the horse could make it and I could stand the severe cold, and my *cabeza* was twisted about where I was, I'd just say, "Come on, Bob. Let's go home." A man never needs to be lost riding a gentle horse.

Storm stranded is another matter. I've been in snow so thick with whirlwinds in those mountains I couldn't see ten feet in front of my nose, and blizzards howling for three days without letup. In a storm like that there's no use trying to go on; you have to make some kind of shelter for yourself. A hatchet was always part of my equipment.

I'd unload my pack horse and unsaddle my horse and leave the stock to shift for themselves. Then I'd stretch my rope from one pine to another, cut branches from the small pines and lean them slantwise on each side of the rope. When I was done, there was a cozy shelter. Next I'd collect dry wood—and a forest man can always find it—and pile the wood inside, build me a fire. There I'd lie snug with my fire and wait for the storm to run itself down.

When Pinchot came for his inspection of the Black Mesa Forest, I took him along a trail I'd blazed some time before beyond Alpine southward toward Clifton. We came to the place the Blue Range breaks off almost sheer, and down below the mountains roll away toward Clifton.

Pinchot said: "Guess we'll have to turn around and go back. We can't get down off this mountain, Joe."

Then I told him I'd blazed the trail down there so that a rider could get through to Clifton. To prove it, we went down, leading our horses.

That evening in camp I asked him: "Do you think there'll ever be a wagon road there, down the Blue Range to the flats?"

He got a laugh out of that. "There'll never even be a good horse trail," he said. "The only way a man'll ever get down there easily is to grow wings and fly down."

That was forty years ago. And now every day automobiles go along through there and roll down the slopes of the Blue Range following almost exact the trail I blazed in 1899, now the Coronado Trail.

Indian Trader at Keams Canyon

Joseph Schmedding

In contrast to the cowboy, the cavalryman, and the settler, the Indian trader is probably the least-known participant in the saga of the southwestern frontier. Bridging the gulf between Indians and whites, the trader was a controversial but often positive figure.

Spending one's days in a remote Indian trading post might have been nothing more than "clerking" in the desert or some isolated canyon, but for Joseph Schmedding it was a fascinating and profitable mercantile adventure as well as a unique opportunity to live within the Navajo culture. As the trader at Keams Canyon from 1916 to 1923, Schmedding observed and recorded daily life with the combined skills of an amateur anthropologist and essayist.

Although his formal education ended at the tenth grade, this German immigrant had special preparation outside the classroom. At sixteen he succumbed to the lure of cowboy mythology and headed West. With incredible good fortune he became associated with two of the most able and respected men in ranching in the Southwest. His first job was as a bronc buster for William Calhoun McDonald, the manager of the El Capitan Land and Cattle Company empire in New Mexico Territory and later New Mexico's first elected governor. At eighteen Schmedding went to work for Richard Wetherill, the well-known horse rancher, trader, explorer, and amateur archaeologist. From both these men Schmedding learned the cowboy's craft. And especially under Wetherill's tutelage, he developed the absorbing interests, attitudes, and habits of mind that enriched his adult life.

Schmedding relinquished his trader's license in 1923. At thirty-seven he began another series of careers that took him from the J. Walter Thompson Advertising Agency in New York to a medical laboratory in Hollywood, California, with sojourns in West Africa, Mexico, and Cuba along the way. Written late in Schmedding's life when he was confined to a wheelchair, these memoirs re-create a world and a way of life that vanished with the frontier.

The trading post in Keams Canyon is one of the oldest and best known in the entire Navajo country, dating its establishment back to Kit Carson's time. Prior to my taking over the place, it had had but two other owners—I was the third proprietor and trader in that particular store. Every Indian family within a radius of some two hundred miles was acquainted with the Keams Canyon trading post. Through successive generations of trading [with] Indians, it had become well and favorably known. The accumulated good will of a large clientele was something intangible, but very valuable.

I arrived at the post in the middle of winter, coming from Gallup, New Mexico, by way of St. Michaels, Ganado, and Steamboat Canyon, riding in a heavy-duty, open buckboard. The trip consumed two days, and in many places the road was obliterated by the snowdrifts. From Gallup to Ganado, it was fairly easy traveling, the road being kept open by the mail stages. After stopping overnight at Ganado, where Lorenzo Hubbell, Sr., was a gracious host, [we continued the trip] early in the morning, but instead of having just a two-horse team, the second stage of the journey was behind a doubled-up outfit, the buckboard now drawn by four horses.

• • •

A slight bend in the road prevented us from seeing the lights which could have told us that we had about reached the goal. The trader's residence was upon a knoll and some fifty feet to the upper side of the trail, and the trading post itself on the opposite side of a depression, hence we did not realize that we had arrived until we were practically upon the very doorsteps of the store. Our driver's shout brought several men to the door, and when that

From Joseph Schmedding, *Cowboy and Indian Trader* (Caldwell, Idaho: The Caxton Printers, Ltd., 1951), 309–346. Used with permission from The Caxton Printers, Ltd.

136

swung wide and let out a bright stream of light, we began untangling ourselves from the robes and blankets wound about us. Cold-stiffened fingers made that a difficult job, but there were willing hands to assist us.

We were pretty well frozen, a tired and hungry lot by the time the stage pulled up in front of the Keams Canyon trading post. However, once being assisted from the buckboard, and supported for a moment or two to allow the numbed bodies to regain their own abilities, we thawed out quickly. One of the store clerks led the way to the residence. There, a Hopi girl, who was both cook and housekeeper, showed us to a bedroom. It boasted a fireplace, with a fire already laid and waiting the touch of a match. In a short while the flames dispersed the refrigerator-like chill of the unused room and spread welcome warmth.

Lorenzo Hubbell, Jr., the trader, had remained at the store to take care of the unloading of the mail and our baggage, assisted in that by one of the clerks and his bookkeeper, Elias Amrijo. The Indian driver, and, of course, the teams, were looked after and properly provided for. Then Mr. Hubbell joined us at the residence to make sure that we were comfortable. By then, thoroughly thawed out, and after putting the baby to bed, we were ready to enjoy a hot supper prepared by the young Hopi woman. Soon after having refreshed ourselves, we retired to our bedroom and a much-needed and most welcome rest.

The general terms and conditions of the sale of the trading post had been agreed upon in Gallup some weeks previous to our coming, but the evaluation of the stock on hand was, of necessity, postponed until our arrival. With that work, Mr. Hubbell and I started early the following morning, and for two days we continued listing the amounts of goods in the store, basement cellar, in the warehouse and adjacent storage spaces. Then the completed inventory had to be priced and figured, which required an additional two days. After that was done, we spent another day arranging the matter of several thousands of dollars' worth of Indian pawns. Between the various matters to be attended to, it took nearly a week in which to complete the business of turning over the post and residence with all stocks and other possessions.

While I was familiar with the usual assortment of trade items to be found in trading posts, I was dumbfounded when confronted by Mr. Hubbell's stock of Hopi Indian pottery. He had stored the accumulation of years of trading in a long, shedlike room, putting the pieces as he received them into cases of every shape and size, and when he showed me this immense quantity of pottery there were at least thirty or more large containers filled to the very top. He had taken large dry-goods packing cases and used them to store away the pottery. From the floor to the roof of the room, every square foot of space was occupied, leaving just enough room to walk.

There must have been tens of thousands of pieces in that lot—I never learned the exact amount. In size and shape they ranged from small pieces of finger-bowl shape to large ollas; others resembled punch bowls and urns, and many pieces were of tall vaselike appearance. Several large cases were filled completely with shallow, platelike plaques. For many I could not find a suitable description; Mark Twain might have classified them as Etruscan tear jugs. All were decorated by hand with the characteristic Hopi designs; many were real showpieces, and of decided artistic value. But what to do with a stock of that size, in a place remote from the railroad, without any regular tourist trade or other means of selling the stuff? It would have been a wearisome job just to count the lot, or to segregate the mass into respective cost values and appraise the accumulation in its entirety.

Hubbell, who was moving to a new location, some forty miles away from Keams Canyon, did not relish the prospect of carting the fragile pottery over badly rutted winter roads and then cluttering up his new post with it.

That was quite evident, and helped to bring about his resolve to turn the whole lot over to me at a round sum, a nominal valuation of just a few hundred dollars for all of it. To that offer I agreed, figuring that I should surely be able to turn the pottery at a profit, even if some time might be required to do so.

In that I was not mistaken, as each year at Snake Dance time, the visitors from the outside world would pick up dozens of pieces, to take with them as mementos of their trip to the Hopi Indians. Throughout the year a steady sale disposed of single pieces, or just a few at a time, to tourists, salesmen, government employees, and others. The biggest sale of pottery, however, was made to B. Altman & Co., New York, whose vice-president came to Keams Canyon one day and bought three thousand assorted pieces, all sizes, leaving the selection to me. That one transaction netted me twice the original cost of the entire stock, and still left thousands of pieces of pottery in my possession.

138

Eventually, the work of inventorying was accomplished, the figuring completed, and the final papers signed. Mr. Hubbell, accompanied by Elias, the bookkeeper, and another one of his clerks left for the Hopi pueblo of Oraibi, where he meant to continue in his trading activities, and I was, at last, in full possession of Keams Canyon, one of the best-known and most influential Indian trading posts in the country.

Many Indians had flocked to Keams Canyon while we were engaged with the work of making the transfer of ownership—all were curious to see what was going on, to take a look at the prospective new owner, and to learn about the disposition of their valuables, left as pawn in the past. Hubbell introduced us to each other, bespeaking their continued patronage for the newcomer and assuring them that their silver, buckskins, beads, and other pledged items were in safe hands and would not be sold by me, but guarded carefully until such time as they could redeem them.

That same guaranty was given the Indian agent, to whom I was introduced, and who had already been approached by several Indians who were uneasy over the possibility of losing their family jewelry and other valuables among the pawned articles.

• • •

An Indian trading post's stock of merchandise makes one think of the old-time country store, where just about everything was to be had. The post is not merely a grocery store, but also a hardware store. Too, it carries dry goods, clothing, hats, shoes, notions, patent medicines, harness, saddlery items, fencing, nails, horseshoes, and stock salt. The larger posts, such as Keams Canyon, also have on hand several types of wagons, suited to the country, up to and including the heavy freighters. Thus, anything the Indian customers may want, from a needle to a big freight wagon, is to be found at the trading post.

One item of Hubbell's stock which was turned over to me was something I had not previously seen in an Indian trading post: several wooden cases with nursing bottles, and a corresponding number of rubber nipples!

I did not know what to make of that, knowing that the Indian mothers had no scruples about nursing their babies, and were not conscious of having to "save their figures." But here were hundreds of bottles and nipples, in a country that recognized no wet nurse.

139

When Hubbell saw my astonishment over the presence of these items, he explained that the Navajos trading in Keams Canyon were steady customers for bottles and nipples, using them to feed lambs which had lost their mothers. This I found to be true, and over the course of years brought in many more cases of those nursing utensils. Apparently, loss and breakage was high in the lambing camps, which helped swell the turnover of bottles in the store.

• • •

Both the brave and the squaw are good shoppers, and as "brand conscious" as the whites. It is difficult to introduce new brands, particularly in the food and dry-good lines, and I learned through costly experience that it does not pay to go against the stream in the matter of attempting to substitute unknown goods for articles in long-established demand.

To make this clearer, I shall name some of the preferred brands, although this is not to imply that other goods are not just as good, and possibly even better. However, the Navajo shopper insists upon certain brands, and the trader simply must supply them.

That applies to Arbuckle's "Ariosa" coffee, both the whole bean and the ground product. Navajos and Hopis alike prefer this particular brand above all others. At different times I tried to introduce other coffees, packaged in a similar manner, but had no success. For the occasional white trade, the post carried Hills Bros., Maxwell House, Iris, Edwards, Folger's, Sanka, and one or two other coffees, but those brands did not appeal to the Indians. If for some reason or other they could not get "Ariosa," they would take none. Incidentally, price did not influence the customers. At different times, less expensive brands were tried, but "Ariosa" remained the preference.

The men would not buy any other but either "Star" or "Horseshoe" chewing tobacco, and only "Bull Durham" suited them for smoking.

The squaws had similar well-defined preferences for the brands of flour and baking powder. At one time we were forced to resack several hundred bags of flour because the mill had stamped a wolf's head on the white bags. To the Navajos it looked like a coyote's head—enough to make that flour taboo!

140

The accepted brands included Stetson hats from Philadelphia, Levi Strauss overalls from San Francisco, and Indian robes
and shawls bearing the blue and gold label of the Pendleton Wool-
en Mills in Pendleton, Oregon. The latter consisted of the selvage
robes worn by the men, and the gorgeously fringed shawls which
were bought by and for the squaws.

Heavy stock saddles, both plain and hand-tooled, came from
famous makers in Miles City, Montana, and Pueblo, Colorado. They
had to be "double-rigged," meaning that they were equipped with
both front and rear cinches, and not too large-skirted, as the Indian
ponies were mostly short coupled. The round-skirted, three-quarter
rig, favored by many cowboys in that section of the Southwest, did
not appeal to the Indians. The saddle horn had to be leather- or
rawhide-covered. When a saddlery had shipped several saddles
with bright, nickled horns, I had to hire an Indian to cover them by
braiding rawhide over them. Those smooth, shiny metal surfaces do
not allow a satisfactory grip to the reata when roping stock. Still
more objectionable is the blinding reflection upon the eyes when
the rider is under the sun's rays.

• • •

Goods purchased from the more distant supply houses
were sent by freight, express, or parcel post. If freight or express,
they would be addressed to Holbrook or Winslow in Arizona; or to
Gallup, New Mexico, as requested in the order. From the respective freight stations or express offices, the packages would be
picked up by the first freighter sent into town, and brought out to
the canyon with other freight.

Generally the Indian teams would go into Gallup, or
Holbrook or Winslow—all of these points being approximately
equally distant from Keams Canyon. There they would unload the
wool, hides, or other goods they had taken in, then load up with
the merchandise ordered from the wholesaler. That would include
calicos, unbleached muslin, canned goods, notions, gloves, quilts,
wool cards (for carding wool, preparatory to spinning), hardware
items, stock salt, dyes, and the thousand and one other items in
regular demand in the trading post. Sometimes, wagons were loaded with just one single item, as once when an order included four
thousand pounds of salt. At different times, the wagons carried

141

solid loads of lumber, used for repairs, rebuilding of counters and shelves, and for the erection of new buildings.

I recall one time when the wagons coming from the railroad carried two hundred cases of one hundred pounds each of Arbuckle's "Ariosa"—ten tons of coffee! The total weight, in fact, exceeded that because each wooden case added some twenty-eight pounds to the weight of the contents.

Many staple grocery items, both dry and canned, had to be bought in large quantities to insure a stock supply through those months when weather and road conditions made freighting impossible. The heaviest freighting took place in late summer and early fall, when the summer cloudbursts had ended, insuring good grazing and plentiful water along the trail, and before the coming of snowstorms. After the first snows, freighting came, automatically, to a standstill.

• • •

The interior of the Keams Canyon post did not differ from the conventional arrangement of other trading stores. Upon entering, one saw counters running the full length of the store at both right and left sides, and also at the rear, forming a large U. Back of the counters, shelves ranged upward to about eight feet from the floor, while the space above the shelves was used for suspending various articles of merchandise. From nails and pegs driven into the walls, and also into the exposed roof beams, dangled pots and pans, pails, galvanized tubs, slickers, assorted saddlery and harness items, lengths of rope, wool cards, tanned buckskins, whips, quirts, canvas water bags, a piece of oil-tanned calfskin from which are cut narrow strips for latigos, and in one section a bar made of an old broom handle holding "dead" pawn, the designation for unredeemed pledges.

When pledged silver belts, beads, bracelets, saddle blankets, or other articles are not redeemed after a specified period, or after wool season or sheep-selling season, the trader will take out of his pawn closet the items which are "dead." Those he will string up or otherwise put on display in the store, which action automatically notifies the owner that unless he redeems his valuables quickly, they will be sold. Friends, acquaintances, or members of his family or relations, who happen to see the display,

142

promptly inform the owner that his treasurers are now offered for sale. Usually he comes to the trading post in a hurry, either to redeem the pledges, or to persuade the trader to grant him an extension.

The trader holds the pawns with the understanding that they be redeemed when the sale of rugs, wool, or livestock gives the Indian enough cash to take care of his obligations. However, if he finds that his faith has been misplaced and that the customer who used him for a convenience when broke, goes to some other trader when he has a load of wool to sell, then the trader is justified in disposing of the "dead" pawn. Generally, such pawned articles are snapped up by other Navajos, since the trader does not sell them at a profit, but at the actual amount of the loan. Of course, if unredeemed pledges are disposed of to chance tourists, or sent to some of the wholesalers or Indian-craft specialty shops which are always on the lookout for such items, they bring their legitimate market value. However, traders generally "lean backward" in the matter of holding pawns, and often carry some article for a long time, taking on-account payments, and increasing the loan through additional advances if the owner finds it necessary to ask for more credit. The Indian considers the collateral a sort of bank account, drawing against it, when need arises, and paying off in convenient installments as he is able.

It is impossible to carry on a trading business without handling pawns, although that means tying up considerable sums. The capital invested does not accumulate interest, since a trader is not permitted to charge that. The sole benefit the trader derives from the pawn business is the profit from the sale of the merchandise (since no cash is advanced on pawns) and whatever good will accrues to him for accommodating the Indians. At all times the trader has to be careful that the pawn is not "sold" to him. If he advances too much credit against the value of the article, he will find that the Indian who pledged it does not come back, either as a customer or as a redeemer of the pawn. The trader is simply stuck with something that he finds has been overvalued.

The counters in the store were about forty inches high, and fully three feet wide. That was to discourage shoplifting and pilfering from the shelves. It was virtually impossible for anyone to reach across the high and wide counters and span the equally wide aisle back of the counters to grasp any of the merchandise displayed

143

on the shelves. Experience had proved that these precautions were necessary, virtually all of the Indians being kleptomaniacs, to use a polite term.

In a number of trading posts some sections of the counters were protected by close-mesh wire screens. All posts that I ever visited had heavy iron bars across the window opening to discourage burglary. The store in Keams Canyon was similarly protected. Doors were double locked and equipped with stout drop bars, all of which demonstrated that the traders did not place too much reliance in the nobility of the red man. In the James Fenimore Cooper "Leatherstocking" tales and in the Karl May series of "Old Shatterhand" Western stories, we are introduced to some noble redskins endowed with wonderful qualities and characteristics. It is unlikely that any Indian trader ever encountered the living counterparts of those Cooper and May heroes. After some disappointing and disillusioning experiences, the trader discovers that the milk of human kindness is about to turn to clabber in his breast. Thereafter he puts his trust in divine protection and strengthens that faith by employing stout bars and strong locks.

The trader has to trust in the iron bars, heavy padlocks, the barred doors to safeguard his goods against burglary, but that still leaves him without the comfort of fire insurance. In those isolated posts, far away from organized fire departments, without adequate water supply and in the absence of hydrants and sprinkler systems, fire insurance companies do not issue policies. If they did, the premiums would be so high as to be prohibitive.

• • •

The trader is both buyer and seller. In order to sell his trade goods to the Indian, who but seldom has money, it becomes necessary first to buy whatever the Indian offers for sale. That may include a wide variety of commodities and articles. Throughout the entire year the Navajos have blankets used for rugs. Too, there is a steady trade in sheep pelts and goatskins, since the meat of those animals is part of the staple foods of the Navajos. The pelts and skins of the slaughtered animals are pegged out, or hung up to dry, and later taken to the most convenient trading post where they are exchanged for coffee, sugar, flour, and other necessities.

In years when the piñons produce a good crop of piñon nuts, the trader will take in varying amounts of those delicious

144

nuts. At the end of good seasons, the Hopis may take large quantities of shelled Indian corn to the trader. While the piñon nuts are shipped to the railroad towns and sold to the supply houses, the trader usually stores the corn and resells it to the Indians in smaller amounts through the winter months, both for human consumption and for stock feed.

The Navajo silversmiths trade the products of their forges and anvils; the Hopis bring in many specimens of their pottery. Wildcat and mountain lion skins are brought in by hunters, baskets and plaques by the Hopi squaws who are experts in basketry.

The really big trading seasons are the periods during which the wool clip is brought in, and the one which sees the sale of sheep, lambs, horses, or cattle. At those times the Indian receives hundreds of dollars in a lump sum, and as a rule will spend virtually the entire amount in the trading post. First, he redeems his pawns, then he loads up his wagon with quantities of foodstuffs. After that, he may buy a new wagon or saddle, or make other purchases of the more expensive goods, such as Pendleton robes and shawls, Stetson hats, many yards of velveteen for squaw skirts and shirts for both men and women, and other items bought rarely at ordinary times.

The trader purchases all and everything that is brought to him, paying for it in silver dollars. Paper money is held in disfavor by the Indians. Many do not know the difference between the various denominations of bills, and paper is too easily destroyed. Therefore, silver is the universal medium of exchange. However, since the Indian has no safe place in his hogan, he is inclined to spend nearly all of the money received, keeping only a nominal amount for future needs.

In times past some traders made use of so-called "seco" money, which designated brass trade chips, stamped with the name of the trading post, and saying: "Good for fifty cents," or whatever value it might have at that particular store. This practice is now outlawed. To persuade the Indian to accept this one-store "money," it was customary to offer a premium for trade in "seco." For example, the trader might offer eight dollars for a blanket if taken in silver, but would go to ten dollars if the Indian agreed to accept "seco."

The usual procedure of a big transaction is something like this: After the price has been agreed upon, trader and customer return from the warehouse, where the wool was weighed, to the store. If he has a private room or office, the trader goes to that—the Indian preferring to do business where hungry onlookers cannot watch over every phase of the deal. The amount due him for the wool (or whatever else it may be) is counted out to him in stacks of silver dollars. Often the money is divided between the brave and squaw, and maybe even into three or more parts, each taking his or her share. Just how the division is arrived at is difficult to understand since it is not on a fifty-fifty or other proportionate basis.

After the money has been paid over, the Indian will take it into the store and begin buying, or he may, as happened often, shove a stack or two of the silver back toward me, and say: "Flour!" On a memorandum I would mark the number of sacks of flour the money would buy, and tell him just how much he had bought. Another stack of dollar pieces would come, and the single word "Sugar," which meant another notation on the shopping slip. More stacks followed for coffee, baking powder, canned goods of various kinds, all noted down on the slip. Eventually, the Indian and his squaw and family would follow me into the store and begin looking over the dry goods or other articles they might wish to buy. The slip prepared in the office was then taken care of by one of the clerks. All goods listed thereon as already purchased were piled on the counter, from where the buyer, assisted by his family, would take them to his wagon.

However, the first matter to be disposed of would always be the redemption of the pawns. Even well-to-do Indians, owners of large herds and other worldly goods, pawn jewelry and other items of value through the winter months. The pawning of pledges does not cast any derogatory reflection upon the Indian—it is an accepted and legitimate business procedure, free from the social stigma that ordinarily accompanies the white man's transactions in a pawnshop.

If the Indian receives his money over the counter, he may, and usually does, give a few dollars to any of the onlookers present in the store. He will take two or three dollars and hand them to the man or woman standing at his elbow, and everybody in the store usually shares in the returns from his sale. And it is not an infrequent occurrence that in the end the just-redeemed pawns are pledged anew to cover purchases for which there does not remain sufficient cash!

The trader must, of necessity, have an accurate knowledge of the values of wool, pelts, skins, livestock, and other things or

146

commodities offered in trade by the Indian. Unless he buys right, and is able to dispose of his accumulated stock at a profit, he will lose money. He has to take chances on market fluctuations that govern the price of wool and skins, which are likely to change rapidly. It is humanly impossible always to buy at the bottom and sell at the top, hence the trader will incur losses and may even go bankrupt, unless he is exceptionally careful.

Navajo rugs and other products of Indian handicraft are a fairly stable investment of trading funds. Those things possess an intrinsic value not affected by stock market or commodity market fluctuations. For the finer grades of rugs there has always been a steady demand—in fact, the supply of the best-grade Navajo rugs is insufficient to take care of the orders.

In summer as well as in winter, a large pail with fresh water stands at one end of the counter, with a long-handled enamelware dipper resting alongside or standing in the pail. That is drinking water for the Indians, and every man, woman, and child coming into the store refreshes himself. There are no individual cups—the Indians make use of the common dipper, but are clean and careful in drinking.

During the winter the store must be warm and cozy. Most of the trading in inclement or stormy weather is done by the men. They do not like it if they have to transact business in a cold place after riding through chilling rains or stinging snows. The trader sees to it that the big cast-iron stove in the middle of the floor between the counters holds a good fire, to welcome the frozen fellows when they enter the place. Quite often they unwrap strips of cloth or sacking or pelts wound about the moccasins (which will absorb water like a dry sponge), to dry out by the stove while they attend to the shopping.

Canned salmon and sardines were part of the stock, but only the white trade would buy them. Occasionally, someone would open a can of the canned fish and eat it in the store, and might offer an Indian part of the contents of the can. That, however, was something he would not eat—not he! In fact, he was astounded to see the white man relish the "snake meat"—he could not be convinced it was anything but canned reptile.

On the counter of the store was to be found a shallow wooden box, fastened down by screws, and holding some loose smoking tobacco, cigarette papers, and a few matches. Long, slender nails had been driven to about half their length through

147

the bottom of the box into the counter. That was not to hold the box more securely to its place but to prevent the Indians from scooping up handfuls of tobacco. The nails allowed thumb and forefinger to take a pinch or two of tobacco, enough to fill the cigarette paper, but did not permit a cleaning out of the box, as would have happened quickly if it were not for obstructing nails. A trader learns many tricks!

At every trading post can be found a substantial hogan, which is a camping place for the Indians who stay at the post overnight. It has been built by the Indians, is constructed in accord with their own ideas, door opening facing east, and has been properly blessed by a medicine man. If the customers arrive at the post late in the afternoon, or weather conditions force them to remain overnight, that hogan becomes the guesthouse.

The trader furnishes firewood for the hogan, and is also expected to supply such camping equipment as coffeepot, tin cups, fry pan and water bucket. He is often "touched" for coffee and sugar, or anything else the Indian can persuade him to donate.

The cooking utensils require frequent replacement—for some reason or other they disappear, piece by piece, until out of the entire assortment there remains perhaps one battered tin cup!

During my trading years in Sanders and in Keams Canyon, Arizona, I developed a steadily increasing mail-order business in Indian arts and crafts. Choice pieces of Navajo silverware, Hopi basketry and pottery, and—foremost—Navajo rugs, were sent by me to all parts of the country. The major portion of the business was with New York, where B. Altman & Co., the Fifth Avenue department store, was one of my largest customers. Specialty shops on Madison Avenue were always in the market for the finely made old-time Navajo silver jewelry, and eagerly bought any "dead" pawn of that nature.

Elbert Hubbard furnished all rooms, the lobby and recreation hall, and so-called chapel of his Roycroft Inn at East Aurora, New York, with fine Navajo rugs purchase from me. He also had me send him several large shipments of rugs to be sold by his Roycrofters to the many visitors to the inn.

• • •

Invariably, the eastern visitors would arrive at the question: "Don't you get terribly lonesome, out here all by yourselves and away from civilization?" Most of them failed to differentiate between lonesomeness and solitude, and did not appreciate the fact that our lives were so full as to leave no time in which to feel loneliness. True, we lacked the conveniences of modern towns, such as electricity, gas, telegraph and telephone, daily news and mail service, and, most missed of all, modern plumbing. But those hardships, as they appeared to others, were not considered too tough by us, but were put up with and taken in stride. We consoled ourselves with the thought that all pioneering involves the giving up of certain comforts, and we reflected that the builders of this nation and the western-bound travelers who crossed the prairies and mountains in ox-drawn wagons managed very nicely without tiled bathrooms and electric switches.

At Christmastime, Indians from far and wide make the post their rendezvous. For days prior to the great event, everyone, including the wife, has been busy with preparations. Paper bags are filled with candies and apples and peanuts, chewing gum and similar confections and sweets. Other bags hold smoking tobacco and cigarette papers. Several cases of Cracker Jack have been opened, and the little cartons with their prizes are piled with the other things. There are larger packages, especially put up for the regular customers, containing some coffee, sugar, soda crackers, a can or two of fruit or tomatoes, and perhaps some Nabisco, Fig Newtons or other packaged cookies.

Everybody that comes to the store on Christmas Day receives a gift of candy and other delectables; the Indians who are the regular patrons of the post get the bigger packages which were made ready for them. In addition, those of the children who may be in need of them are fitted out with new stockings, or little sweaters, and any and everything that can be spared from our own wardrobe—used, it is true, but still very acceptable because clean, warm, and serviceable.

It is a day of little trade—the object of the Indians is to receive gifts, and, if time allows, to make a hurried trip to the nearest mission or other trading post to repeat the performance and share in the gifts offered at those places. If that means a ride of twenty or thirty miles, it does not discourage anyone—distance must lend enchantment!

The missions maintained through Navajoland by the different churches also prepare for the Christmas holidays. Usually they distribute large quantities of clothing, shoes, overcoats, and other

149

wearables which have been donated by the denominations supporting the missions. They call upon the nearest traders to help out
with assortments of fruits, candies, cookies, and peanuts, which
means that the trader near a mission carries a double burden.
However, nobody frets over that—the yuletide spirit is strong, and
to play Santa Claus is about the only chance the trader has to do
something for his friends and customers.

• • •

Yes, a trader's life is not just standing behind a store counter and selling merchandise at exorbitant prices to untutored savages, as some people seem to believe. It embodies many other
phases, but from whatever angle it is viewed, the trader sees life in
capital letters. There is fun and pleasure and profit, to be sure, but
also pathos, misery, and tragedy. The trader has to be an adaptable
person—he is called upon to face many situations that never trouble one off the reservation. At all times he must be self-reliant;
there simply is no one else to whom he can delegate unpleasant
and dangerous tasks. Unless he is willing, ready, and qualified to
do his share, and to accept the responsibilities, he had better look
for some less exacting calling.

Teacher to the Navajos

Minnie Braithwaite Jenkins

For many an ambitious young man of the late nineteenth
century, the American frontier was the place to launch a career
or fulfill a dream that had been stifled in the more constricted
society east of the Mississippi. For some women also, the frontier
offered a chance for adventure, romance, entrepreneurship, and
independence.

Minnie Braithwaite Jenkins was one of scores of well-bred,
educated young women who found an escape valve for their
ambitions in a teaching career in the Indian Service. As a young
girl growing up near the campus of the College of William and
Mary in Williamsburg, Virginia, Minnie longed to study there.
When she was refused admittance to the all-male school, she
resolved to "go West to teach the Indians."

Horrified at the prospect of her fragile Southern daughter
stranded among savages on some remote reservation, Minnie's
mother maneuvered to scotch her plans. Through the intervention
of a sympathetic Congressman and a Bureau of Indian Affairs
official, Minnie was offered a position at a new school in an
isolated and inaccessible northern Arizona canyon. The well-
meaning Congressman assured Mrs. Braithwaite that "all
appointments to the school have been declined, and she also will
turn it down." To their consternation, she immediately accepted!
With a modest loan from a family friend, a railroad pass to
Chicago, and a bulging picnic basket, Minnie departed the
orderly society of tidewater Virginia for the Enchanted Mesa and
Blue Canyon regions of Arizona's vast Navajo country.

This young woman from Williamsburg was an instinctive
and gifted teacher. Within days of her arrival at the Blue Canyon
School, listless and dispirited Navajo children seemed
transformed into eager and attentive learners. Her love of the
Navajo children fostered a love for the Navajo landscape.
Although she never lost her longing for the lush, green comforts

of her girlhood home, she continued to accept new positions in Indian schools until her marriage to a fellow teacher.

These recollections are representative of the lives of women who found in the American West opportunities beyond the traditional duties of family, household, and church. Although a teaching position offered little security, long hours, and primitive living and working conditions, for many women it was an opportunity to test their confidence, their minds, and their bodies. Some were quickly discouraged by the harsh conditions and the excruciating toil of frontier existence, yet others, like the girl from Williamsburg, flourished.

As I lay shivering, crowded into the narrow single cot with my roommate, I could not help thinking of my home and of my mother—of the large bedroom that was mine, the window seat in the bay window, the dainty frilled curtains, the towel rack with its spotless towels by the washstand, the rugs on the floor, and best of all the wide spacious bed that I had all to myself.

To turn my thoughts from that luxury, I dwelt on the tulips, hyacinths, and roses of our garden, the dear old apple orchard with its family tradition of the first little trees brought over from England in tubs. Should I ever again see the little pond in the beloved ravine or swing over it on grapevines? Should I ever again see the lovely dogwood blossoms like lace against the evergreens?

For now here I was, imprisoned in bleakness in the barren desolation of this stony canyon.

• • •

When I opened my eyes in the cold, dim dawn, Mildred was up and quietly dressing. When she saw I was awake, she said again, "Return with the sheriff. If you don't, you will regret it."

Though her earnestness made me unhappy, I had no intention of taking her advice.

"Come what may," I assured her, "I am going to stay."

She went on quickly in a breathless, frightened way, "Oh, how I have wanted to get away from here! They have been devilish to me; but I did not have money enough to get to the railroad and pay my way home. You see, they had put up the money for my ticket here, so I was caught in a trap." She paused, trying to get

From Minnie Braithwaite Jenkins, *Girl from Williamsburg* (Richmond, Virginia: The Dietz Press, Incorporated, 1951), 26–39. Used with permission from Dorothy Jenkins Ross.

control of herself, then asked, "How did it happen that you wanted to come?"

I told her the whole story, ending with, "A man on the train begged me to turn back. Miss Sue, too, warned me that sometimes the schools were bitterly cruel places. And now you are saying the same thing." I added indignantly, "How can these people treat you so cruelly?"

Mildred began to weep. "Oh, my God," she cried, "yours are the first kind words I have heard since I came here!" I saw she was wan and thin, her gray eyes sad. She lifted up the hem of her long apron dress and wiped her eyes as she tried to compose herself and tell me something of her work.

"I am fond of the children and I like the old Indians," she told me. "I do not mind the work, which, however, is very, very hard. But we no sooner got settled after our arrival than the Hammers began to be mean and cruel. I soon found that I was trapped in a wily spider's web. I was here only to be used as a servant for their benefit, to relieve the work pressure, and they had only contempt for me because I was so easily caught."

Mildred twisted the hem of her apron while she was telling me this, every once in a while wiping her eyes. She said she had been very lonely and if, after her duties, she went to the Hammers' quarters; they ran to the door when they heard her coming and turned the key in the lock. Then, at the table, Mrs. Hammer would not speak except to say things intended to humiliate her. Mildred could say unkind things, too, and matters went from bad to worse, until these three white employees lived like cats and dogs.

Mildred was school cook. She had to rise early to oversee the preparation of the children's breakfast. Our talk had delayed her. As she left the room, she said that when the employees' breakfast was ready, an Indian boy who spoke English would come for me. "I have," she said, "an Indian assistant, Chonto, and a detail of Indian children to assist in the routine work."

When she was gone, I stretched out in the narrow cot with its hard horse-hair pillow. My very bones ached from the wagon trip across the desert, and my face was raw from the sunburn. The coarse sheets on the bed were so short that if the top sheet was pulled up to my shoulders my feet stuck out at the bottom.

The room was tiny, with a log ceiling, and the walls, plastered with adobe mud, were bare. In one side wall there was an open fireplace; otherwise the room was more like a little cave than

154

a room. There were the single iron cot, a cheap golden oak bureau on which stood a comb and a jar of salve, one chair, and an up-ended box which held a tin water basin and pitcher.

High up above the box was a small window with four tiny panes of glass, not made to open, and so high that only a bit of blue sky could be seen. I flinched as I stepped out on the cold bare floor.

I dressed. Someone banged on the door. When I turned the white china door-knob and pulled back the heavy homemade door (I later learned that the door and window frames were made from packing cases), a boy of about twelve stood there. He had a pleasant, intelligent face and close-cropped head. His garments were worn but clean. I could not fail to note that his shoes were without soles as in staring at the new teacher he unconsciously kept turning one foot over and back.

He gestured wildly for me to come, and thrust his finger down his throat exclaiming, "Eat, eat." Then he led me around to the back of the building to the employees' kitchen. This was the boy who spoke English!

As I followed him I glanced around. This stark barren de-solation might have been on the moon. Such a spot surely did not belong to our earth: the ugly, low mud-rock building, the small windows that looked like stark, staring eyes, the cold, bare rocks, and the hard-beaten earth with nowhere the least sign of living green.

The boy pointed to the door I was to enter, then he went on to the shed where the clatter of dishes made me aware the children were eating there.

I entered the bare homely room with its well-scrubbed floor, its one small unshaded window. There were a cook-stove and a kitchen table, oilcloth covered, set for breakfast.

A short, stout man stood up, puffed out his cheeks before he spoke, then introduced himself as Mr. Hammer, teacher-in-charge, and Mrs. Hammer as matron. He was fair and ruddy. Mrs. Hammer was big and stout, with snapping blue eyes, red cheeks, and smoothly parted brown hair. She wore a voluminous calico Mother Hubbard.

The breakfast consisted of porridge and milk served in yellow crockery bowls, thick puffy biscuits that Mildred had warned me were made without shortening, fried salt pork, a bit rancid, and a drink they called coffee, which was brown but de-void of any flavor.

Mrs. Hammer, in a voluminous Mother Hubbard, had been giving my white shirtwaist and navy serge skirt a sharp inspection. Without formality, she informed me with clipped emphasis, "Your style of dress is all wrong for this country." She shot a sharp look of disapproval toward Mildred and added, "Mother Hubbards are the proper thing for this country."

I could see that she resented Mildred's high-necked, long-sleeved apron dress. I realized that she was practically issuing an ultimatum as to how I should dress. I dismissed her despotic assertion with a careless, "Oh, this is my regular school costume."

The matron's face flamed with anger and sudden animosity. I sensed her determination to combat my judgment. She swelled up and pouted in silence, her eyes flashing resentment. I came to know later that had the Sheriff not been present this occasion would have ended in a terrible outburst of anger.

• • •

Up to the time of my arrival, over sixty Indian children had been taken into the reservation school and entered as pupils. They were listless and bored, as there was nothing to interest them except the novelty of plenty of food three times a day.

Mildred told me that the Hammers had formerly been in well-established schools, but had had so much trouble with other employees that they had been shifted from one place to another. Each time strife and dissension had followed them. I was beginning to understand the reason for the poor girl's emotional state.

At last there had been a drastic official investigation, and the Hammers had been discharged from the Service they liked so well. With pleadings and hysterics they pestered the Department for reinstatement, until, to put a stop to it, the officials had notified them that they might come to this location, gather some children if they could, and start a school.

Breakfast over, . . . Mr. Hammer then wanted to know if I desired the schoolbooks from the commissary.

"If they have pictures in them, yes," I replied.

"The children are put into four classes," Mr. Hammer explained, "and you will have each class two hours. Also, you will have all the children for an hour in the evening, when they are not to study but to be entertained."

156

This meant that my work began at a quarter to eight in the morning and lasted until five in the afternoon. The hour in the evening dismayed me, as I surely should need that time to prepare the plans for the four classes the next day.

"I told you they were devils," said Mildred, as we met at the side of the building when I was coming from our room and she was going to it.

In addition to the heavy teaching schedule, I had to take my turn every third week at cooking for the employees. Of course, I had to do my own washing and ironing. Brought up in the manner of a Virginia girl of that time, I had never gone to our kitchen except to take a message from my Mother to our cook.

. . . At a quarter to eight, Mr. Hammer conducted me out to the school bell. This big bell was meant to be hung in a cupola, but there was none. It stood in a plank floor on the ground. It was big and heavy. To be rung, it had to be pushed back and forth with a crank by main strength and awkwardness.

Mr. Hammer rang the bell. The children assembled, and he called the names of those children who were to be in the first section. In one hand he held a piece of broomstick with a hole in the end through which a length of leather thong had been thrust and tied, making a sort of policeman's billy. When he was not using this billy to point with, he wore the loop over his wrist, letting the stick dangle.

The pupils who lined up were half of the oldest boys and girls, some of them nearly grown. Mr. Hammer pointed with his billy and made them toe an imaginary mark until the line was straight. He then had them hold out their hands while he inspected them and their faces for cleanliness. One boy was ordered back to wash.

I noticed that the children were slender and had bright, intelligent faces; I was later told that they were from the Navajo and Hopi tribes.

None of the boys had sufficient clothing and they were a ragged and pitiful lot. Not only were their garments inadequate, but only a few had shoes. As I stood there before these children who were to be my charges, it seemed to me that the Government might furnish them at least sufficient clothing, for the February weather was cold.

As they stood facing me, their dark eyes gazed at me fearfully. They must have felt that they were on the verge of some strange and startling experience. Actually, I was as much afraid as they were. However, I looked them in the eye confidently, although I was far from feeling either confidence or pleasure.

Mr. Hammer said to them in Navajo, "Watch my feet and do just as I do. Face front!" Then he swung forward to face me. "Turn! Forward march!" And he began to mark time, "Left, right, left, right," then went forward, motioning them to do the same. He marched them around the building and into the temporary schoolroom.

In one corner of the boys' big dormitory, single iron cots had been pushed aside and desks moved in. This space was to be used for school. Mr. Hammer motioned with his billy for the larger boys and girls to stand by the larger desks. When all were in position, he said in Navajo, "Be seated."

Then he explained that I was the teacher that the Great Father in Washington had sent to them, and that each day they would come to school for a short time, also that they would come at night for a while. Then, informing me that hereafter I should ring the school bells, inspect the children for cleanliness when in line, and march them in, Mr. Hammer gave me a list of the four classes, turned the billy over to me as the badge of my authority, and left.

The one word in English that each child knew was his name, as the roll had been called at bedtime often enough for that.

I gave slates and pencils to a boy to distribute down one row and books to a girl to distribute down the other. I indicated by signs that those who had books might look at the pictures.

Although the children knew enough to answer to their names, they had never seen them written. I now took the first child's slate, asked him his name and wrote it at the top, Mark, while he watched with excited interest. Handing the slate to him I said, "You write it," motioning to make my meaning clear. The boy was enthusiastic. This was what his father had told him he was coming to school for . . . to learn to read and write marks. How happy Mark and Guy and Isaac were!

I went down the line, writing each child's name while he watched, saying as I handed him the slate, "You write it." Knox, Posey, and Tilden, named for the three officials who had selected the site for the school, were especially interested.

Those who had books enjoyed looking at the pictures, but the ones writing their names were indeed thrilled. The others were very envious. "Bye and bye, soon," I said, and the children repeated the words after me.

I busily inspected the writing, showing each child how to make the curves. I went to the small tilting blackboard and indicated that, as written, "A" was closed at the top, and "U" was open. Then I wrote the vowels on the blackboard. The youngsters went on a vowel hunt in their names, and were as excited as if they were hunting rabbits. What bright children they were!

A boy pointed at an "O" and said, "Name?" He meant "Has this letter a name?"

"Yes," I said, "sometime soon, but not now."

After ten minutes of this, some of the children could write their names without looking at the copy, and those whose names were longer were distressed that they could not. I praised them and said, "Soon, tomorrow perhaps," and smiled encouragingly.

At the end of fifteen minutes, I wiped the slates clean with a wet cloth, and the books and slates were exchanged across the aisle. After listlessly hanging around the buildings all day long, they found school a thrilling experience.

This teaching of children who were of a different race and did not speak English was to me a real problem, for which I was in no way prepared. How should I proceed? However, . . . I had given the matter thought. I had determined that if I were placed in such a situation, in teaching language and numbers, I would do it in the simplest way possible. Giving these children their names to write was a happy inspiration of the moment and it had won their immediate interest.

This period over, I drilled them on head, hand, foot, touching my head, holding out my hand, putting out my foot, and having them do the same over and over. Then it was stand up, and sit down. We stood and sat down until they knew these phrases perfectly.

After fifteen minutes of language drill, we had fifteen minutes of number drill, counting rocks and fingers, boys and girls. Then we had reading.

There was a primer chart. The first page had a lesson on the cat. I pointed to the cat; the children repeated the word until they knew it.

Then I pointed to the words under the picture and read slowly, pointing to each word, "This-is-a-cat."

Pretending I was eating something, I asked Guy, the boy who knew one English word, "What am I doing?"

"Eat," he proudly called out. So I ate an imaginary slice of bread, taking bites, chewing and swallowing. "Bread," I said, "I eat—bread and meat. At dinner (they knew 'dinner') you tell Mildred, Chonto, 'I want bread—and meat.'"

Time was up. "Stand up! Forward march!" and I marched them out, waving my hand and saying "good-bye" as I hurried to ring the bell for the second division, to go through the identical procedure again—three more times, as the first task was to teach each class English.

Since the work was entirely oral it was extremely fatiguing. By noon I was trembling with weakness. But I had to hasten to our kitchen where Mildred was cooking, to learn all that I could before my turn came to cook. Seeing that I was trembling, Mildred made me sit down and brought me a cup of goat's milk to drink.

At the noon meal Mrs. Hammer complained of the mutton, declaring that it was not cooked enough. Mildred insisted that it was. Mrs. Hammer stared critically at the potatoes, which Mildred had not had time to mash, turning them over with her fork gingerly, as if she were afraid they would bite her. As for the canned tomatoes, Mrs. Hammer "told the world" she was tired of them. "Why couldn't one have a decent meal?"

The matron's work was certainly no sinecure. To see that the children were up, dressed and washed for breakfast, for school and work, beds made and rooms cleaned, was a real task.

Yet Mildred's work was much more difficult: the huge tubs of bread to be made each day—great wash-boilers of stew and beans to cook, with the children to be fed three times a day—on time—and the whole job performed with insufficient and primitive equipment.

At the end of the first afternoon session, Mildred gave me another cup of milk. "Now don't you dare tell anyone about this milk," she warned, "or they will think you are ill and ask to have you removed so Mrs. Hammer can be teacher."

After the last afternoon session, I was ill with prostration and unable to go to the mess kitchen again. I was thoroughly fatigued from the long train trip, the ache from three days of hard desert journey, and then this cruelly hard day. I hastened to my room to rest.

160

At supper, I forced myself to sit erect and pretend to eat. There were cold sliced mutton, hard cold biscuits, and canned corn this time instead of canned tomatoes.

Came the evening session! All the pupils were present. I could only pass out the books and slates. They could look at the pictures and draw. I sat from sheer fatigue. The children were very appreciative of the books and slates, quiet and well-behaved.

A very few of the wee ones were plump, but most were very slender. A tiny little plump girl named Lily was beautiful and carried herself like a royal princess. Most of the children were attractive and good-looking and seemed to have a great deal of pride.

Little Fanny was blind, but I found that she was even happier in school than the others. She had a teacher to love, and each day she could learn wonderful things. Her rapture shone in her face.

More to bolster my courage than anything else, I began to hum softly over and over:

"My country, 'tis of thee . . . ."

One child began to hum with me, then looked at me, startled. I smiled and nodded. Others began to hum softly with us, and soon all joined in.

A child said, "Name?" He wanted to know what it was and what it meant.

"You know—Blue Canyon, school, mesa, desert—all," waving my arms to take in everything. They nodded vigorously that they got the idea. I said "Name is 'My country!'" They repeated the words I sang:

My country, 'tis of thee
Sweet land of liberty, of thee I sing.

And we tra-la-la'd through the rest. The children had sweet voices and loved to sing. We sang it over and over and louder.

The Hammers and Mildred were astonished; they opened their doors unbelievingly to make sure they did hear us singing a song the very first day of school. At that distance they did not know we were not singing the words also.

The children dismissed, I began to wash the slates for the next day, but was shocked by the pictures drawn upon some of them, of animals in the most intimate of corral animal life.

In my distress and exhaustion, I felt I could not stay. I wanted to go home and at once! But Mildred comforted me. "Of course they know the facts of life. They grow up in the corral among the animals; all phases are familiar to them. Their father or mother calmly nods and says 'That's all right; by and by a baby horse—a baby sheep—or goat!' They are taught to take these things as the natural course of nature."

"Fiddlesticks!" cried Mildred as my distress continued, "shut up and go to bed and get some of the sleep you have been missing these many days. You are completely tired out!"

162

Advice to the Health Seeker

George B. Price

Diseases of the respiratory system, especially tuberculosis, were among the most widespread and dreaded afflictions of the nineteenth century. Images of the fading consumptive clutching a blood-stained handkerchief, coughing discreetly, and growing more pale and wan each day filled the popular literature and haunted the imagination. The scientific community's inability to discover a cure for tuberculosis led to dependence on the theory that a change in the environment and life-style could be beneficial. So physicians prescribed long sea voyages or leisurely overland travel for their patients. Those without sufficient means for luxurious travel tried moving to a different climate in the hope they would recover quickly enough to work. The essential ingredients of this environmental cure were rest, simple, nourishing foods, exercise, and fresh air. As a result the westward road to health was littered with hundreds of unmarked graves of persons who were too ill or too poor to regain their health. But the remarkable fact was that for many the cure worked, and worked in ways which modern medicine cannot fully explain.

In spite of early descriptions of the Colorado and Gila country as "earthly Edens" where a man might "revel in perennial spring or luxuriate amid unfading summer,"* Arizona did not begin to attract large numbers of health seekers until the late 1870s. The completion of the railroad and the cessation of Indian hostilities made travel and life there much more appealing. Once started, these migrations became so enormous that the years up to the end of the century were aptly dubbed the era of the "sunshine rush."

Arizona's arid environment was particularly attractive to persons afflicted with any ailment which dampness aggravated—

---

*Rufus B. Sage, *Scenes in the Rocky Mountains and in Oregon, California, New Mexico, Texas and the Grand Prairies* (Philadelphia: Carey and Hart, 1846), 237. Sage was an invalid who traveled to regain his health.

respiratory ills, arthritis, and rheumatism. As the tide of invalids swelled, various types of establishments sprang up to provide lodging and care. Facilities ran the gamut from luxurious sanatoriums with large medical staffs and gourmet chefs to squalid tent camps at the edges of cities and towns where invalids huddled awaiting nature's cure or summons.

The search for personal health was an uncertain and frightening quest devoid of the adventure and excitement that accompanied gold rushes and homesteading. As thousands began to trek westward in search of a cure, "how-to" literature appeared. Much of this was propaganda. Yet, in the midst of the competititon for the health seeker's dollars, informative and reliable publications advised the invalid on a variety of subjects from lodging and nutrition to the medical importance of a cheery disposition. The following selection is representative of the kind of advice that a health seeker would have welcomed.

One of the earliest questions to be settled is where and how to live.

No matter what your ultimate destination, it is better to go first to one of the larger towns or cities and stay for a few days at a hotel there, whence you can look around for a boarding place or whatever else you may have in mind.

There is a wide range as to expense of living and several alternatives as to manner and location.

A ranch in Western parlance may mean anything from an unenclosed area of thousands of acres of wild country with branded cattle and broncos, presided over by the nomadic cowboy, down to a two-room shanty on a half-acre lot, with chickens and a dog.

So there are ranches and ranches, and if you strike a really good one, conducted on intelligent business principles for the benefit, not of the proprietor only, but of the invalid as well, you may be quite happy in realizing that you are getting that abundance of fresh air and nourishment which has been pictured in your mind as belonging to ranch life.

But do not assume that you will find it all to your liking. The average ranch is not nearly so good a place to live in as the average boardinghouse, and it is much to be doubted whether the average results to the invalid are as good.

The food is too often coarse or carelessly cooked and not sufficiently nourishing or abundant, while as to milk and cream, the best of it has probably gone to be sold to the city trade.

Ranch houses are not supposed to be fitted to modern comfort, and you may have to "put up with things" relating to insuffi-

From George B. Price, *Gaining Health in the West* (New York: B. W. Huebsch, 1907), 39–62; 81–91.

165

ciently heated or ground-floor rooms, poor plumbing or none at all, limited supply of hot water—and that by special arrangement with "cook"—no indoor toilet accommodation, or bathroom, miles of distance between you and the post office, the nearest doctor and the druggist, and likely no telephone or telegraph office near. If you become ill suddenly and need medical attention it may be hours reaching you, while sympathetic care and scientific nursing may be less obtainable than if you were a wounded soldier on a battlefield.

Thoughts of early rising, of riding the farm horse daily to the post office, of watching the seeds grow and of making friends with the pigs and chickens may form quite an idealistic picture, for a limited time, in the brain of the wearied invalid; but at best these things are apt to be overestimated as means to health, and are certainly not to be seriously entertained as compensation for the aforesaid disadvantages.

Again, you may be either a lone boarder at this ranch, having practically no companionship and left to eat out your heart in wearisome dejection, or you may be one among a community of invalids seeking health like yourself, and drawn thither by the reputation of that particular ranch.

The notion that one can get better air and cheaper board at a ranch is largely overdrawn. As to air, the populations are relatively so small and non-compact, even in the towns, as to have little appreciable effect in contaminating the air; while as to board, if a ranchman takes you at all he will want quite as much out of your finances as the average town boardinghouse keeper.

There is a great deal of overestimation and delusion about the superiority of ranch life, and if you are sensible you will first take up your abode within the precincts of some town, to get your bearings and view the possible allurements of ranch life from a nearer vantage ground. Doubtless a few weeks of it, in the warm and open time of the year, may be quite pleasant, even jolly if you happen to be with "your own crowd," and provided you are strong enough to enjoy several miles' walk or a ten-mile horseback ride daily; but there are more suitable places for the real invalid.

Boardinghouses are more usually chosen by the sojourners in the West, and there are several good reasons why this is so.

There are plenty of them to be found in almost any Western community, which in itself tends to produce that kind of business competition productive of comfort to the boarder.

They are of all kinds and in towns of, say, ten thousand inhabitants or over. They range from houses fitted with the most modern plumbing, electricity, telephones, and a very excellent style of domestic service down to the simple but comfortable home of the ordinary mechanic's family, with its "home cooking," the price of room and board correspondingly varying from twenty-five dollars to five dollars a week.

A very satisfactory room and board can be had in such cities as Denver or Colorado Springs at from thirty-five dollars to fifty dollars a month. At such houses the invalid is likely to get a good table and a cozy, comfortable room, and have his wants generally looked after by his landlady. He will usually not lack, either, for more or less agreeable companionship to help while away the hours.

A boardinghouse home, as contrasted with a ranch home, gives you the advantage of easy access to your physician or other helps, if emergency arises, while the larger community affords change of thought and scene because of its more varied opportunities.

As to sanatorium life: People in general entertain a sort of primitive aversion to going into a sanatorium as a place to regain health. They regard it somehow as a kind of prison, and feel as Dante felt when he read that alarming sentence over the portal to hell, "All hope abandon, ye who enter here." But no prejudice can be less founded in reason or experience, and the timorous individual who has crossed that dreadful Rubicon of superstition and found, by blessed personal experience, the physical helpfulness and mental rest which come of a residence in one of these well-appointed sanatoria for consumptives, looks back upon his earlier fears as having occurred in a period when he "felt as a child and thought as a child."

I acknowledge the weakness, or rather ignorance, of having felt the same sort of timidity when I first went West. A friend, perhaps wiser than I, had mentioned to me the name of a sanatorium in Colorado Springs, as probably a good place for me to go to. "Very likely," thought I, "a good enough place for one who is quite hopeless—but for myself, no, I thank you." After living out there some months I had occasion to spend a week at this sanatorium. Those few days dispelled my prejudices.

It were difficult to find a more contented lot of people anywhere. Why not? There was food of excellent quality, daintily

167

served at tables spread with spotless linen in a large, well-lighted dining room; bedrooms as neat as a pin, and cozy and comfortable as your own at home; sanitary appliances as perfect as art can produce, and the scrupulous enforcement of sanitary rules throughout the house and grounds, which results in making such a sanatorium a much safer place, so far as contagion is concerned, than any hotel in the world. Beside all this, a doctor, an apothecary shop, every emergency appliance, and skilled nurses always near; cozy parlors, with piano and open fireplace, well-stocked book shelves, an amusement room for games, perhaps a billiard room. Often there are individual tents about the grounds where those who prefer to can sleep nearer to earth and sky. What is there not in such a sanatorium to provide one's comfort? The whole building, with its every appointment and particular, is the embodiment of all that the most advanced science has discovered for the welfare and cure of the consumptive. Why should it not, then, be the best place and the quickest means for restoring the invalid?

Accumulating statistics are proving it to be so: a larger percentage of cures is being effected through the ordered life, treatment and methods of the sanatorium than by any other known course. I believe it is not questionable that whatever the patient's condition—and all the better if he is not very ill—he will gain far more steadily if he spends his first months in such a place than he is likely to gain in twice the time, if left to his own undisciplined guidance.

This fact is worth thinking about seriously. Investigate it a little for yourself. Get the opinion of your physician on it, and of others—who haven't ideas simply, but who know without prejudice.

Perhaps it will cost you a little more to live in a sanatorium (their rates are usually from ten to fifteen dollars a week, without extras) than in a medium-priced boardinghouse; but if the living is better and your gain is to be faster, the probability is that it will prove the most economical kind of an investment.

In order to adopt the sanatorium life, it appears that about all you have to overcome is that first feeling of repugnance to making one of a company who sit around in steamer chairs and wraps and whose occasional coughing isn't quite musical. But, my dear fellow, whether or not you wish to disguise the fact and try to fool yourself with forced delusions, you are already, by circumstances beyond your control, in that same category; so instead of foolishly fighting that invincible fact you might save your strength and courage for better purposes by gracefully admitting it and letting a more amiable logic aid your recovery.

You are not the only fellow who has had a "knock-out," neither has fate been particularly unkind to you alone, as you will learn presently when you get to exchanging confidences with some in that company. Very likely there will be a slow, silent effect upon your heart that will do you good, just as every sorrow is gradually made easier to bear through the undefined sympathy of closer contact with those who have drunk from the same wine-press. Yes, when you come to know them you will find men and women among that steamer-chair community, from which you so lately turned away in aversion, whose patience will make you ashamed of your restlessness; men of reputation, of education, of scientific learning; men and women who can discuss your chosen hobby, or pleasantly while away your idle hours with discourse of travels and experiences and past acquaintanceships, leading you to realize anew that friends and friendships are not of one place and time alone, but are as broad as life's pilgrimage.

Day by day that once formidable sanatorium community will resolve itself into a large family whose characteristics will interest you increasingly, as you learn who and what and whence they are and your own heart opens more to their already willing helpfulness for you. You may discover, after a little, that you never before were in a company so varied: among them, personalities whose culture represents the best homes in the land; strong characters and weak; noble souls, generous, tender and sympathetic, often entertaining and gracious; all of them broadened and made more sensible of the true brotherhood of man through having their several temptations to petty jealousy and grosser overreaching burned away by the cleansing, leveling, purifying fire that has borne them, severally, from the activities of life's feverish rush. A silent voice is teaching their souls the philosophy of an inner life. Then do not look askance at the invalids in a sanatorium, or regard too lightly the claims which such as institution may rightly prefer, as being both a home and a means to restore you to health; for many have proved them true.

I have known people who, after spending some months at one of these places, have tried boarding elsewhere, have longed for the sanatorium again, and have gone back to it simply as boarders, for it appealed to them finally as the most homelike place to be found.

This is my advice: if you are very sick, go straight to a sanatorium; there is no question of its being the best place for you, because your case is serious and you simply cannot afford to trifle with experiments or waste your most valuable asset, time, in getting rid of prejudices by trying everything else first. If you are "not at all sick"—only a little scratch on your lung—you certainly will lose nothing and will be allowing yourself a wider margin of safety by early applying for board at a first-class sanatorium.

Living in a tent—which generally means sleeping in one at night and spending the daytime out-of-doors—is much in vogue, being frequently prescribed by physicians. Under certain conditions and restrictions it has the advantages of cheapness, but this is not necessarily implied, as tent-life may be carried on in a manner quite as expensive as any other.

The matter of providing good meals is not to be overlooked, since suitable food, and plenty of it, is as important as fresh air, and since you are very apt to slight your diet if you have to prepare and cook the food yourself, it is much better to pitch your tent in proximity to a boardinghouse, where you can and will eat your three square meals a day. Don't try living on canned foods and the numerous wheat and hay preparations only, or even chiefly. Every day you will need some hot, well-cooked meat and other food, quite likely plenty of milk and some raw eggs. Whatever you do, don't try to skimp on your diet! Remember that the food you put into your human boiler is the only thing that can keep up your strength and also repair the now unusual waste, and unless your system can renew itself and gradually gain over the daily depletion going on, the disease will gain on you!

Sanatoria quite often have a few tents on some part of their premises, in which those patients who prefer to, or for whom it is ordered, can sleep out and at the same time have all the advantages of the institution, eating in the dining room, using the croquet grounds, porches, etc.

It is also not unusual for boardinghouses to have one or more tents, tent-houses, or tent-porches to be used in conjunction with the regular house and table and other domestic facilities. A tent-porch is either a small floor balcony extending outside of one of the bedrooms, enclosed by canvas and just big enough to hold

170

one or two iron bedsteads, or it is a section of the general porch, set apart and enclosed by canvas. In either case, ingress and egress are customarily through a door or window to the adjoining room in which the occupant dresses and undresses, going thence out into the porch-tent to sleep. These tents have one advantage over the ground tents, especially for those of rheumatic tendency, in being higher off the earth. They are, however, necessarily limited in numbers, as few houses can spare their porches for such exclusive use.

The usual tent is the familiar A-type of canvas covering, built upon the ground. For this purpose a thoroughly dry piece of ground must be selected, sandy soil if possible, and there must always be a good board floor within, raised from four to six inches off the ground, so that there may be a free circulation of air underneath to insure dryness.

Since a tent must lack water and sanitary facilities, it is desirable that it be pitched within easy access of a house, or at least of some pure water supply. By the way, don't trust running brooks, even mountain brooks, too implicitly without inquiring as to their purity, especially if there be houses, camps or picnic grounds in the neighborhood. I have known of cases of typhoid fever contracted from sparkling mountain brooks, very innocent-looking but befouled by careless campers.

Don't forget, either, the importance to your comfort of pitching your tent where it will get the east shadow of a tree or some other object during the hotter hours of the afternoon, for a tent out in the blazing sun of a July or August afternoon is nearly an impossible place to stay in during just those hours when you might wish to lie down in seclusion. Every tent should be provided with an over-cover of canvas, called a "fly," which is stretched several inches above the true tent roof. The use of this fly is to break the force both of the sun's rays and of occasional hard rains which otherwise would penetrate the single canvas wall. Sometimes another smaller fly is projected outward from the tent doorway, under which you can sit on a camp chair enjoying the quiet scenery or a good book and feel that you are quite a monarch on a small scale.

The chief value in tenting is that you sleep out-of-doors (you are supposed to keep out-of-doors in the daytime anyway), and get more fresh air than you would sleeping in a bedroom; not that fresh air and plenty of it cannot be had in a bedroom provided enough windows are kept open, but too often the patient cannot be

171

depended upon to keep the windows open, while in a tent he cannot prevent a certain percolation of fresh air through the canvas walls. But this natural percolation is not now considered quite sufficient of itself, so that several improvements have been devised . . . and such improved tents are to be had from the principal tent-makers of the large Western cities. The improvements consist mainly of a ventilation opening in the apex of the tent, covered by a regulating cone, and of a channel-like, screen-covered orifice extending around the inside lowermost edge of the tent wall and open to the outside atmosphere; by which double arrangement air is constantly entering all round the tent, at the floor line, and passing up and out through the top vent.

The patent tents are much more costly than the ordinary form and it may not be expedient to purchase one, but the tent-dweller should at least provide some sort of covered outlet, to be opened or closed at will, at some high point in his tent wall, as this simple expedient will be found to improve ventilation.

There is a modified form of tent known as a tent-house, a kind of cross between a tiny house and a tent, combining the desirable features of both. This is essentially a board floor with a shingle roof extending completely over it. About one-half of the area is enclosed by four board walls, making a complete room about seven by twelve feet, with windows and door, and holding a couch, stove, washstand, chair, small table, clothes-press and bookshelf—really quite an ideal little den. The other half of the area is enclosed by canvas or by wire screens and curtains, and contains the iron bedstead. This arrangement permits of sleeping out-of-doors, screened from flies and other insects, and provides a cozy, warm room for dressing and other uses. It seems much superior in accommodation and comfort to any tent. Its cost, for the size mentioned, would be about one hundred and twenty-five dollars, exclusive of furnishings.

What is known as the "Chicago Portable House" is also convenient, and is the least expensive form of a fully enclosed room. It is built entirely of wood, lined with building-paper for extra warmth, and has doors and windows to suit. Its cost, for a room twelve feet wide is about five dollars per linear foot of depth, making a twelve-by-twelve-foot room cost only about sixty dollars. It is built up and taken apart in sections, making it transportable. A couple can live quite comfortably in such a portable house, and at the minimum of expense.

172

Tenting, however, seems to afford the cheapest opportunity for the really poor man to maintain himself, since an eight-by-ten tent with a fly, poles, ropes, etc., big enough for a single individual, can be bought for about ten dollars. The wooden floor, if he employs a carpenter and uses new lumber, will cost nearly as much as the tent, but might be constructed in homemade style with second-hand lumber for two dollars. A canvas cot costs about one dollar and a half; a small wood-burning, sheet-iron cook-stove (used in cold weather for warmth), three dollars; a camp-chair, fifty cents; plain bedding, say eight dollars. But this would be a rather lonely way to get on for any length of time, and, since food would cost quite three dollars, the saving would be only about two dollars a week over the cheapest boardinghouse. However, it might be preferred for health's sake.

A man and wife together can live in a tent on but little more than it would cost one alone, and the companionship and helpfulness of it would make tenting not only endurable, but happy. The question might be asked here: Is there not danger to the well person from dwelling in such close proximity to the sick one? There need not be if the proper precautions are observed. The tent should be of a somewhat larger size, naturally, to accommodate two single beds, chairs and a closet.

The whole question as to the advisability of living in a tent would better be left until you are on the ground and have the advice of the local physician there. It is not always and everywhere equally advisable for every patient. While some are undoubtedly benefited by tenting, under the right conditions, all are not. Let the doctor decide it for your case.

Housekeeping. Of course the ideal way to live in a Western community, as anywhere else on earth, is for the married man or woman and the family to live regularly in their own comfortable home. This home may be only a rented house; no matter, it is yours for the time being and may be enjoyed no less than if you held the title-deed. Indeed, on the whole it is rather better to rent a home before owning one: it gives opportunity to test conditions and environment before pledging yourself to a permanent investment. Sometimes desirable furnished houses can be rented for a few months, while the owners are away, at from fifty to one hundred dollars or more a month. In the larger towns you may find one or more apartment houses, where flats or suites of rooms—usually unfurnished—may be rented for housekeeping. The average rent

173

of such unfurnished suites is from forty to seventy-five dollars per month, including steam heat and janitor service.

Furnished rooms without board can often be rented in semi-private houses, desirably located, and may sometimes be had in suites as well as singly. This plan implies going out to meals, but meals of a good quality can usually be obtained in the near neighborhood, at from five to eight dollars per week. The rooms would cost from eight to twenty-five dollars apiece per month, including linen and service, ordinary lighting and heating.

• • •

One of the most valuable assets to the recovery of health is the possession of a cheery disposition.

If you don't possess one naturally, try to cultivate one.

In the first place, rid yourself at once of that uncomfortable state of mind which sees only profound misfortune in your having to go away from home to get well. It may prove, in the end, one of the most fortunate necessities of your life, as it has proved to be for others.

Get rid of the feeling that "now you are in for it you will try to endure it." It is possible to do much better than endure; it is perfectly possible to enjoy it.

Antagonism of all sorts is to be put in a bag and dumped overboard.

Look at things philosophically and you may soon learn to be happy. Don't permit your thoughts to dwell regretfully on your lost opportunities in the East, or sarcastically compare the simpler life of your new abode with the rush and glamour of a great metropolis. When you stop to reflect that those wider opportunities, as you consider them, and all commingling with metropolitan life had already been forfeited by reason of your invalidism which, had you remained there, would speedily have put you forever out of the realm of mortals, the comparison is no longer a just one. You have reason to feel thankful that under restricted conditions your life is yet spared you and that these very restrictions may ultimately prove the means whereby you shall find other avenues of usefulness and enlargement of your prosperity.

Do not fret yourself, either, because of a present lack of "business." After all, have you not simply substituted another business of a different kind? Instead of a business having money-getting

174

as its chief object, you now have on hand the business of getting well! And isn't that quite as valuable to you personally as any other result? I sometimes think that there is a good deal of the "spoiled child" still remaining in our grown-up natures, which is prone to whimper when everything doesn't go exactly as we want it: we still have the desire to possess both the penny and the cake.

Be sensible! Your body needs rest and your mind needs relief from worry and regret; it needs also pleasant diversion. Perhaps you have been needing these things for many months past, and you wouldn't give up and take them. Now Nature has taken the matter in hand and, with a sound metaphorical cuff to wake you up, has said: "Get out and learn something else than the errors in which you have been living. Learn now that all your business, your profession, your successes, are not worth a picayune without health! Get that back, and while doing it learn the delights of relaxation!"

Continue to fight against your lot, keep yourself in a melancholy, cross, crabbed humor, and such stupidity will bring its further sorrows; you might as well have stayed at home. Be courageous and hopeful, come out of your shell, put on a smile, make everybody your friend, read good light literature, talk cheerily with others trying the same prescription, and the effect is bound to be beneficial. It will not be many weeks before you begin to feel it is quite a picnic!

But you will surely want diversions: let's see what you can do to make the hours pass pleasantly.

In the first place, choose your environment, as nearly as possible, to put yourself among people who will probably be companionable. We all need companionship and favorable environment, and when we are invalided and otherwise dependent we especially need them.

Of course your permitted indulgences will be somewhat abbreviated for a while. The doctor will probably prohibit the theater and perhaps church, too, to prevent your getting into crowded rooms or close atmosphere. It must be early to bed, and not too early to rise, with window open top and bottom (curtain and shade removed) all night, and out-of-doors all day, not exercising much, but mostly sitting in the sun, wrapped, if need be, for extra warmth.

Now is a time for good reading (but not sitting with your book in the sun), for outdoor sketching, for writing, for photography, for genial conversation.

175

If you haven't yet learned the fascination of drawing and coloring try it now, with pencil, with brush, in pastels, or in pen-and-ink. Possibly a latent talent may develop into no mean artistic ability.

Or, with pen, paper, and thoughts, what is to prevent your becoming an author?

How about that long-cherished hobby which you have been promising yourself for years past that you would some day ride, when you found the time? Well, here is the time now; why not begin?

During college days wasn't there a subject that particularly interested you?—pursue it further.

Or perhaps you never went to college, but wanted to: what is to prevent your taking up now some subject there offered? If you happen to be located in a college town this will be easy to do, attending some one course as a special student with no fear of examinations to harass you. This would pleasantly employ much time and would cost very little.

Aside from such study, think of all the delightful branches of knowledge easily within your grasp for the cost of a few books or a share in a library. Are you already well-versed in the wonderful things in astronomy, in botany, in chemistry, in geology, in mineralogy or in the interesting fields of zoology, of physics, of anatomy and hygiene, of secular and religious history? Have you ever experienced what an antidote to the blues there is in mathematics?—what a range of thought in philosophy?—what a mine of useful knowledge in the study of mechanics?—what fascination in electricity?—what pleasure in studying architecture; in learning how to design buildings and figure out strains and stresses in the materials used?

Such studies, investigations and analyses may develop you into an inventor or a discoverer. Why not? Because some of these brain possibilities have never been used, is that any reason why they cannot be?

Come to think it over, you have thus far been playing upon only a very few chords of your possible being, with whole ranges of its possibility not yet touched into vibration. You really don't know your entire self. Explore your brain a little, let down some grappling-hooks into its unknown depths and see what sort of pearls may be there.

176

Very likely you got a fit of the doldrums when that little accident to your lungs or throat blew you out of your wonted sailing; but that was only an incident, perhaps to show what kind of a skipper you are. Besides if everybody kept on sailing forever in his little narrow channel who would ever discover that "gem of purest ray serene the dark, unfathom'd caves of ocean bear"? What that mountainside would forever keep locked the precious metals hidden beneath its rough and ordinary-looking surface, unless the explorer came.

If you are aesthetic in feeling there are the magnificant fields of art, poetry, literature, music, as inexhaustible studies and delightful diversions. The study of historic ornament, embodying history, legend, art, is only one of the related branches in this field, yet this study alone might develop you into a practical designer of fabrics, ornaments or wall decorations.

If none of these things interests a man, it is a bad sign and needs treatment. It means either that his intellect has never yet been truly cultivated (and now is the chance to pull up another rung on the intellectual ladder), or else it means that he is discouraged and sees no good or usefulness in anything.

If you are hipped about yourself there is nothing so wholesome as to shift the mind off to the purest and best thoughts engaging the attention of the best type of manhood. In one who is "down" the process may have to be forced a little at first; but try it.

Most of your diversions and occupations must be mental rather than physical, for a while, since your physical nature particularly needs resting and building. Exercise must be limited and watched that it produce only healthy reaction and not exhaustion.

Driving or trolley-car rides, with short walks, are permitted enjoyments.

Bicycle riding and horseback riding should be enjoyed only with the doctor's permission, since these forms of exercise are often too violent and may be even dangerous for those with tendency to hemorrhage. Tennis, for the same reason, must be avoided.

Picnics in the cañons are pleasant half-day diversions, while golf opens a field for both diversion and health to those who are fairly strong. Golf and country clubs are popular and their membership embraces the "best" people in the community, although sometimes a very fast set. But apart from dissipation, which is always foolish for the "lunger," one may live very comfortably,

177

healthily and happily, with ample diversion, especially if the pocketbook be not too cramped.

A good club, with its hospitable fireside and easy chair for an hour's rest and coziness, card parties as often as one cares to play (if you don't sit in a closed room), occasional musicales or performances by traveling theatrical companies, sometimes a grand opera, are among the possible diversions.

The ladies are particularly genial and apparently never lack for entertainment among themselves—afternoon teas, card parties, luncheons, and frequent meetings of women's clubs with discussions of all sorts of things interesting to womankind, keep up an endless round of "something to do."

Then there are all sorts of fads, fancies and "isms" which you may find diverting or study seriously, according to your mood and temperament.

It will take a few weeks to get acclimated and realize your surroundings; but no one need lack pleasant diversion who makes himself agreeable in return.

A Trip into the Grand Canyon

George Harris Collingwood

Since the beginning of Arizona's recorded history, the Grand Canyon has been the symbol of the state's spectacular natural beauty. But the Grand Canyon is more than a gigantic fissure in the earth. It is a pageantry of undulating bands of color that play over sheer walls, ruddy buttes, distant knobs, and eroded promontories. It is a huge geological phenomenon of the Colorado Plateau carved over millions of years by the slow erosive powers of flood, heat, wind, and cold. One author has described the Canyon as a "mountain in an abyss, a wildly baroque expansion on the essences of canyons, a world in itself."*

From the first glimpse into the chasm until the day when the experience finally enters and settles into memory, the visitor to the Grand Canyon is always trying to give words to what has been seen and felt. Generations of travelers have tried to express their sense of wonder at its immensity, to depict the symmetry of its geological formations, and to recall the chaos of its colors.

In the following selection a young man hired to work in the forest service in the summer of 1910 writes to his family to tell them of an overnight trip to the bottom of the Grand Canyon. His letter is brief. The tone is forthright, even jaunty, but there can be no mistaking that he, too, experienced the canyon's spell. In a single sentence he summed up how scores of travelers have felt in the canyon country: "It is worthwhile getting up in the morning here."

Grand Canyon, Arizona
July 2, 1910.

Dear Mother:

I am at the bottom of Grand Canyon now about one-eighth of a mile above the Colorado River. You would laugh if you could

---

*Stephen Trimble, *The Bright Edge: A Guide to the National Parks of the Colorado Plateau* (Flagstaff: The Museum of Northern Arizona Press, 1979), 33.

see me now. I'm pushed up in a little niche in the side of a big rock that rises at the rate of seventy-five or eighty degrees. It is in the shade, but just the same it is hot, because of the reflection, and a hot wind is coming down the valley. Just the same it is better than no wind at all. Every little while one of these little lizards will scoot by me. I don't mind them, but Cliff who is sitting above me makes quite a fuss.

I think I told you in a postal card that we saw the Forest Supervisor and he told us that we need not start work until July [illegible] and that we might take a day and a half leave of absence which will be due us at the end of the month and combine it with Sunday and the Fourth and go to Crand Canyon now. So we did it. We are all three assigned to the Apache Forest Reserve with head-quarters at Springerville, Arizona. We have to go to Holbrook from Williams and then go by stage to Springerville. In our stage ride we will go thru the Petrified Forest.

We arrived at Williams yesterday morning, got a small camping outfit and then ate dinner at a Chinese restaurant. (That's all they have out here.) We took a little train out from Williams at 1:30 p.m. and arrived at Grand Canyon at about 4:30. It was a mighty nice train, a chair car free, & a smoking car, we *took the chair car.* There was also a private car attached. It seems to be the business of the people here to make everyone believe that they are weaklings and must stay in a hotel and must have a guide to take them around, and must ride wherever they go. They didn't fool us tho! We changed our clothes in the baggage room because it was the only place we could store our trunk. Then we rolled up our blankets and camped just off the brink of the canyon and about a mile from "El Tovar." "El Tovar" is Fred Harvey's big hotel, made of logs very large and rambling, and beautifully furnished inside. Yet it seems altogether out of place in this wonderful canyon. Bright Angel Trail Camp is also managed by the Harveys but is cheaper and more like a resort. Lots of tents put in rows like a little city and a cheap frame building. There is also a post office here.

We had a peach of a place to camp, within sight of the can-yon, and with nut pines and junipers growing all round us.

From the George Harris Collingwood Collection, Special Collections, Northern Arizona University Library, Flagstaff, Arizona. Used with permission from The Forest History Society.

You should have seen us when we first looked down on the canyon. (But then, probably you would have been so absorbed that you wouldn't have noticed us.) All we could do was to look, and then we all swore sort of softly, and in between the curses we would speak of the wonders of God. It was all so wonderful we didn't know just what we were doing. Then Wales broke the spell for a moment when he remarked, "I wonder how far my straw hat would sail out over that hole." He didn't break it up for long tho, because we seemed to be sort of hypnotised. It is so enormous and yet so beautiful, with the wonderful colors and the awful shapes all mixed in together. There is a certain symmetry about it, and yet when you try to define it, it is gone and there is nothing but chaos left.

We looked at it then, we looked at it while we were getting supper, and we looked at it before we went to bed. Each time it was different and each time it seemed more wonderful than before.

This morning we were on the trail at seven o'clock and came to the Colorado River at eleven o'clock. We carried our bedding about half way and then hid it. If it is there yet we will probably camp somewhere in the canyon tonight and see the sun rise from the bottom tomorrow. It is worthwhile getting up in the morning here. It is getting late, and we want to take a plunge in a little pool we found just above the Colorado River. The river itself is too dirty and too swift to think of bathing in although it did feel mighty good to soak our feet in it after our long hot walk.

Tell father that the "tarp" is great; the three of us slept together last night with the stars for a roof. The brightest stars I ever saw, I believe. I slept between the other two and I felt like a cogwheel before rising. It was a mighty cold night but we kept plenty warm enough.

I must close now because it is getting late, and it is too hot to stick up here and write too.

Your loving son,

Harris.

P.S. Will you please send me some stationery, that "official" stuff in the bottom drawer of my dresser will be good enough.

July 3, [1910]

Well we made the ascent. It was a hard one but we did her. We got back as far as the "half-way house" last night and were pretty dry, so we each got a lemonade at twenty-five cents per. It was pretty high, but I believe it was the best lemonade I ever drank.

The people are mighty nice out here tho. Even if they do charge high for everything. We spread our blankets out on a grassy plot a little way above this house and slept under the stars. It was great down in the canyon with the stars shining down, and a warm wind blowing over us. We did not put our blankets over us until nearly midnight. This morning we were up at five and all packed and started shortly after six. This alkali water and the heat of yesterday seemed to have hit us all. We made the trip up in about five hours, the same which we did going down in less than two. Wales was rather sick, and Cliff and I had to carry his packs, too. It was pretty hard work, but about half way up we met a couple of fellows and discouraged them, so that they came back with us and helped us with our packs. It was the hardest forenoon I ever spent. When we reached the top we all lay down on the tarp and rested for about two hours. At a little after two, Cliff and I went over to "El Tovar" and got what will probably shock you, but which has made us feel like new men,—a glass of Schlitz Blue Ribbon.

Tomorrow morning we will go back to Williams and leave at night for Holbrook that night. We expect to see a real western Fourth. We will stage from Holbrook Tuesday morning.

Frank Phillips is here at the Bright Angel Camp. He is looking fine. We met him on the trail as we were coming up. He was trying his old trick of trying to make a record. This time it was to make record time from the rim to the Colorado River and back again. It's a pretty stiff pull, and I doubt if he makes it in less than four hours.

My paper is getting short so I must come to a close. I came pretty near getting homesick this noon when I looked at the clock and realized that you were just getting dinner ready. I thought about beef steak and it almost made my lips moist. (That trip this morning dried me up.) Aside from getting acclimated we are all well.

Harris

July Fourth Celebrations, 1910

George Harris Collingwood

Americans have always loved summer holidays filled with parades, speeches, fireworks, and colorful banners streaming in the wind. And, to top it all off, dinner on the grounds. On the agricultural frontier the urge to turn routine work into a community celebration produced barn-raisings, corn huskings, and quilting bees that helped relieve the monotony and crushing toil of farm labor, particularly in the era before steampowered machinery became widespread.

In Arizona where the population was sparse and people lived on isolated ranches, at remote mines or in small settlements, Independence Day provided the perfect opportunity to gather in the nearest town. Instead of the traditional parades, patriotic speeches, and fireworks displays, frontier people often celebrated with contests of skill and endurance. July Fourth was a day when both sexes, and all races, participated with gusto. Cowboys arrayed in fringed shirts, tight-fitting trousers, colorful silk bandanas, Stetson hats, chaps, high-heeled boots, and jingling spurs were the main attraction. And legends were even then in the making.

In a brief letter written in 1910 to his family before assuming his duties as a forest ranger at Springerville, George Harris Collingwood captures the color and pageantry of such a day.

Williams, Arizona, July 4, 1910

My dear Rebecca!—

We came back from Grand Canyon this morning and now we are spending the Fourth here in Williams. It is just like Buffalo Bill's Wild West Show. The town is full of Indians, and Mexicans,

From the George Harris Collingwood Collection, Special Collections, Northern Arizona University Library, Flagstaff, Arizona. Used with permission from the Forest History Society.

and cowboys. There are also lots of Negroes and Chinamen, and they are all celebrating the Fourth together. They do not fire very many crackers out here, nor do the men fire their guns, but they are having an awfully good time. This morning they had a squaw race between a couple of young squaws. Each was dressed in bright colors, and had bandanas on their heads, and moccasins on their feet and their hair hung loose. It was very funny because as soon as one squaw began to lead, the other covered her face with her hands and ran off the track. They also had Indian boy races, between the Moci and the Loci.—I don't know which won. The best of all was a pole raising contest between the Western Union linemen, and those from the Postal Telegraph and Overland Telephone companies. The men raced each other to see who could put their poles up quickest and then one man from each team raced to see who could climb up and put the cross arms on first. The last part was very exciting, especially when the men came down. It seemed as tho' they only touched the pole in about two places before they hit the ground.

After that they had a grand free barbecue. It was like the barbecues at the college only they roasted the steers on steel rails laid across a pit. It was very good and that was all we had for dinner this noon.

You probably never saw a town like this. About all there is here is a big Harvey hotel called the "Frey Marcos," a couple of depots,—one for the Santa Fe and the other for the Grand Canyon line. There is one main street with a few stores and saloons on it and a few little cottages. There is also this hotel. All the restaurants and laundries are run by Chinamen, who have their queues all wound round their heads. The town is full of Mexicans and Indians, and men and women go galloping up and down the streets as fast as they please. There are also a lot of cowboys and one or two cowgirls. California Red just went galloping by. I am going to write Laura a letter and tell her about a most frightful experience we had in the Grand Canyon yesterday, so I will have to stop. Don't forget that my address is Springerville, Arizona, c/o of the Forest Supervisor.

Your *little* brother,
Harris.

The Street Vendors of
My Childhood Days

Arnulfo D. Trejo

*The City of Tucson sprawls beneath the sun in the Santa
Cruz valley at the base of the Santa Catalina mountains. One of
the oldest towns in the United States, Tucson is a modern
metropolis with deep roots in Indian and Spanish colonial history.
Spaciousness and color lend distinctiveness to the physical
setting. Low foothills ring the city and jagged peaks float in the
distance. At every hour of the day they appear to change color as
brown turns to lavender and then to deep blue at twilight. Amid
the muted neutral colors of the desert the green palo verde,
greasewood, and saguaro appear. As more and more winter
visitors linger to become permanent residents, more building,
increased planting, and greater effort to "civilize" the
environment follow. But deserts, mountains, and climate are
formidable obstacles in the way of change, and for the present, at
least, the magnificent landscape continues to survive and
dominate.*

*With the remarkable growth and development since World
War II, Tucson's appearance has altered. Undistinguished, multi-
storied buildings of stone and glass dwarf low adobe landmarks.
Sleek, huge shopping centers have replaced jumbled marketplaces
and tiny shops. Wide, straight manicured boulevards carry the
traffic around and away from the twisting streets of the Old
Pueblo. Honking horns, exhaust fumes, and rock music have
drowned and driven out the predominant sights and smells of the
barrio of fifty years ago.*

*In the following selection, a former Tucson resident
vividly recreates the colorful street vendors of his childhood. The
aroma of steaming tamales and freshly baked bread seems
literally to rise from these recollections. And the voices of the*

street vendors hawking their wares seem to be coming from some place nearby. Nostalgia for the carefree days of boyhood may have caused the author to embellish these recollections somewhat and to ignore the economic and social injustices often hidden from us in childhood. Yet remnants of the rich customs and beautiful traditions of life in the barrio still survive and recalling them may help to safeguard and preserve the best of them.

Almost a year ago business took me back to Tucson for a short sojourn. My, how that place has changed! It's just not the Tucson of my childhood days anymore. Like almost all American cities, it has grown in length and breadth, and its population has more than doubled. It now has a freeway which, in avoiding the heart of the city, has severed one of its main arteries. Then there are the block-long shopping centers, and countless modern buildings that have replaced many of the old adobe landmarks that dated back to the colonial days of the Southwest.

With these innovations the Mexican barrio, which for scores of years had clung to the customs and traditions of old Mexico, has fast disappeared. Oh, there are still areas where my paisanos (fellow countrymen) predominate, but they are the new generations who in the process of acculturation have left behind large portions of the heritage which our parents brought to this country. A discussion of this topic could be the subject of a book, but right now I only wish to share with you my reminiscences of yesteryear. More specifically, I wish to acquaint you with the colorful street vendors who were so much a part of the Tucson which I associate with those delightful years of my early life. When I revisited my old tramping grounds I looked for them. I even optimistically cocked my ear to see if perchance I could hear their once familiar calls. They are no more. Those vendors are now history. They had to give way to the drive-ins, the supermarkets, or, let us say, to the jet age.

"Tamaleees! Tamaleees calientes!" This was the call with which Doña Ramona lured her customers to her delicious homemade tamales in the late afternoons as she drove through the streets where so many of the Spanish-speaking people resided. She

From Arnulfo D. Trejo, *Arizona Highways* 39 (August 1963): 37–41. Used with permission from Arnulfo D. Trejo.

187

was a woman in her late fifties and sort of mannish in appearance. Some of the older boys used to say that she had to shave, same as a man. With her dark rebozo (shawl), however, which she wore over her head both in summer and winter, she seemed to regain much of her femininity.

Her transportation was furnished by an obedient, not-too-well-fed, old mare that lazily pulled a light-weight wagon on which Doña Ramona stately sat up front not too far from her tamales. The horse had been on the job for so many years that it automatically stopped as soon as a customer would come out so that Doña Ramona could attend to the sale. Then it would be off on its course again as soon as the purchase was made and it heard the lid being placed back on the steaming pot of tamales.

Doña Ramona was not the only vendor that provided the Mexican colony with tamales. There were other vendors whose tamales were just as good and whose lungs were just as strong. Yet this old lady was the dean of them all. The secret of her trade was that with each sale she always managed to share with her customers choice bits of neighborhood gossip. Whenever my mother would buy tamales from Doña Ramona, she always felt as if she had read the newspaper for the week. To her competitors she was *la vieja chismosa* (the gossipy old lady), but to her regular customers she was simply Doña Ramona or, jokingly, *la señora periódico* (Madam Newspaper).

Some of Doña Ramona's envious competitors were always trying to undermine her successful occupation. One of them, I recall, once circulated the rumor that she was using cat meat in her tamales. I do not know how much this hurt her business, but it became a known fact that she finally got rid of the ten or twelve cats that she used to keep.

The most colorful vendors of all were the *Arabes*, as they were called, who in broken Spanish were heard calling out their "specials" of the day. I don't know why they were called Arabs, for years later when I grew up I discovered that most of them were Jewish. Their stores were on Meyer Street, but on Saturday mornings, or whenever the workmen from the Round House received their paychecks, these vendors would load up and peddle their goods along the streets where the Spanish-speaking people lived.

One of these peripatetic merchants who particularly stands out in my mind was a man called *San Dimas*. Nobody knew his real name, but it was said that one of his early unsatisfied customers,

188

upon seeing him coming her way again, made the sign of the cross and exclaimed: *"Ahí viene San Demonios."* (There comes Saint Demon.) Thereafter, not wanting to call him Saint Demon to his face, the people decided in favor of *San Dimas*. Like a good businessman that he was, he accepted his new name in good spirit. He even adopted it as part of his call. *"Aquí viene San Dimas, marchante,"* he used to say with a strong Yiddish accent.

When *San Dimas* went on a selling mission he was a sight to see. He would put on as many hats as he could carry—all sizes, shapes, and colors. Dangling from his coat, or shirt on a hot day, were combs, curlers for the ladies, rattles for the babies, watches, pins, buttons, and even a few rosaries. You name it; he had it. The only problem was getting to these items, because over all this merchandise, thrown over his shoulders, were multicolored bolts of cloth. As if this was not enough, on both hands he carried dresses for both women and girls and sometimes even a man's suit. In the summertime it was almost pitiful to see the plump, round, little man walking the streets in the blazing Tucson sun.

An important part of his paraphernalia was a stack of lined cards about ten inches in length by three inches in width. Since most of his sales were on a credit basis, he had a card for each one of his customers. The grapevine had it that once you were entered in the deficit column on one of his cards, the amount never seemed to diminish no matter how much you paid on your account. Maybe he was appropriately named after all.

Fridays and Saturdays were the days when the Papago Indians from nearby San Xavier or far-away Sells were expected in town with their wagon-loads of wood. They were the ones that provided the fuel for our stoves and our fireplaces. Unlike the other vendors these were the silent type. About the only way that one could tell when they were in town was through the squeaky wheels of their wagons and the clippety-clop of their horses. During the winter months people were seen anxiously waiting for them, but during the summer the wagons would roll over and over again through the same streets.

The Papagos from San Xavier usually arrived on Friday, but despite their lead on their blood-brothers from Sells they apparently had a harder time selling their wood. This might be explained by the fact that the quality of their wood was not as good as that brought in from Sells. The Papagos from Sells specialized in palo verde, which was just what the housewives wanted. It lasted longer

189

and gave a more intense heat, but palo verde was more expensive. Then, too, the Papagos from San Xavier had the reputation of stacking their loads; that is, they camouflaged the green mesquite wood, which nobody wanted, by neatly covering it with selected pieces of dry wood.

Buying wood from the Papagos was an art in itself. To begin with, they spoke very little, either in English or in Spanish or in their native tongue. Usually they just sat on their wagons until the right price was offered to them. When the Indians from San Xavier were willing to bargain they would invariably say *"lena seca"* (dry wood) in their slow, quiet manner of speaking. The ones from Sells, who were not any more loquacious than the Indians from San Xavier, simply said "palo verde." This was sometimes amusing, because they would consistently say the same thing even when all they had to sell was mesquite. In the wintertime when wood was in demand and the price offered to them was not to their liking, they would nonchalantly drive off saying *"mañana vengo"* (I'll come tomorrow). Interestingly enough, once they put their wagons in motion they very seldom stopped. Instead, they circled the block and, if in the process of doing this they did not get a better offer, they would return and station themselves right in front of the place where they had heard the best bid. In a tough bargain the number of times that the wood vendors went around the block usually depended on the buyer's stock of patience.

The *menuderos* were the early risers. As early as five o'clock in the morning one could hear them calling: *"Menudooo! Menudooo!"* Then they would stop and wait beside their two-wheel, hand-pushed carts in the hope that someone would come out to buy their product which they carried in extra-large pots. If no one came out, the vendor would let out a couple of less-animated calls and continue with his route.

Menudo is a kind of soup consisting of tripe, the cow's hoofs after they have been especially prepared for cooking, and hominy. People with a weak stomach may find the ingredients a bit offensive, but in effect they make a very nourishing and tasty dish, particularly when spiced with a little chili, chopped onion, and a pinch of oregano. Those who have had one too many the night before may discover that a bowl of this hot soup can be more effective than a glass of Alka Seltzer.

In my neighborhood the two best-known *menuderos* were Don Pedro and Don Angel. The latter lived up to his name. He used to dress in white and was immaculately clean, but Don Pedro, well . . .

Don Pedro was about fifty years of age, a bit younger than Don Angel and heavier built. Sometimes Don Pedro wore a hat, sometimes a cap, and many times he just displayed a shock of curly hair which was foreign to a comb. During the summer he appeared only half dressed, and it seemed that the only water that ever touched the rags he wore was that which came from the infrequent Tucson rains. In winter he wore a long, threadbare overcoat that some said originally belonged to Father Kino. Don Angel's voice was high pitched and did not carry too well, but when Don Pedro let out with one of his calls he could be heard all over the block.

There was no doubt that Don Angel sold more *menudo* than anyone else, but Don Pedro had the most fun doing it. Sometimes when he did not get a response to his call, or should we say roars, he would direct a barrage of insults to his customers that went something like this: *"Levantense, viejas feas, que no tengo todo el día para esperales!"* This was the summons to those who had imbibed too freely the night before. "Get up, you drunkards, I've got the cure here for you!" he used to say.

Although Don Pedro's appearance was unsightly and the salesmanship methods that he used were unorthodox, to say the least, he stayed in business thanks to the kind people who bought his menudo, although it may have been in self-defense.

In the late afternoons the bakers took their turn on the streets. *"Paaan, pan caliente!"* they used to shout as they carried on their heads baskets full of freshly made bread. It must have been the load on their heads that precipitated their walk, or maybe they just thought it was good business to keep one step ahead of their competitors. Their call was not always a simple one.

El Canario, who had a rather pleasant voice, as one might suspect from the name that was given to him, used to sing out the names of the different kinds of "goodies" that he had for sale. No, that is not quite true, because his lyrics really depended more on his mood and the time of day than on what he actually had for sale. At the start of his rounds, and if he happened to be in a jovial mood, there seemed to be no end to the extensive variety of Mexican pastries that he had available. My mind does not serve me well to recall his complete repertory, but here is a good start: *Pan de huevo, semitas, pastelitos, polvorones, conchitas, roscas, besos, empañadas, chamucos, cuernos, monos, corbatas, and cochinitos.*

191

The way *El Canario* would combine all these terms to give them harmony was truly commendable. The only trouble was that his customers never did know for sure what he really had for sale. Now if this singing baker happened to be in the neighborhood late in the day, by which time he was tired and perhaps even low in spirit if business had not gone well for him, there was no reason to disbelieve his call. By that time his previously lively song was reduced to a mere chant of *paaan, paaan, paaan.*

One of these wandering bakers, however, was neither swift nor melodious. He croaked like a frog and moved like a turtle. Ironically, he was called *El Venadito* (the Little Deer). A handicap which was attributed to polio had left his mouth pointing in two different directions but also had made a cripple of him. Some people found him so repulsive to look at that doors were slammed shut and window blinds pulled down at the sight of him. Nonetheless, he had more than his share of devoted customers.

El Venadito used devious methods to promote the sale of his merchandise. For example, the boy or girl that first saw him coming in the afternoon always received a *cochinito* (a small gingerbread cookie in the shape of a pig) as a reward. As soon as the children would see him coming they invariably stampeded, shouting: "*El Venadito, El Venadito, El Venadito!*" With this kind of reception, how could the neighborhood fail to know that he was around?

When the children were in school he would knock on the door of one of his steady customers. This person would then be asked to call out her neighbors. Usually this produced the right results for him, particularly if he was able to find someone like our neighbor from across the street. My, how that woman could yell!

But the success of El Venadito was in knowing how to make use of the local Spanish idiom *dar madera,* (the act of praising, to compliment, to laud.) Yes, he could really flatter the women, who, incidentally, were the ones who usually bought from the street vendors. To him, the fat ones were slender, the skinny, well-filled-out; the old ones, young; and the young, grown up. To his eyes there was not a homely woman in the world. The Spanish language is rich in adjectives to describe beauty. He knew them all, and at one time or another even the unsightly, shapeless, misproportioned, haggard, and ill-looking women that bought his *pan dulce* (sweet bread) must have been thrilled to have these descriptive terms applied to them. So while his competitors tired themselves walking

192

the streets of the neighborhood, this handicapped but clever man probably made more money in his business than all the other bakers put together. As in the race between the tortoise and the hare, speed did not prove to be an advantage over astuteness.

This work would be incomplete if I did not include *Palillo* (the Stick), a seasonal vendor who hibernated during the winter months and made his appearance only in summer. His business was selling *leche nevade* (ice cream), *Paletas* (popsicles), and *cimarronas* (snow cones).

Palillo, as his name implies, was on the skinny side. To tell the truth, his ribs seemed to merge with his spinal cord. But he was strong. He had to be to control the spirited horse that pulled his white wagon shaped in the form of a box car. An important piece of equipment that was installed on this strange-looking vehicle was a bell that could be heard for miles. Why, it was so loud that the neighbors used to say that *Palillo* had to change horses every year, because by the end of the season his horse was completely "shell-shocked."

One thing that could be said for the bell was that it gave the children plenty of advance notice so that they could work on their parents for a nickel. However, there was always the problem of getting *Palillo* to stop for a sale. He did not like to make frequent stops, so we had to chase him for blocks before he would stop. *"Palillo, Palillo, Palillo!"* the children used to yell as they ran as fast as they could after the ice cream man. Perhaps it was the challenge of getting him to stop that made the youngsters want to patronize him that much more.

And so end these portraits which are a part of my impressionable years. I hope that I have captured the life and spirit of those people who have now passed into the realm of folklore.

The Doctor of Roosevelt Dam

Ralph F. Palmer, M.D.

Water dominates the Arizona story. Water, for domestic use and for agriculture, has been the single most important element in Arizona's growth and development. The historic problem was not lack of moisture but control and storage of runoff from snowmelt and spring rains at higher elevations for use in the valleys below. The solution was to impound excess water behind dams and, through a series of canals, direct it to fertile farmlands and to growing cities.

The early Indian settlers had mastered desert farming. Although pioneer farmers in the Salt River Valley had irrigated their crops using canals the Hohokam Indians had originally constructed, the system was unstable. Brush and log dams were swept away during floods, and in summer, when the Salt River dwindled, crops withered. Promoters of extended settlement in the valley knew that a more efficient way of harnessing the river's flow must be developed if Arizona were to prosper.

Beginning in 1889, the Phoenix Chamber of Commerce took the lead with a series of surveys, expeditions, fund drives, bond sales, and tax levies which culminated in the federal-state partnership to construct Roosevelt Dam. Located at the point where Tonto Creek flows into the Salt River, Roosevelt Dam was the first major irrigation project the federal government financed. Completed in 1911, the eleven-million-dollar project was debt free when the government loan was fully repaid in 1955.

Preparations to erect the dam were as monumental as the actual construction. Prior to the start of building, Apache workmen cut sixty miles of wagon road through precipitous mountains for the hundreds of mule trains needed to haul men and material to the remote site. A sawmill, an intake dam to generate electricity, and a cement plant were built on-site to supply construction needs. Building this huge dam virtually by

195

hand before modern construction equipment was available was a tribute to human ingenuity, energy, and will.

The Roosevelt Dam campsite was a miniature city with offices, dining and sleeping tents, an icehouse, a blacksmith shop, a carpenter's shop, a sewage treatment plant, and a field hospital. The chief surgeon selected to serve the project was Ralph Fleetwood Palmer, a pioneer physician who had arrived in Arizona in 1902. He was reared in a Michigan family of comfortable means and educated at the College of Physicians and Surgeons at the University of Illinois. Dr. Palmer traveled to Arizona for a visit with a brother who was trying to regain his health. He remained to establish a "horseback practice" first at Prescott, then at Camp Verde. After his years of service at Roosevelt Dam, he settled in Mesa.

Dr. Palmer thrived on the invigorating climate. He accepted the occupational hazards of riding all night over crude mountain trails to attend a patient as easily as a modern doctor steps from consulting office to examining room. The medical problems he encountered without benefit of antibiotics and sophisticated diagnostic techniques seem incredible, but his healing skills were widely sought.

In addition to his medical prowess, Dr. Palmer was a sharp observer of daily life. His recollections are an important contribution to Arizona's historical record.

196

At the time of our arrival these projects were mostly on paper on the drafting tables at Livingston. My first job was to assist the acting superintendent, Charles Olberg, in laying out the camp at the damsite, and we started on this immediately. On a low bluff on the south side of the Salt our survey gang staked out the location for a large corral, an engineers' mess tent on a higher level, a field hospital tent, sleeping tents for engineers and guests and numerous tent sites for working men, a blacksmith shop, carpenter shop, etc.

As the work progressed, we laid out a townsite adjoining on the east, the lots to be leased to individuals on permit for business purposes at no rental but under restriction as to conduct, especially in regard to liquor, which was prohibited within a three-mile limit over the entire project. We also located an excellent spring and brought water in by gravity to a large storage tank supplying the entire camp and town, and later the contractor's camp to be established on a high bluff across the river on the Tonto side. Of the early tents set up were two in a cottonwood grove across the Salt and on the Tonto where Mr. Olberg had them placed—one for himself and one for us.

These tents were canvas stretched on board frames with board floors, mostly of dark canvas with an additional fly. When furnished they were very comfortable. Later on, a number of houses were erected on a hilltop south of the camp, also an office building and a septic tank to dispose of sewage. In the beginning, we used latrines throughout the camp and town with a sanitary squad to lime them daily.

From Ralph F. Palmer, M.D., *Doctor on Horseback* (Mesa: Mesa Historical and Archaeological Society: 1979), 80–129. Used with permission from the Mesa Historical and Archaelogical Society.

197

Eventually, Roosevelt became quite a well-organized camp with electric lights, a large icehouse, running water and sewage disposal and a number of business houses. At its prime it had a post office with daily mail and a population approaching 5,000 persons. As the dam walls started up and the water began to back up, all the business houses had to move to higher ground and a location half a mile above the office building was chosen. It was first called New Town and later Roosevelt.

• • •

With later construction of storage dams at Horse Mesa, Mormon Flat and Stewart Mountain, Roosevelt has become almost entirely a power dam, supplying together with the other dams lower down the river power to the Salt River Valley Water Users' Association (S.R.V.W.U.A.) which distributes it throughout the Salt River Valley and to the mines at Superior and Miami.

• • •

During the first few weeks on the Roosevelt project we continued to live with the Harrises. With Mr. Olberg I made daily trips to the campsite at the dam, driving my horses mostly. The road crossed the Salt River several times. At one crossing in particular there was a good-sized pond and usually there were many ducks on it. The country was also alive with quail and wild turkeys and as Charlie and I both liked to shoot, we managed to keep the camp well supplied with game. At the end of the first month, however, our two tents in Cottonwood Canyon were ready, Mrs. Olberg had arrived, the hospital tent had been set up, a hundred or more workmen were on the job. We moved to Roosevelt.

As appropriations from Washington began to come in, the various preliminary projects developed rapidly and so did my practice since medical service to workmen was provided without charge to them. Road camps had been established at various points on the Apache Trail from Government Wells on the desert to Fish Creek, seventeen miles west of Roosevelt. Also at the intake dam-site and at the sawmill in the Sierra Anchas. I had set up a first-aid station in each of these camps and made each station once a week, a round trip of about two hundred miles horseback. As the Reclamation Service had horses in each camp, I was able to get a change every thirty miles or so and save my own mounts.

One of my early experiences at Roosevelt happened on a Saturday evening when I was riding up the river looking for ducks. A man from the sawmill caught up with me and said the wife of the boss was dying. We were just opposite Sally May Canyon, where a horseback trail went up the mountain to the sawmill camp, a distance of about twelve miles instead of thirty-five by road.

I gave the man my gun, and told him to go back to the hospital and get my saddlebags and follow me up the trail. I was wearing a sweater vest and in one of the pockets happened to have two vials of placebo tablets, one pink and one white. By the time I was well up the mountain it started to snow on top of the eight to ten inches already on the ground, and by the time I reached the sawmill it was quite dark.

The boss's tent was a big one, about sixteen by twenty feet. There were four double beds in it and a red-hot box stove in one corner. The sawmill was run on a contract basis by a group of Arkansawians [sic] and there must have been fifteen or twenty of them in the tent, more people than air. On one of the beds lay the boss's wife, apparently unconscious.

On cursory examination, however, she had a normal pulse and apparently normal temperature. There was no swelling anywhere and, as far as I could tell without a stethoscope, she was perfectly normal except for her apparent unconsciousness and breathing. The breathing was quite remarkable and rhythmic. From apparent cessation entirely, respiration would very gradually increase in both volume and rate till a climax was reached when she would give a little gurgle and "cough up the death phlegm" (pronounced "fleem" by one of the women who explained it to me).

I watched her through several of these cycles and noted no more than a normal change of pulse during them before concluding that it was a case of pure hysteria. I stage-whispered to the husband and a woman or two beside the bed that although his wife was apparently near the end I had a very powerful remedy with me which might either bring her back to life or on the other hand might end it quickly. Personally, I would not take the responsibility. It was up to them to decide.

After considerable discussion beside the bed, they decided that she was going to die anyway and they would take the chance.

199

So we got a couple of spoons and dissolved one of the placebo tablets in hot water and one in cold water. At the apex of the next cycle, and just as the "death fleem" was coming up and her mouth was open, I slipped the hot pink one well back in her throat and as she started into a spasm followed it with the cold white one. The spasms and shudders gradually subsided and she passed into a natural sleep.

After a while we went down to the cook tent and had some Arkansaw [sic] food and coffee. We sat around till midnight when the patient woke up from her sleep and said she had had a terrible dream where she was crossing a dark river and there were many winged creatures flying about!

Another interesting trip during that first winter at Roosevelt was made to see a patient at Young with a cattleman named Ed Gilliland who had ridden down from there to get me.

Young was a small center with a post office and general store situated in a high mountain valley about forty miles north of the sawmill but only sixty miles from Roosevelt by trail. We started up Tonto Creek late in the afternoon and at Cline took off up Greenback Canyon trail to get up on the mountain. Along after dark it had started to rain and we came to a one-room cabin beside the trail. We were invited in by Florence Packard, who was a lion hunter.

In the cabin besides Florence were a half a dozen bloodhounds. Florence must have been in his late sixties for his long hair and full beard were gray. The chief furnishings were a small wooden table and a couple of three-legged stools. In the corner was a small fireplace with a coffeepot and a pot of beans on the coals. Several rifles and a saddle were in another corner. A board bunk against one wall was provided with lion skins for both mattress and covers.

Florence, for all his fierce appearance and surroundings, was a genial host; and when he learned where we were heading he said the trail up would be bad in the dark and rain and it would be snowing on top, so that we had better stay with him overnight. Ed thanked him but said Mrs. Young was powerful sick and he thought we could make the Steward ranch on top without trouble and maybe get all the way through to Young.

We did, however, accept a cup of coffee and a plate of beans. There was only one cup so we took turns pouring the cup full of water into the coffeepot, which was full of grounds, and after it came to a boil poured it back into the cup to drink. Not much for coffee, but it was hot. There were two spoons so we could both eat beans at the same time directly out of the bean pot. After an hour or so when thoroughly warm and dry, we started out. As Florence had warned us, the trail was slippery and rough and finally covered with snow.

At the top, the snow was well over the horses' knees, but Ed seemed to know the way and followed it through timber till finally about midnight we descended a little slope. Ed got off his horse and, after digging in the snow a bit, found a wire gate which he managed to get open enough to get through. A few hundred feet inside we came to a good-sized log cabin.

Ed found some paper and wood and got a fire started in the fireplace. As soon as we were warmed up a bit, he unsaddled the horses and brought them in to a sort of woodshed on the side of the house. He also found and lit a coal-oil lantern and in rummaging around finally found a little coffee left in a can and a couple of cans of beans. With melted snow we made coffee and, after defrosting the beans, had our midnight supper. It was very cold outside, probably close to zero. There was plenty of wood in the shed, however, so we sat on the floor and talked until daylight.

Ed told me this was the Jack Steward cattle ranch but in the winter the cattle and cowboys were down on the lower ranges. He also told me it was about the south end of the district which was the scene of the Tewksbury-Graham cattle and sheep war which was described in Zane Grey's *To the Last Man*. About the war itself he would not say much, either because he didn't know or because he wouldn't talk on the subject. The main trouble was but a few years back and individuals were still feuding.

At daybreak we saddled up and rode the ten miles down a gradual grade to Young, where we found a good breakfast. Mrs. Young at the time was in her seventies and had been bedridden for several months. She was greatly emaciated and having severe hemorrhages from a cancer. There was not much to be done except to give her what ease I could with morphine of which, fortunately, I had a goodly supply and, fortunately too for her, she did not have much longer to live.

Word of a doctor visiting a patient in these remote regions seems to spread rapidly and, as usual during my day there, I saw several other patients. Also had a request to visit another bedridden woman, a Mrs. Holder, some ten or twelve miles east. So after

201

spending the night at the Youngs', I started out next morning with the Holder boy.

The Holders were goat herders. While the house was not in the center of a goat corral like the Sullivan ranch, there was the same general atmosphere and the same kind of goaty food. Mrs. Holder was also well along in the advanced stages of cancer with nothing to do except relieve pain while she lived.

The Holders, like all the goat herders I met, were poor but honest. During the following years the boys used to come into Roosevelt once a month or so and bring me a young kid. We found these kids to be excellent meat, and quite in demand by our friends at Roosevelt.

• • •

Along in February Mr. Louis C. Hill—Chief Engineer on the project, appointed by the Reclamation Service to carry out the plans and specifications prepared by Mr. Arthur P. Davis—arrived at Livingston to take active charge of the work. Mr. Hill was a graduate of the Engineering College at the University of Michigan and had been teaching mathematics at the Colorado School of Mines at Denver for a few years.

He was a powerful man both physically and mentally, enabling him to take on the arduous duties involved in a project with so many facets and keeping in his retentive mind the many details associated with it. Frequently in our visitations to the various camps our routes would coincide, and we would often drive together when there was a road or ride together when there was not.

• • •

[On one trip] I mentioned to Mr. Hill that I understood there had been some fifty or more applications from within and without the Territory for the position as surgeon on the project and asked him how come I had been selected.

"Well," he said. "It was at a meeting in Phoenix with Mr. Newell, Chief Hydrographer of the U.S. Geological Survey, and Mr. Davis, the Chief Engineer, when the applications were discussed. A month before that the qualifications of the various applicants and their references had been investigated and yours seemed to be the only one where no political or other influences was sug-

202

gested. Your references were entirely on medical qualifications and were satisfactory. You were also in the Territory in active practice and, on these bases, you were offered the appointment."

Mrs. Hill and their two children did not come to Roosevelt until late summer when the houses on the hill were constructed, so on his overnight stops at the damsite camp Mr. Hill usually occupied a tent next to the hospital at the engineers' camp. Here after supper in the mess tent he would discuss the various engineering problems with the engineers and outline specific problems for them to take up.

• • •

Mr. Hill had set up his first office at the engineers' headquarters in Livingston. He had a desk in the open drafting room and anyone who wanted to talk with him simply walked up to the desk. One of his many problems was talking with ranchers along the two rivers whose property would be inundated when the dam backed up the water. The surveys showed the lake would have a total length of twenty-five miles: fifteen on the Salt and ten on the Tonto. These ranchers would crowd in on him all talking at once.

One day I had been in Phoenix and, in company with Dr. Craig, had gone into the Connolly bar on Adams Street for a glass of beer. While we were sitting in a booth, Mr. Connolly came in and said he had a patient in the back room. We went out with him and found a young man on the floor coughing up a considerable amount of blood. We got him into bed at the Adams Hotel and when I saw him the next day he was quite cheerful and said his name was Finley McGuire, that he had been private secretary to Mr. Charles Schwab at Gary, Indiana, when he developed tuberculosis and Mr. Schwab had sent him to Arizona.

I told him I thought I could get him a job at Roosevelt. The road was quite passable by that time so he went to the dam with me, I explained Mr. Hill's situation and said I thought he really needed a secretary. When he looked Mr. Hill's office arrangements over, Finley said that it would be easy to fix so we arranged for a carpenter to build a rail fence around Mr. Hill's desk during the night. The fence had a gate in it and a small table outside the gate.

When Mr. Hill came in the next morning and came to the gate, Finley, whom he had not met, stopped him and said, "Mr. Hill is not in yet, please give your name and sit down. You will be first as there are no other appointments ahead of you." "Well! I'm Mr. Hill and who in ---- are you." "Oh, Mr. Hill," said Finley, rising with his hand out. "I'm Finley McGuire, your new secretary that Dr. Palmer brought up from Phoenix." "I didn't know I needed a secretary, but it might be a good idea. I'll try you out for a day or two and see how it works."

It worked, and Mr. Hill had no further trouble dealing with more than one visitor at a time for no one got past the gate without the secretary's permission, and usually his name and business were provided before getting to Mr. Hill. Later Mr. Hill told me I had a lot of nerve hiring him a secretary without his permission, but after he learned Finley's proficiency, he was duly appreciative.

Although my appointment as surgeon to the Roosevelt Project contemplated my principal activities would be taking care of employees, I was also permitted to have private patients. As the nearest available physician to the remote areas more or less adjacent to the project, I was frequently called on to treat patients in the backcountry. One of these calls that first winter involved the most strenuous seventy-two hours of my horseback practice.

Joe Zacharie, a cattleman living just under the Mogollon Rim seventy-five miles north of Roosevelt, came in one evening. He had ridden into Payson some thirty miles to get a doctor who had located there. The doctor, however, had left the country, so Joe rode on an additional sixty miles to Roosevelt. He said his sister had been in to see this doctor at Payson a month before because of a rupture and that the doctor had put some kind of a contraption in her vagina. A few days ago when her next period started she had terrible cramps and had become much swollen and they thought she was going to die because the contraption would not permit any blood to come out.

Joe had left his horse at Cline some 12 miles up Tonto Creek and I told him I would meet him there next morning. From Cline we went up into Greenback Canyon but up a trail on the north side instead of past the lion hunter's cabin on the south side. On top we came to a small clearing and house about thirty-five minutes from Roosevelt. The owner, Jake Lauffer, was plowing a field with two mules. After a brief conversation Jake unharnessed the mules and threw my saddle on one of them and I left Raccadoni in his barn.

About ten miles further we came to another cow ranch and here Joe got a fresh mount but I stayed with Jake's mule, though, because of the mule's narrow withers and my single cinch saddle, I was frequently riding on his neck going downhill into the washes and on his hind end climbing out. However, we had not crossed any deep canyons until after we left this last ranch. Then for the next twenty miles or so to Potato Butte the drainage was east and west and the canyons were from zero to two hundred feet deep and we had to cross one after the other so that by the time we got on the open ground I was well nigh all in and so was the mule.

On a high mesa opposite the Butte we met a cowman named Paul Sell. I didn't know him, but Joe did. Paul was riding a large black horse and said he was but a few miles from his ranch, so he generously loaned me his horse and rode the mule home. Joe, of course, was anxious about his sister and had been forcing the pace all day long, but for the next ten miles to the ranch he had a hard time keeping up. The last two miles were down a steep side hill into the canyon of Willow Creek. The black horse with high step-ping front feet and sliding hind feet almost pranced down the hill, while Joe's tired horse had to stumble down.

The Zacharies were a Danish cattle family and had a log cabin, white-washed inside and out. We found the sister, Dalgmar, sitting up in bed singing Danish songs to her own accompaniment on a guitar. She was much better of her cramps and swelling and when I fished out an occlusive-type of pessary, she was all right. It was dark by that time and Mrs. Zacharie had a roast chicken with other good things for supper.

In the morning we started back, stopping at the Sell Ranch to return Paul's horse and get Jake's mule, and again that grinding ride over one ridge after another and up and down to cross the canyons. Along in the afternoon it had started to snow, which made it worse. We finally picked up Joe's horse and reached Lauffer's Ranch about five in the afternoon. By that time it had really started to snow and a considerable blizzard was making.

During the day for all of our covering plenty of territory we had seen no one except Paul Sell and the man where Joe had changed horses, but within the next two or three hours after we had holed in at Jake's no less than five other men came in for shel-ter. They must have known the country well and that the door of Jake's cabin was always open for shelter. Two of them were forest rangers, one was a deputy sheriff from Globe with a cattle thief whom he had under arrest, and one was a prospector with his two burros. So with Joe and me the Lauffers had seven visitors.

205

There were beans and salt pork with biscuits, honey, and coffee, however, and Mrs. Lauffer fed us all including herself and Jake and two boys both under ten years. They also had plenty of blankets and wood in the house, and though we all lined up on the floor to sleep, it was not so bad. Jake had been shot through the back during the Tewksbury-Graham war a few years before, but, except for some tingling in his lower limbs, was not having much trouble with it at the time. . . .

The blizzard lasted through the night and in the morning, although the wind had subsided, it was still snowing with about twelve inches of snow on the ground. After breakfast I told Joe to go on home as it was only eight or ten miles to Greenback and Raccadoni would take me home. When we came out of the timber on the rim above Greenback, neither Raccadoni nor I could locate the trail down the canyon. After a vain search I picked out a point about opposite the lower ridge which divided Greenback into two canyons and, taking my lead rope, got off and started to slide down the side of the canyon leading my horse, for I wanted to be sure to have him at the bottom. The bottom of the canyon was at least fifteen hundred feet below the rim and as we slid and scrambled down we got out of the big timber and into manzanita and later mesquite. The dry snow on the top gradually changed to wet snow, then slush and then mud, while the snowfall itself changed into sleet and then rain. At last we made the bottom and picked up the north trail leading to the Tonto.

It was about five o'clock when I reached the corral and there I found a call from Livingston, where the paymaster had fallen off a haystack and broken his arm. I took a buckboard and team with a driver for this trip. After setting the arm and putting it in a splint, I finally reached home about nine p.m.

But there was no rest for the weary doctor. I found a man there waiting with an emergency call to Payson with instructions to pick up a horse at Judge Howell's at the foot of Tonto Hill for the last twenty-mile stretch into Payson. So, with a fresh horse I started off again. At Judge Howell's I found the horse and turned mine into the corral. The ride up the grade into Payson went from three thousand to fifty-five hundred feet in elevation and the last of it up a ridge with a fifteen to twenty percent grade.

It was just daylight when I reached the Postmaster's house and found a ten-year-old girl with a double pneumonia. We did not have antibiotics in those days and had to do what we could with stimulants, expectorants and antiphlogistines or other types of chest poultices.

After breakfast, when the child was more comfortable and I had seen a few other patients who came to the house, a cowman named Bud Armer came over and took me home with him for a rest. Mrs. Armer put me in bed with a two-year-old daughter who in later years when I met her at a dance in Phoenix told me that I had been the first man who had ever slept with her. They woke me up about five o'clock and I went back to see my patient. She was markedly improved. After leaving medicine and instruction, I was ready to leave.

When I had gone out with Bud earlier I had noticed a good-looking pole buggy in the barn and asked Bud if he could dig up a team and take me down to Judge Howell's where I had left my horse. Sure enough when I came out there was Bud with several cowboys at the gate. They had the buggy out on the road and a team with harness on.

Bud and I got into the buggy before they hooked the team up. They finally managed this with a cowboy on each side with short ropes on the horses. After some plunging the team got started on a run. A quarter mile down the road through town we had to make a right angle turn to get on our road. As the cowboys swung the team around with the buggy on two wheels we started up a hill about a mile long. The cowboys cast off their ropes and we were on our own on a dead run up the hill.

The team, two range horses never broken to drive or mind the reins, did keep to the road, and by the time they reached the top of the grade had simmered down to a trot. During the ten miles to the top of Tonto Hill they became pretty well broken in. The road down Tonto Hill at that time was down a long gravelly ridge with a very steep grade, especially at the bottom where it dropped into a sand wash. There was no breeching on the harness and the light brakes on the buggy would not hold much, so all the horses had to hold back with were their collars.

While we started down on a walk and Bud held their heads up with the reins, we were not more than half-way down when the team broke into a run. When we hit the sand wash we should have tipped over, but Bud held the horses straight while I hung on to the buggy. At the foot of the hill was a roadhouse with a barn. In order to stop Bud ran the pole of the buggy right into the side of the barn.

207

After we got the horses quieted down and tied to the hitching rack, we went into the bar and had a much-needed bottle of Red Top, a favorite brand of whiskey in Arizona bars at that time. We also found some food there and after an hour's rest Bud drove me on to Judge Howell's with a well-broken team of driving horses.

It was a nice moonlight night and I jogged down Tonto Creek, meeting a freight outfit on the road about daylight. I had coffee and biscuits with them and got home for breakfast.

• • •

Work went as usual until along in July several cases of typhoid fever developed. They were all in the engineers' camps and, although never definitely proved, the suspicion was that it came from raw milk supplied by a man up on Tonto Creek, where there had been a case of typhoid the year before. Mr. Olberg and I were among the victims. Before coming down myself, however, I had shut off the milk supply to the mess hall and with my cow and two others started a new dairy with Charley Hill, who had a small pasture up the Salt River. There were no further typhoid cases in camp.

When I took to bed, Dr. Richard D. Kennedy, a physician with the Old Dominion Mine Hospital at Globe, came out to look after me and my work. He gave the typhoid patients the same antipyretic treatment I had inaugurated. This was to put the patient in a canvas tarp with several inches of water in it and a cake of ice at the head and foot. Then four to six men would hold the sides and ends up and swish the cold water round by rolling the patient in the canvas. It was a very effective treatment from a fever standpoint, but as my 105-degree temperature began to respond I sure wanted to beg off. Anyway, there is an end to all things and all the typhoid cases recovered.

• • •

On returning to duty after my experience with typhoid I gave particular attention to sanitation. Our milk problem was apparently safe for we had no further cases of typhoid after starting Charley Hill on the new dairy. He increased his herd by several additional fresh cows, arranged his milking pens to keep milk clean

208

and, while the milk was not pasteurized, the buckets were thoroughly scalded and the milk continued good.

I appointed Joe Zacharie as chief of the sanitary squad, and he did an efficient job during the latrine period. They made a complete daily inspection and report not only on the latrines but on all garbage and refuse. On the hill as the cottages were nearing completion I made a study of septic tanks and we developed one to take care of the sewage on the hill.

This was a concrete structure with a two- by six- by four-foot settling tank with a trapdoor to remove sand or dirt if it filled up, which it never did. Then the main tank was forty feet long by twenty feet wide with a depth of six feet arranged with projections from alternate sides to slow the flow and permit prolonged anaerobic decomposition. The outlet went over the bank on to an aerating rock filter. This filter was some fifteen feet high with a circular base about 4 feet in diameter. An aerobic film formed on the boulders, and by the time the water came out at the bottom it was perfectly clear and odorless.

• • •

Our spring and storage tank proved adequate to supply water to the entire camp and town and later, by suspending a pipe across the canyon, also supplied the contractor's camp.

• • •

While still without an assistant, I had two rather serious surgical cases that fall. One of them was a Mexican with a chronic osteomyelitis of the tibia with several discharging sinuses. In my senior year at the County we had started using spinal anesthesia, mainly because the warden had issued an edict that no intern would be permitted to do a major operation without the presence of a member of the attending staff. We asked for a definition of a major operation and learned that it was any operation requiring a general anesthetic. Since we interpreted spinal anesthetic as a local we got the technique from Morton of San Francisco and began using it.

As I had no anesthetist at Roosevelt, I prepared to give my Mexican patient a spinal. I didn't have a platinum needle in my outfit so used a steel spinal needle with the patient sitting on the side of the table bent over. The needle went in nicely but just as it entered the foramen, the Mexican suddenly straightened up and broke the needle off with the broken end just outside the canal. It wouldn't do to leave it there so I lay him on his face and put him under with choloroform, getting Tommy, the mess hall flunky next door, to come over and continue with ether while I did a partial laminectomy sufficient to reach the needle and get it out. We finished the bone operation on the leg under ether.

The other case was a Cherokee Indian boy from Oklahoma who had a strangulated hernia when I found him in a tent at Livingston. The hernia had been strangulated for some seventy-two hours and, though I had but a few instruments in my bag, I was afraid to ride him over the rough road to Roosevelt. Under a local I cut down the mass and severed the constricting ring.

The strangulated loop of gut about the size of a cantaloupe was very black. For perhaps an hour we kept it covered with hot boiled dish towels till finally his circulation returned in all but a few isolated spots and I felt fairly safe in returning the damaged gut to the abdomen, leaving a rubber drain with the skin partly closed.

I took the patient back to the hospital with me and next morning he had a temperature running up to 105 degrees plus which lasted for several days. The skin of the entire abdomen and flanks became discolored and crackled to the touch with emphysema, giving all the appearance of a gas bacillus infection. I figured that perhaps the colon bacilli could do the same thing, and sincerely hoped so. At any rate the wound was well drained and, after several days of hot bichloride wet dressings, the temperature finally subsided. No peritonitis developed and there was apparently enough inflammatory reaction locally to close the sac and cure the hernia. At least there was no recurrence during the three or four years I kept him under observation.

• • •

As the preliminary work got into full swing, my practice both with the Reclamation Service employees and private cases became unduly heavy, so I was greatly relieved one day to have a fellow named Bush come to the field hospital looking for a job. He had walked out from Globe and had all the appearances of a genuine tramp, and, as far as I ever found out, that had been his chief

210

occupation following the Spanish-American War. He claimed, how-ever, without any written support of his contention, that he had served as a hospital steward with the U.S. forces in the Philippines. At any rate, I really needed some help and took him on as steward.

Shortly after we had found a pair of shoes for him and enough clothes to make him look respectable, he entered upon his duties. He did keep the place clean and the canvas cots neatly made up. A Mexican came in one day with a toothache. In the back country tooth pulling was a part of the practice of medicine, for to send an aching tooth to a dentist in Globe or Phoenix meant the loss of two or three days work for the tooth and another week to sober up. I said, "Bush, can you pull teeth?" He said, "Sure, that's the first thing we learned in de army."

The tooth was a lower left molar. The Mexican did not speak English and Bush did not savvy Español, but he got the fel-low backed up with his mouth open and, seeing a bad-looking tooth on the right side, got the forceps on it and twisted it out in spite of the Mexican's attempts at protesting, which Bush of course thought was due to the natural discomfort associated with the pulling of a tooth. When the Mexican finally quieted down enough to explain that it was the wrong tooth, I showed him how bad the pulled tooth was and if he would get back on the table, we would pull the aching one also.

In spite of his many eccentricities Bush made a good stew-ard and was quite popular with the young engineers with whom we messed. He was also good at serving trays to our patients so that he saved Tommy, the mess flunky, many steps and so was popular in the kitchen where he often helped Tommy with the dishes.

• • •

During the year Bush acted as hospital steward he was val-uable in many ways, but I was unable to instill any knowledge of medicine into him, though he did learn to administer ether for anesthesia in a safe if not expert manner.

On one occasion we were up against a ruptured extra-uterine pregnancy in extreme shock from hemorrhage and, al-though our provisions for major abdominal surgery were rather meager, Bush gave a good anesthetic and watched the normal sa-line solution after I got a needle in the vein. The operation itself was, of course, not too difficult for a surgeon, even without a nurse or assistant, for it simply meant getting through the abdominal wall and clamping off the bleeding vessels and ending the emergency.

At any rate, the case made me realize that with the increasing population both in the camps and in the rapidly growing business district and with the contractor soon coming in, I would likely get into similar difficulty more or less frequently and I determined to get a regular assistant. I wrote to Dr. William Schroeder, a Chicago surgeon and professor of surgery at Northwestern Medical School.

Dr. Schroeder selected and sent out a third-year medical student named Tim Hinchion. While Tim didn't have his M.D., it was proper at that time in Arizona to use an undergraduate medical student as far as his capabilities would go. During the three years Dr. Tim was with me he became very proficient. Following his graduation he studied in Dublin for a year and then continued with industrial surgery at the stockyards in Chicago with the Morris Packing Company.

During the hot weather the following summer I took my family to Los Angeles and Long Beach to stay for a while and I commuted back and forth. Incidentally, our second daughter, Harriet, had come along the October before. I was away from the project for a week or more at a time, and during my absences Tim and Bush took good care of the hospital work.

On one of my trips to the coast I looked up Dr. Edwin H. Wylie, who had been on the Cook County house staff with me and later became police surgeon in Los Angeles. During the evening in the Jonathan Club someone proposed a poker game, but as it was against the club rules a real estate man named Ellingwood suggested that we go to his office across the street on Sixth and Main. There were five and sometimes six in the game, which went on until after midnight when Mr. Ellingwood had some refreshments sent up.

During the intermission he took us into an adjoining office room and demonstrated an X-ray machine. This was a Rose coil (one of the very early coil X-rays) invented by a man named Rose in Los Angeles. Ellingwood was financing him and was acting as agent in selling the machine at $250. After returning to the game where I had previously accumulated a goodly stack of chips, the pots went along no one winning very much till we came to a jackpot which woke things up.

212

I was under the gun and picked up three little threes and opened the pot for the size of it, probably five or six dollars. The next man passed, but the third one boosted my opener by five dollars. Then it passed around to Ellingwood, who called and raised another five dollars. The dealer passed and, after hesitating a little, I stayed in to see what the next man would do. Instead of calling or dropping out he called and raised another five dollars and Ellingwood did the same. I figured the man next to me would call on that round so I stayed along another ten dollars for the percentage.

I had first draw and took two cards; the next man and Ellingwood both stood pat. I naturally checked the bet but the next man bet ten dollars and Ellingwood raised it another ten dollars. I looked at my draw then and found I had caught the fourth three so I just called figuring the next man would make another raise. He did, a twenty-five-dollar one this time. Ellingwood, still confident, called the twenty-five dollars and raised it fifty dollars more. I was afraid to risk the other man for another raise so I called and made a small raise to give Ellingwood another chance. The next man dropped out with a flush and Ellingwood, with a full house, fell for my come-on and raised another fifty dollars.

I took out my wallet, for it was an open game, called the $50 and threw the wallet in the center announcing a raise of $250 against his X-ray machine. As Ellingwood had a high full house and was in considerable, he said O.K., he would call. So I had an X-ray machine to take back to camp with me.

When one of the electricians got the generator set up we were able to get plates of our fractures, besides having high-frequency current through vacuum glass tubes available.

In the early spring of 1905 with the power canal completed, the cement mill well along and the Apache Trail available for freight teams, Concord stages and buckboards, the contract for the actual dam construction was awarded to John M. O'Rourke & Company, who had completed the Sea Wall at Galveston, Texas, just the year before.

They set up their headquarters on a high bluff on the north side of the Salt River just below its junction with the Tonto. A suspension footbridge across the box canyon gave access to their camp during high water. Their preliminary work was to develop a stone quarry as the plans called for a stone masonry construction

213

for the dam. Also, to construct a coffer dam and ditch to carry river water around the damsite while excavating the riverbed to bedrock and several feet into the solid rock. They strung two steel wire cables across the canyon to handle equipment and material. This work started slowly and it was fall before they had much of a crew, then they imported several hundred colored laborers from Texas.

My contract for medical services was on the basis of one dollar per man per month, which was to include all professional service, hospitalization and material. With the added personnel to look after we needed a larger hospital, so Mr. Hill had the new hospital constructed, still a canvas-covered structure but with capacity for twenty patients besides an examining and treatment room.

In return for hospitalization for my contract patients, I agreed to furnish all medicines and dressings required for Government employees. This arrangement proved very satisfactory and continued during the construction period. The advent of the colored population for labor also helped the domestic situation on the hill, for a number of wives came with them and one of these at least was a very good cook and nurse as she took care of Harriet, our second child, when she came along in October of 1905.

• • •

About the time the contractors had their first coffer dam in and a lot of heavy equipment down in the canyon, the rivers put up a rather considerable flood with water in the canyon reaching the bottom of the suspension bridge, which meant about fifteen feet of water. The heavy equipment was buried in the sand and everything movable, including the coffer dam, went down the river. The flood started late on a Saturday night, and Sunday morning with Walter Lubkin, the official photographer on the project, I went down the trail to the turbine plant which was just above water level.

We found Mr. O'Rourke down there sitting on a boulder, looking at the river. "Good morning, Mr. O'Rourke," said Walter. "What do you think of our little river now?" "Oh, that little bit of water doesn't amount to anything," he replied. "You know, we just completed the Sea Wall at Galveston where we really had some water." However, I think Mr. O'Rourke changed his mind about our river to some extent as time went on, for before they got into

214

bedrock and had the dam up above the level of the riverbed, they experienced two more floods, each time losing their coffer dam and considerable equipment.

While the colored men were efficient laborers, they were not so good on rock work. The contractors imported a few hundred coal miners from Pennsylvania for this job. These were mostly double-jack miners and did well on open quarry work, but when it came to opening the penstock tunnel where they had to do single-jack drilling, the medical department became flooded with cases of tenosynovitis of the forearm and wrist. Forty or fifty of these fellows were laid off at a time until they finally got used to swinging a four-pound hammer in one hand while holding a drill in the other. In later years, when feeling and listening to the squeak of tenosynovitis cases, I have often thought of these Italian miners and wondered if we did not have compressed air-jack hammers in those days and, if so, why they were not used in the tunnel.

While the contractors' camp provided the usual number of fractures and minor accidents, there was almost no sickness among the employees and only one death during my time there. This was a colored man who fell from a cliff some forty feet and was killed.

The most serious accident happened on one of the cables when the wheel had gotten jammed. The repairman had gone up the chains and was hanging with left arm on the cable suspended some two-hundred feet above the riverbed. When the jam came loose, the wheel ran up his forearm from his hand to his elbow and he was pinned there for some ten minutes before a rescuer could get out and support him while the hoist man ran the wheel off his arm. While amputation was not done, the tissues and nerves were so badly crushed that the hand and forearm later atrophied and were not much use.

The first stone of the dam was laid in bedrock in September 1906, a year and a half after the contractors started to work; and the last one was fitted into place in February 1911, four-and-a-half years later. Formal dedication and naming of the dam took place on March 18, 1911, with Theodore Roosevelt present and speaking.

After making a few remarks on his satisfaction over the large degree of success of the Reclamation Act which he had signed while president, he expressed his appreciation to those who had named the dam after him, as follows:

"I wish to congratulate all who have taken part in this extraordinary work here; and gentlemen, first of all, I want to thank

215

you for having named the dam after me. I do not know if it is of any consequence to a man whether he has a monument; I know it is of mighty little consequence whether he has a statue after he is dead. If there could be any monument which would appeal to any man, surely it is this. You could not have done anything which would have pleased and touched me more than to name this great dam, this great reservoir site after me, and I thank you from my heart for having done so."

Mr. Roosevelt then pressed an electric switch which opened the sluice gates, letting through a gushing, roaring torrent of water to the riverbed below, so long dry. During his visit in the valley, Mr. Roosevelt, with his wife Edith and daughter Alice, stayed at the Evans School in Mesa as guests of Professor Harry Evans, where son Archie was in school at the time. Besides his speech at the dam, the ex-president made a number of other speeches in the State.

He had a rather severe laryngitis at the time, and when he found that spraying with cocaine and adrenalin solution relieved it to an extent where he could go on speechifying, he had me following him around with a portable compressed air tank and a nebulizer. I also had the privilege of treating an ingrown toenail for Mrs. Roosevelt, so there are compensations for practicing in out-of-the-way places.

Recollections of a Chinese-Immigration Inspector

Clifford Alan Perkins

Clifford Alan Perkins was a small town Wisconsin boy with dreams of a professional baseball career when a suspected case of tuberculosis forced him to move to a drier climate. After two years at a monotonous job with the postal service in El Paso, Texas, he secured an appointment as an inspector in the Chinese division of the Immigration Service with orders to assume his duties in Tucson, Arizona.

When Perkins arrived in Tucson in January 1911, it was the largest town in the Arizona Territory, boasting a population of thirteen thousand. But to the young man from Wisconsin the low, flat-roofed adobe buildings situated in the sun-baked desert looked like "some sort of jumping-off place to oblivion."

The Chinese Exclusion Acts which Perkins was to enforce prohibited the immigration of all Chinese and persons of Chinese descent. But since the 1870s, thousands had arrived on the West Coast to provide manual labor for western mines and railroad construction. As antipathy toward Orientals intensified in coastal cities and towns in the last quarter of the nineteenth century, many Chinese moved into the interior. As a result, Tucson had a large and thriving Oriental community when Perkins arrived. Many who had entered the U.S. originally as laborers now operated restaurants, laundries, and other service industries; some had begun to acquire real estate. Other industrious Chinese maintained gardens in the city's outlying areas which Anglos considered undesirable. These gardeners provided most of the fresh vegetables, poultry, and eggs which Tucson's housewives purchased every day.

This Oriental colony became the major focus of Perkins' activities. Although he performed his official duties in strict adherence to the law, Perkins was aware of the cruel irony of the situation. He felt a genuine sympathy for these people who had come so far and whose "wants were so few in a land of so much opportunity." As it turned out, he was the last inspector to enforce the Chinese Exclusion Acts.

217

O ver the years, many laws have been passed to regulate or re-strict immigration into this country. . . . In 1882 the first Chinese Exclusion Act suspended for ten years the immigration of Chinese employed in mining and other skilled or unskilled occupations. This, in effect, barred the entrance of practically all Chinese, for few if any professional men were interested in emigrating from China. Those already in the country were entitled to receive from the collector of customs a certificate of identification, evidencing their legal right to go from and come to the United States.

This act was succeeded by the Act of September 13, 1888, prohibiting the immigration of all Chinese except officials, teachers, students, merchants or travelers for pleasure. Laborers who had returned to China were forbidden to reenter unless they had wives, children or parents in the United States, property therein valued at one thousand dollars, or debts of like amount due them and pending settlement.

As a matter of practice, few Chinese who left the country tried to qualify for reentry. If they had a fairly good stake here and wanted to go back to China for a visit, they just went. Legally, they could not return without a certificate of identification, so those who did come back shipped to Mexico and were smuggled into the country with the idea of making our government prove they had been away. They even concealed their right names when they left for China so it would not be possible to establish by a ship's passenger list that they had gone.

In October 1888, all certificates of identity were declared void and of no effect, legally eliminating any possibility of reentry. This was followed in 1893 by an act which required every Chinese in the United States to apply within six months to the collector of

From Clifford Alan Perkins, *Border Patrol*, compiled by Nancy Dickey, edited by C. L. Sonnichsen (El Paso: Texas Western Press, 1978), 7–24. Used with permission from Texas Western Press.

internal revenue for a certificate of residence and to carry it at all times. The certificate bore a photograph as well as a detailed identification of the individual and was to be surrendered if and when he left the country.

The second and final Chinese Exclusion Act, passed in 1902, prohibited the immigration of all Chinese and persons of Chinese descent until otherwise provided by law. The "otherwise" did not come to pass until 1943, when immigration restrictions for Chinese were liberalized.

During the time that these progressively restrictive measures were being passed, word was reaching men in China that it was possible to accumulate in the American West "fortunes" (by Chinese standards) of several thousand dollars. This caused a corresponding increase in the number trying to get into the country surreptitiously. All who came wanted to make enough money to return home and marry, if they did not already have wives there, live out their remaining years in what would be relative luxury, and be buried properly. They had no intention of staying in the United States permanently, and families of numerous men who died here eventually made arrangements to have their bones shipped back to China, for it was believed their souls would not be at peace so long as their remains were interred in other than Chinese soil.

• • •

Responsibility for dealing with illegal aliens was assumed by the Immigration Service in 1908 with the creation of a section called the Chinese Division, officers being designated as Chinese inspectors. The Customs Service line riders, however, having had jurisdiction for so long and being on the job, continued to pick up any suspects they ran into. Until that patrol was abolished, the two services always cooperated in the enforcement of federal statutes.

Chinese inspectors and immigrant inspectors, working with Customs line riders, made it increasingly difficult for Chinese to get into the country via busy ports and populated areas, and as a result smuggling activities shifted to the sparsely inhabited sections of southern New Mexico, Arizona and California. By the time I joined the Service, few Chinese were coming in east of El Paso. Some continued to enter through Gulf and West coast ports, but by far the greatest numbers were entering in the vicinity of towns on or near the Mexican border and, for a while, through Canada. This border phase of law enforcement [was] carried on by a comparatively small number of inspectors working twelve to fifteen hours a day, seven days a week. . . .

After 1893 every Chinese alien was required to carry identification, including a photograph. Such procedures invariably led to forgeries and duplications. Photography in 1893 was rather rudimentary, and many pictures on certificates of residence faded with time. Also, most of the Chinese who were required to register were adults, since the immigrants up to that point had consisted almost entirely of males over twenty-one years of age. Eighteen to twenty years later, it was almost impossible to be sure the photograph on a certificate of residence was of the person presenting it. Copies of the originals, with photographs, were supposed to have been filed in the office of the U.S. collector of internal revenue of the district where the application was made, but records were sketchy. Additionally, the forms varied from one locality to another, so the fact that one document did not look exactly like another meant very little.

When a man in his forties to mid-fifties appeared in one of Tucson's Chinese establishments, it was fairly easy for us to ascertain that he was a new arrival from Mexico since we had records of all Chinese entering by train. There was very little travel except by train, and our record books already contained the names and addresses of all local Chinese residents. Proving he came from Mexico following an unlawful trip to China, however, was more difficult, for some recent arrivals went to great lengths to hide the illegality of their entry. We had cases where the description contained in the certificate presented by a man picked up for questioning indicated that the possessor had certain scars. In one or two instances we were able to prove that the holder of the certificate was not the individual who had originally applied for it, and that his scars had actually been added so his appearance would conform to certificate details.

It was important to prove that a suspect picked up coming into the United States after a trip to China had actually been out of the country and was here illegally. Of course when he was apprehended at Tucson, Phoenix, or some other point near the border and was suspected of having just reentered the country from Mexico, he was thoroughly searched and his clothing was examined. In some cases identifying marks were found, but the Chinese soon learned to remove all such markings. Strangely enough,

220

it was sometimes possible to trap them by making a casual comment to them in Spanish. This they might answer unthinkingly, though they would not respond to questions put to them in English. This was not prima facie evidence, but it often served as a lever to cause a suspect to confess where he had been.

For a time the Service hired Mexicans in Nogales, Sonora, to photograph Chinese on their arrival by train from the south and, if possible, to take pictures of new arrivals living in Nogales. Such pictures were supplied to the Tucson and other border Immigration offices, where they were filed by approximate age, shape of face, and body type. This reference material was often useful in establishing the fact that apprehended Chinese had been in Mexico as recently as a few weeks or months previously.

We also arranged to have pictures taken in Tucson of persons suspected of illegal entry from Mexico and sent to ports and agents on the border for referral to residents and officials in or near Mexico. In a number of instances we were able to secure witnesses who could swear in court that the alien had been in Mexico on a certain date. Bringing witnesses in from Mexico to testify in court had to be discontinued after a couple of years, however; they got to making a good thing of it since they received money to cover their expenses up and back. Their credibility suffered when one witness identified our Chinese interpreter, maintained in the office full-time by the Service, as a man he had seen getting off a train in Mexico.

The Chinese apprehended while I was in Arizona were all males, and usually in one of two age groups: young men in their late teens to twenties and old men who had lived here at one time, registered, and gone back to China without reporting their departure. Those who had been here before could usually print their names and carried their old papers, knowing that once they reached San Francisco or one of the larger inland cities with a sizeable Chinese colony, no one would be able to prove they had ever left the country. To avoid deportation, younger men had to claim they had been born here and prove it in court if they were picked up, which was relatively easy for several years if they were brought in by a corporation known as the Chinese Six Companies.

At the turn of the century this organization was one of the richest in the world. With head offices in San Francisco, the members engaged in all sorts of importing and exporting and were reportedly behind the white slave trade as well as the smuggling of opium and Chinese. As I understood their procedure, if a Chinese here had a relative or friend for whom he was willing to pay to have brought from China, he got in touch with the local representative of the Chinese Six Companies. The individual's name would be passed to the Company agent in, say, Shanghai, while the relative or friend living here would notify him to go to Shanghai. The Six Companies also brought in many young men to work for Chinese already established here. These aliens were expected to repay the Company for their expenses, which amounted to several hundred dollars, and many a so-called tong war in which Chinese hatchetmen left mute evidence of their existence was merely the result of some alien's attempt to run out on his debt to the Six Companies. Often the killing was not sanctioned by any tong, but by arranging for it to appear so, the killer could easily place responsibility elsewhere.

An alien brought in by the Six Companies was given preliminary instruction in English and deportment in China, after which arrangements would be made for him to be taken to Mexico, usually aboard a Chinese ship destined for Mazatlán, Guaymas or Manzanillo. On arrival, he would be met at the docks by a Company agent who would take him in a tow and see that he was put to work in a restaurant or laundry. There he could be weaned further away from some of his Chinese mannerisms and learn something of the business in which he would eventually be working. When his indoctrination was completed, he would be put on the train for Nogales, Sonora. From that city he would travel by stage (later by bus) to Naco, Agua Prieta or possibly Mexicali. There he would be turned over to a Mexican hired to take him across the border and deliver him to a contact in some nearby American town. In the United States his Americanization was continued. He would also memorize a complete description of the house where he supposedly had been born and an account of who his parents were, who the neighbors were, who lived upstairs and down, the school he attended, the names of his teachers, and the names of children he could claim to have played with—all individuals who could establish their identity in this country.

The San Francisco earthquake and fire in 1906 destroyed all records in the city hall and in all of Chinatown, so most of the younger Chinese aliens claimed to have been born there. The Six Companies management was well aware that government representatives would be unable to prove otherwise if the alien was properly trained, schooled in his cover story, and suitably dressed. If by some chance the alien was picked up, then released on bail pending a deportation hearing, the Company would arrange for delays in the hearing while he was given clothing and additional instruction. A year or so later, when he appeared in court, he would be very Americanized. Witnesses, including a few Anglos, would be brought in from San Francisco to swear he was the child born to Mr. and Mrs. So-and-So, who lived in the apartment next to them, and it would be almost impossible to disprove their stories. This procedure became so widespread that the Service stopped bothering to file charges against Chinese aliens. In the end, inability to prove they were illegal entrants made citizens out of them. At one time it was estimated that if all of those who claimed to have been born in San Francisco had actually been born there, each Chinese woman then in the United States would have had to produce something like 150 children.

To enforce laws applicable to the admission of aliens and to supervise border crossings, Immigration officers known as immigrant inspectors were and are stationed at major coastal and border sea and air ports, at rail terminals, and along vehicular access routes to inspect all incoming traffic. They also maintain surveillance of backcountry areas according to the possibility and probability of encountering illegal entrants, for the number of persons trying to cross into this country is so much greater than the force attempting to prevent them from doing so that officers must concentrate their efforts where they can do the most good. They depend for their high degree of success upon knowledge of people's habits and instinctive reactions to certain circumstances, familiarity with local topography and transportation facilities, and the fact that they are trained and equipped to survive in unexpected and potentially serious situations.

• • •

As the newest (and youngest) appointee in the office, it very quickly came to my attention that I was low man on the totem pole and, because I had grown up with horses, qualified to be sent out on horseback details with the least amount of notice, or sleep, when I was not checking railroad cars in the freight yards. Otherwise, my duties and status were exactly the same as those of the immigrant inspectors, for it had become apparent in the years following establishment of the Chinese Division that it was not practical to have some inspectors involved only with Chinese and others only with immigrants. All subsequent appointments at Tucson and elsewhere on the border were made as immigrant inspectors, and with my first promotion my title was changed to Immigrant Inspector.

The other part of my indoctrination, which came as something of a shock, was that we were expected to provide our own uniforms and guns within thirty days after we were sworn into office. We were allowed to wear casual work clothes—soft brimmed Stetson hats and high-heeled riding boots—on scouting details. Also we put on our oldest clothing and heavy-soled army boots to inspect freight cars as the work was arduous, dirty, and most of the time in weather either extremely hot or bitterly cold. During the inspection of passenger trains, while working in town and in the office, however, we had to wear uniforms and carry guns, although I do not recall shooting at a single person during my two-and-a-half years in Arizona.

Our winter uniforms were olive drab double-breasted woolen suits cut along the lines of the uniform worn by U.S. Navy officers with a badge on the left breast and an olive drab cap bearing the letters USIS over an eagle insignia above the cap bill. In summer we wore similarly cut cotton shirts and trousers, but no coat. Several companies made uniforms to order for us, and a few of the men had theirs tailor-made. The badge, buttons and cap insignia were furnished, but the government did not begin supplying anything else and the Sam Brown belt did not become part of the uniform until after the Border Patrol was established in 1924.

With only ten inspectors to cover Tucson and the surrounding countryside for forty or fifty miles, we were on duty twelve to fifteen hours a shift, seven days a week, alternating from days to nights and back every two weeks. Train inspection was the most arduous work because each car in every train destined for the interior had to be checked thoroughly for Chinese. My room was close enough to the depot so when a passenger train was due I could clean up a little before putting on my uniform without wasting too much time, but there was many a day when one more change of clothing would have finished me with the Service. Sometimes, in addition to inspecting two or three passenger trains, we opened as many as three hundred freight cars on a shift, regular loaded freights usually having from fifty to sixty cars and empties as many as seventy.

224

Chinese attempting to reach inland cities undetected hid in every conceivable place on trains: in box cars loaded with freight, under the tenders of the locomotives, in the space above the entryway in the old passenger cars, in staterooms rented for them by accomplices, and even in the four-foot-wide ice vents across each end of the insulated Pacific Fruit Express refrigerated cars, iced or not. We also had to check the passenger cars in the depot for traveling Chinese, making a record of their names, where they had boarded, their destinations, and any documents they carried. The information was then verified with the conductors to be sure it was correct insofar as they knew it. They were familiar with our work and told us right away whenever they had seen a Chinese board the train at a small station, especially if it had been on the side of the car away from the platform or under other circumstances that might indicate he was being put aboard by smugglers.

As soon as a passenger train had pulled out and I was back in my old clothes, I took off for the freight yards, which extended for half to three-quarters of a mile east of the depot to the roundhouse and shops and would handle seven or eight trains at one time. During our inspections we were assisted by a railroad watchman who went along to pen and close the heavy car doors and by a clerk who recorded the number of each seal broken on a loaded car and, after the inspection, applied another. They were also supposed to make sure we did not take anything out of the cars, although I was always too busy, hot and dirty to think much about carrying off something.

The Los Angeles–bound banana specials from Galveston gave us the most trouble. Because the railroad wanted to move them faster than regular freights, they operated on the same schedules as passenger trains and often as sections of passenger trains. Temperatures inside the twenty-five to thirty refrigerated cars in each train had to be regulated carefully; if they were once allowed to rise above a certain point, nothing could be done to keep the bananas from spoiling as the ripening fruit would generate enough heat to literally burn itself up. Each of these trains was accompanied by a "banana messenger" to prevent such an occurrence. His job was to see that proper temperatures were maintained and they all strongly resented our opening the cars, especially to inspect the ice vents through the two lift-up trap doors on top. There was no leeway in our work for consideration of temperature variations, inside or outside the cars, and as a consequence we had more

225

than a few arguments and once or twice a knockdown, drag-out fight with a banana messenger.

It would have been easy to skip over a few cars, and one inspector was discharged for doing just that, but the government sometimes took steps to make sure we did our work properly. One plainclothes agent tied the hasps on all doors of the loaded freight cars in a train with black silk thread at a stop east of Tucson, then checked the train again in Yuma. The man who was supposed to have inspected the train in Tucson passed every car as opened and examined and recorded its number without breaking a thread.

Once in a while a government plainclothesman would hide in one of the freight cars we were due to inspect. That was a very risky procedure, however, because cargo sometimes shifted en route or during switching operations. One day I entered a car loaded with steel pipe after the train conductor told me a man was in there. Sure enough I found him lying down at one end of the car in a small space left by some short pipe. A quick jerk by the locomotive could have caused the load to move and crush the man instantly. Such methods of spying were fairly pointless since the brakemen and the firemen usually saw the agent enter one of the cars and tipped us off. Besides, it put these men in a bad position with us. No matter how we roughed them up (we were inclined to think they were not too smart or they would have been more concerned about their personal safety), reporting us was pointless because the government did not want to acknowledge what it was doing.

When we were not inspecting railroad cars or out on scouting trips, we had to check out the establishments in and around town which were operated by Chinese for "temporary guests." Eventually I reached the point where I recognized most of the four hundred or so local Chinese citizens by sight, as did several of the other inspectors, and got to know rather well a few of the older men who worked in the laundry and restaurants I frequented. For the most part they led rather solitary lives and responded readily to the slightest friendly overture.

It must have been difficult for them to become more than casually acquainted with me, for they knew I was always on the lookout for any of their countrymen who might be laying over on their way to the interior. Perhaps my visits with them just never happened to coincide with the presence of an alien in the back of their shops, for they always acted glad to see me, especially after one dinner during which my cup was filled with boiling hot tea while my attention was elsewhere. After spilling most of the cup's contents down my shirt front into my lap and jumping up in considerable discomfort, I started laughing during the blotting up that followed and from then on several waiters (and sometimes the cook) would gather near my table to observe my enjoyment of the won ton soup and the other tasty dishes. With hands clasped under aprons, or smoking what had to be chains of cigarettes, they would chatter among themselves, indicate amusement by much head nodding, wide grins and restrained, soft laughter whenever something occurred that pleased me, too.

One of our regular calls was by horse and buggy to the Chinese vegetable gardens beyond the ruins of old Fort Lowell. The men who worked in the gardens, cultivating and irrigating vegetables for local sale and use in the restaurants serving Chinese food, wore dark blue or black loose cotton jackets and pajama-type unpressed trousers, sandals and large straw hats. They looked much alike in the harsh glare of the midday sun and unless we knew them, we had to examine their papers and check them against a loose-leaf record we took with us showing the names and types of documents carried by Chinese residing or working in every establishment in town. They called their certificates "*chock chee*," so we would refer to them the same way when asking to examine their papers. We all picked up a few words of Chinese and sometimes they came in handy in finding out where they lived, or in asking, "*Ne gu mot ming ah?*" (which spelling would no doubt cause a language expert to shudder, but that is the way it sounded) to ascertain their names.

Our record books of Chinese residents were all locally prepared for the convenience of the Tucson inspectors and to assist new officers who had to take over the duty of checking for aliens and constituted more or less an up-to-date census. They were not required to be kept by any Service directive, but were logical lists to maintain of persons with whom we were in continuous contact. It was relatively easy to recognize a man when he was always seen working as a gardener. But if, a few weeks later, he was working in a kitchen as a helper, or in a laundry, the fact that he was out of place and dressed differently would make it difficult to recognize him. When we had any doubts about a man, he would be asked to produce his *chock chee* and we would check it and what he told us against our records. If we had no information about him or if what

227

he said did not agree with our files, we would take him to the office for further investigation with the assistance of our Chinese interpreter. If it was found that he was not in the United States legally, he would be held in our detention quarters and arrangements initiated for his deportation.

I had been on duty only a few weeks when I came in contact with my first illegal entry. After my shift was over one morning at seven o'clock, I left the freight yards and started uptown for breakfast. Coming toward me down the street was a two-horse hack carrying two men. I paid no particular attention to it until it pulled to the curb in front of the Shanghai Low Restaurant and I saw that the two passengers were Chinese. It was most unusual for Chinese to be riding in a cab, so I walked closer. I noticed that one was expensively attired and the other was wearing a suit that had obviously been made for a much heavier man.

Following them into the restaurant, I showed my badge to identify myself and demanded to see their papers. The well-dressed Chinese claimed to own the cafe and produced a certificate of residence that had all the earmarks of being genuine. The other did not speak any English. As he had no identification and was wearing clothes of recent make which he obviously was not used to, I took him in. Chinese were so accustomed to the loose clothing they habitually wore that they stood and walked like mannequins the first few times they put on an American suit with a coat which fitted tight across the shoulders. Where an Anglo might swing his arms, and possibly put his hands in his pockets, the alien would try to pull his shoulders in and would hold his arms perfectly straight at his sides.

Chinese aliens were seldom deported to Mexico because there was no way to control their destination or their almost immediate reentry attempts. Agents of the Six Companies were so well-organized in Mexico that Chinese aliens had to be deported by ship from California ports to Asia. Approximately once a month, Service details came through Tucson picking up aliens being held for deportation by officers along their route for delivery to the Immigration office on Angel Island in San Francisco Bay.

Some of our work at the Tucson headquarters, as already noted, involved expeditions on horseback into the surrounding countryside. It used to be a relatively simple matter for aliens to cross the line away from inhabited areas because people who knew the back country avoided it. The real problem faced by the Chi-

228

nese, and later by people from other countries, was to reach the interior without being detected when the only rapid means of transportation was the railroad. Moving objects can be spotted at great distances in clear air by the dust they raise, a man on horseback being visible up to five or six miles. Sitting on the ground to steady our binoculars, we would scan our surroundings, sometimes studying the motion, shadow and dust raised by some unidentified object for ten or fifteen minutes since the heat waves made it hard to be sure we were looking at a horse, a cow, a small animal or a human being. To escape observation, smugglers led aliens along river washes and through brush-covered areas whenever possible. Much of the year, small patches of grass could be found at the bottoms of the arroyos or in the low spots between hills where any available moisture would accumulate from rains higher in the mountains. If the wash was large enough, there would also be a few pools of water, making such locations highly desirable as campsites in an arid land. Chinese coming into the country followed the dry washes until they flattened out and disappeared before they struck out across open country to pick up the trail towards Phoenix.

In a country where water was not readily available and temperatures were often high enough to endanger survival, anyone avoiding places of habitation was assumed to be a smuggler or an alien. Reports from men working on the railroad, outlying ranchers, and the Papago Indians (who seemed to have a natural antipathy for Chinese) were our best sources of information about the movement of aliens.

Loaning horses was a custom of the country, there never being a question of pay for their use or when they would be returned. A borrowed mount could be ridden as far as necessary, swapped for another, and another; as a result, our details were not hampered by lack of stamina of the livery stable horses on which we had to start out. Most of the ranchers, on seeing our credentials, would have their remudas brought in and give us the choice of what they had, with the possible exception of their own and their family's personal horses. Nor could we ever pay for the meals they served us. It was enough to share a drink with the owner, if we had a bottle in our saddlebags, or buy him one when he came to town.

Scouting the country south of Tucson, we rode into the King Ranch late one afternoon. It was unusually well equipped, and had a main house that was luxurious for that area. Dismounting and tying our horses to the hitching rail, we walked up to the main

229

house to discover that everyone was gone except Mrs. King. When we inquired if she had seen any Chinese passing through, she rather hesitantly said, "No," but followed her reluctant response with a cordial invitation to stay for dinner. She had our horses taken care of while we were cleaning up and she offered us the use of her husband's razor since we never carried them on scouting trips and were usually rather scruffy-looking after three or four days.

Toward sundown her husband rode in on a large chestnut stallion. When he walked in the house, she immediately called him to another room and shut the door. He came in to greet us a few moments later. Laughing, he apologized for his wife. She told him that about an hour before we arrived three Chinese had passed by some distance from the ranch house. She had not told us when we inquired because she felt sorry for them and did not want to be the one responsible for their being caught.

We sat down to a wonderful dinner that evening, served with Mrs. King's best dishes and silverware on a damask linen tablecloth. We spent the night, too, going on our way the next morning after another fine meal. In the long run, everything worked out well, for we located the Chinese we were after hiding in a railroad culvert a few miles north of the ranch.

Entering the United States by wagon or on foot through that country was a hazardous, lonely proposition, and must have been a bewildering experience to the majority of Chinese who made the attempt. They had made a long and no doubt miserable ocean voyage, they had to learn a new language, become proficient at unaccustomed work in a foreign land, adapt to different customs, clothing and surroundings. About the time things became familiar, the aliens would be put aboard a mechanical conveyance they probably had never seen before. It would carry them north through uninhabited, barren and sometimes mountainous country and leave them in a sun-baked town of drab adobe buildings.

Nobody wanted them; few people made any attempt to understand them; and detection would make futile all of the effort and money expended. Mexican railroad section hands seldom would help them because they did not want anyone around who might get them in trouble; the native Indians seemed to resent their passage through the harsh land; and uniformed officials who knew the country were sent out on horseback with guns to catch them. It was little wonder so few of the Chinese we apprehended gave us trouble and so many appeared to be almost glad they were going to be

230

sent back to China. Often it was hard not to feel sorry for some of them, even though enforcing immigration laws was our job. They had come so far, and their wants were so few in a land of so much opportunity. I did not know it then, but there would be many times when I would be caught between the natural inclination to help another human being and my responsibilities as an officer, and guided by the conviction that it is far easier not to take the first wrong step than the second.

This was one of many lessons I learned in Arizona. I had begun to evaluate people as individuals and to accept them for what they were, not for the way they looked. My judgment and awareness had been tuned up considerably. For the rest of my career in the Immigration Service I built on the foundation laid in those early years.

Turning Points in the Life of a Hopi Artist

Fred Kabotie

Fred Kabotie's paintings of Hopi Kachinas, ceremonials, and scenes depicting daily life and tribal legends are the artist's response to the urge to preserve and understand the past. In his art he records the tranquility and harmony of Hopi philosophy and religion. But in his autobiography he explores the conflict, alienation, and cultural impoverishment that often resulted from the government's efforts to force the Hopis and other tribes to walk the white man's road.

Caught in the struggle between the conservative and progressive factions of the Hopi tribe, Kabotie's older male relatives were "arrested" and sent to the Carlisle Indian School in distant Pennsylvania. During the five years the family was separated, Fred rebelled against the forced schooling on the reservation which was designed to erase his Indianness.

Ironically, the very educational system that attempted to mold him for white society awakened his artistic talents and eventually drew him back to the Hopi life. At the Santa Fe Indian School before World War I, Elizabeth De Huff, the superintendent's wife, provided Fred with paper and watercolors and a place to paint. Instinctively the lonely boy from Second Mesa painted scenes remembered from home, and soon he attracted notice and encouragement in the artistic climate of Santa Fe.

As his reputation and stature increased, Kabotie took care to nurture his talent. He studied under the auspices of the Guggenheim Foundation. He experimented with different design concepts and perspectives. Soon awards and honors came to him. In the 1960s, Fred Kabotie and his wife represented the United States as goodwill envoys to India. Yet, in spite of his international fame, Kabotie remained faithful to the culture that was the well-spring of his success. Through his own painting as well as his encouragement of silversmithing and native Hopi

crafts, he helped sustain a broader tradition of distinctive
regional styles in the arts going on everywhere.

The following excerpt from his autobiography provides a
glimpse of the artist early in his career. With gentle humor and
lack of pretension, Fred Kabotie reveals his artistry with words as
well as watercolors.

234

I caught a ride west with a fellow from San Juan Pueblo who had a car and was going to Sacaton, Arizona. I didn't get off in Winslow, as I'd planned, but rode as far as Williams. Then I went up to Grand Canyon. Several Hopi friends were working there for the Fred Harvey Company, under Frank Spencer. He gave me a job, too.

Near the Bright Angel Lodge was a rough stone building called the Lookout. It was built on a narrow point that extends out from the rim; there was a souvenir shop inside, and overlooking the canyon, an observation platform with a powerful telescope. My job was to focus the telescope on canyon features for the tourists: the daily mule trains, the lodge being built on the North Rim, deer, wild burros, and an occasional bighorn sheep. I was paid thirty dollars a month plus room and board, but sometimes I made as much as sixteen dollars a day in tips from people who enjoyed my telescope tours.

At the Lookout I worked with a tall, skinny guy who had a wonderful sense of humor, Jack Nagle. He was always kidding the tourists. One day he was talking with some ladies from back East, and they asked where they could see some real cowboys. "Well, Fred, here, and I, we're cowboys," he told them. "Right now we're dressed up, but after work we put on our cowboy clothes and ride down into the canyon to our ranch."

I was making good money at Grand Canyon (I remember how twenty-dollar gold pieces felt in my pocket) and had joined a dance orchestra. But I was still drinking too much. . . . I thought I'd better go home.

I went by way of Phoenix. Leo, who was also from Shungopavi, had saved up some money to send to his sister at Phoenix

From *Fred Kabotie, Hopi Indian Artist: An Autobiography Told With Bill Belknap* (Flagstaff: Museum of Northern Arizona and Northland Press, 1977), 43–44, 48–64, 92. Used with permission from the Museum of Northern Arizona, Flagstaff.

235

Indian School. He didn't trust the mail, and asked if I'd take it down to her. Since I'd never been to Phoenix I was glad to deliver it, and that was how I met Alice, my wife.

At the school I found the building where she lived, and asked for her; Alice came down and met me outside. She was short, still a growing girl, and she asked me for Leo's money right away. I wondered why the hurry, but I gave it to her and we talked for a few minutes. Years later Alice said she'd been afraid of me, that with my city clothes and hat she thought I looked like John Dillinger, the gangster.

From Phoenix I finally came home to Shungopavi. . . . That winter was a difficult time. When the money I'd saved from Grand Canyon ran out, I was broke. And then I was herding sheep, as I used to; but the sheep didn't bring me any money. After that I started hauling wood, harder work than I'd done in years, out in the cold, and I wasn't getting enough food.

I had a lot of time to think, to sort out what was important, and I began to appreciate my Hopi heritage as never before. It had been years since I'd spent winter nights around a stove, hearing the old folks tell about the earliest times they remembered, or listening to the men rehearse a song. Without a written language, this is how our culture and traditions pass from one generation to the next. Taking part in these things again, living the Hopi way, made my *bahana* life in Santa Fe seem less important.

• • •

In 1933 the Santa Fe Railroad completed the famous Watchtower at Desert View on the south rim of the Grand Canyon. It was built mainly as an observation station for visitors, and is operated by the Fred Harvey Company. A large round room on the ground floor represents a prehistoric ceremonial kiva. Inside the tower a circular stairway leads up to its various levels.

Mary Jane Colter, architect and interior decorator for the Fred Harvey Company, asked me to do the murals in the "Hopi Room" on the tower's second level. Since the Colorado River at the bottom of the Grand Canyon is the main feature that people see from the Watchtower, I painted the Snake Legend, showing that the first man to float through the canyon was a Hopi—hundreds of years before Major John Wesley Powell's historic Grand Canyon trip in 1869.

236

According to the legend, at one time there was a Hopi village up near Navajo Mountain, by the Colorado River. The son of the chief had always wondered where the river went, and decided to find out. In the driftwood he found a hollow section of cottonwood log large enough to hold a man. He smoothed up the inside and filled the open end with a door that could be sealed with piñon pitch.

When everything was ready, his father gave him pahos, prayer feathers, and a pouch of sacred cornmeal. His mother and sisters had prepared food and gourds of water which they placed in the log. Before the door was sealed, his father handed him a short club, and advised him that if the log became jammed, pounding from the inside might free it. Then the chief and the head men of the village moved the log into the river and watched it float away.

For many days the young man drifted. He could hear the rushing water outside, and was able to jar the log loose when it lodged against rocks. At last it became stranded and everything was quiet. Carefully he unsealed the door and looked out. He was on a wide beach in open country, beside a large body of water. Some distance offshore he noted a kiva ladder sticking up, which meant that there were people. But how could he reach it?

From his pouch the young man took some sacred cornmeal and made a ball, praying as he shaped it. He then threw the ball toward the kiva ladder. As it rolled across the water, a path formed which he was able to follow, perfectly dry. Descending the ladder, he found himself in the village of the Snake Clan. The people were glad to see him, but were not surprised; they had known he was coming.

The Snake Priest received him graciously, and the young man lived there for many months, learning the secrets of rain-making, and eventually marrying the Snake Priest's daughter. Finally it was time for them to start homeward, and the young couple began the long journey back to the village near Navajo Mountain. Their descendants founded the Snake Clan among the Hopi, and to this day they understand how to bring rain, and are the ones who put on the Snake Dance each summer. This was the legend depicted in the Watchtower mural.

Miss Colter was a very talented decorator with strong opinions, and quite elderly. I admired her work, and we got along well . . . most of the time. But once in a while she could be difficult, especially when it came to matching colors. I remember one

237

day she kept sending me up in the tower with little dabs of oil colors, too small to match. I don't know whether you'd call her thrifty or stingy, but I finally lost my patience. "Let me have that tube," I said, and slashed it open. I squeezed everything out, and stirred in the color I felt was right.

"We're through—you've ruined everything," she gasped. "And you've used up all the paint!"

"But Miss Colter, we haven't tried it yet," I said. I took a little dab and ran back up in the tower. Fortunately it matched, the very color we'd been seeking. So that saved my life—and hers.

When the Watchtower was finally completed, the Fred Harvey Company, the Santa Fe Railroad, and the National Park Service held a dedication ceremony. Hundreds of specially invited guests attended from all over the country, plus Arizona political leaders and everyday canyon visitors. Mr. Spencer had asked Peter Nuvamsa and me to organize a group of Hopis to come over from the villages and present some dances. They were the highlight of the dedication. After the program, Katherine Harvey (of the Fred Harvey family), whom I'd known for several years, came over and talked with me. "Now Fred, this is your place. It's really right for you," she said. "As soon as we can arrange it, you'll be working here." There were so many people around that I didn't think much about it right then. But later I found out she meant it.

• • •

After President Roosevelt took office in 1933 some of his federal job programs reached out into the Hopi Reservation. Like so many people, I was out of a job, although Alice was still working at the day school. The first program that came along in 1934 was for building "natural dams." These were low earthen dams placed across washes to collect water for livestock. I was asked if I'd be interested in supervising the project for our part of the reservation. I accepted, and was sent to a school at Cameron to learn about constructing telephone lines and building roads, as well as digging water holes.

My first assignment on the government's natural dams project was lining up men and boys who wanted to work. Then we started on a big dam out beyond Coyote Springs, using horses and

Fresno scrapers. On that job I worked as a straw boss under the general foreman, but later I became a supervisor.

The last job I worked on was building dams and fences above Keams Canyon. That was when we started getting Navajo workers and their families. They kept coming in because they needed jobs, and I had to go down to Keams Canyon for more tents. We had a regular village then, Hopis on one side, Navajos on the other. I had my own tent.

In the evenings the Navajos would sing and put on dances. The Hopis did, too, and sometimes we'd combine. And that was the first time I'd had a chance to see something of the Navajos and their dancing. I liked to hear them rehearsing; their voices in unison were beautiful. But their dances always seemed disorganized—the music off and their steps not coordinated.

As usual when you get Hopis and Navajos together there were problems. I had one Navajo, a young fellow with a wagon, and I told him, "Your duty is to haul water for the job." When he would go out to load up, the Navajos would give him trouble because he had a Hopi boss. He would come back and report this and I would say, "You go on up there and get the water, and never mind about those Navajos!" And there were raids back and forth between the camps—and a few fights—some in fun, some serious.

Then one day when I was on the job, my boss brought out my old friend Mr. Spencer from Grand Canyon. He was in charge of the Hopis who worked at the canyon, and made frequent trips to the reservation, bringing them back and forth. He was always very nice, very direct. "Say, Fred, I want you to come to work for me out at the Watchtower," he said. He had already seen Alice and she was willing to go, so that was the end of my government dam-building. Alice quit her job at Shungopavi Day School and we moved to Grand Canyon. This was in early 1935.

The Watchtower at Desert View stands on a high point near the east end of Grand Canyon National Park. When we worked there, the community consisted of a few houses for Fred Harvey and Park Service employees, hidden back among the piñons and junipers. All water had to be hauled from Grand Canyon Village, twenty-five miles west. Cameron Trading Post, down by the Little Colorado River, was the next place to the east, thirty-four miles by dirt road. We had no telephone in the tower; the nearest one was at the ranger station five minutes away—the old wooden box type

239

with a hand crank to get the operator. The line was noisy and didn't always work.

Even though it was isolated, the Watchtower was already getting hundreds of visitors a day, most of them traveling by private car, but quite a number on tour buses. Jimmy Ricca, who worked for the Fred Harvey Transportation Department, managed the tower and was responsible for taking care of the tour groups, and for keeping a large punch bowl filled with fruit drink and ice. My job, under Mr. Spencer's department, was to manage the gift shop and, with the help of my Hopi crew to keep the tower in good shape, floors mopped and the big picture windows so clean that you couldn't see the glass.

Those windows were always surprising people; hardly a day went by that somebody didn't try to throw a cigar butt or chewing gum through them. And once I remember a tourist came in carrying a coffeepot half full of water, which he tried to throw outdoors—through one of our windows.

Some days, if we weren't too busy and I had a group of interested visitors, I'd take them up and explain the ceremonial objects and my murals in the "Hopi Room," and then up to the top for a telescope tour of the eastern Grand Canyon, the Painted Desert, and the Indian country.

In the gift shop I learned a lot about selling and the retail business. Fred Harvey had a rigid system of accounting, where every single item you had in stock had to be accounted for. And as the manager of the shop, I was responsible for any losses by shoplifting. But with that many tourists milling around, there was bound to be some, and this worried me . . . until an old-timer in the business taught me about "scaling," or marking the higher-priced items in each shipment slightly higher than the normal markup. With a little practice I got quite good at this, and could make my inventory and sales figures come out to the penny.

The worst experience I remember at the Watchtower came one day when Jimmy Ricca was away, and I was in charge of the whole operation. Early in the morning, right after we opened, a charter bus load of teenage girls came in, with two chaperones. Soon they were all milling around, handling everything in my shop, then several of them asked to see trays of silver and turquoise rings that we kept in the showcase. I put the trays on the counter so they could try on some rings, and turned away to help somebody else. Donald and two other Hopi boys were with me, but there was too

240

big a crowd for us to watch everything carefully. When I went to put the rings away, I could see that quite a number were missing; and I was positive we hadn't sold any. But what could I do? I called the two chaperones aside and explained to them that some expensive rings were missing, and that they must be returned because this was not my store, and if I lost anything, I would have to make it up myself. But they denied strongly that their girls had taken anything. I was really in a spot.

"Well, we'll just have to search everybody," I told them. "Close up the doors," I called to Donald and the boys. "Nobody is to leave!"

The chaperones said that they would be first. So then they all lined up just inside the door, and we began searching them: their hair, their purses, pockets, everywhere that rings might be concealed. But before we had gotten very far, their driver came in and saw what was going on. He protested violently that I was not doing the right thing, searching people like that; if it had been the police, that would have been different. "All right," I told him, "if you want the police, we'll have them out here!" I ran up to the ranger station and told the park ranger that either he should come down, or he should call the police out from Grand Canyon Village. He called the police.

I went back to the tower to wait. It didn't take long. In less than half an hour, a policeman I knew, Bob Fix, arrived with two helpers. "Well, Fred, what's your trouble out here?" he asked.

We still had the girls in the tower, and I explained the situation to him. Bob Fix then began asking questions, and discovered that the bus driver hadn't gotten the proper permission to bring a group into the park. Bob told him that he was under arrest, and would have to bring his bus and the group back to Grand Canyon Village. But apparently there was no way that they could legally search the girls, so we never got our rings back. It was a bad day for me, one of the worst I can remember.

• • •

I didn't do much painting during the two years we spent at the Watchtower. I worked long hours, and when I'd get back to the house there'd be no daylight left. I tried painting at night by gasoline lantern, but that's hard, and the colors never look right the next morning. The orders were piling up, and I think I finished

241

only one painting in all that time—a Kachina I did for Mrs. Harold Ickes, wife of the Secretary of the Interior.

[Years later] Byron Harvey, Jr. asked if I'd do some murals for the new cocktail lounge in the Bright Angel Lodge at Grand Canyon. Not having any other big projects lined up for that summer, I took on the job. I asked if he had anything special in mind. "The walls are yours, Fred," he said. "Paint whatever feels right to you."

In the years I'd worked at the canyon I'd formed a series of mental caricatures of typical tourists—I guess everybody does if they work there long enough—and so that's what I painted. Fat tourists, skinny tourists, young ones, old. Tourists snoozing in front of the lodge. Tourists taking pictures of each other on the rim, kids climbing over the rim. Frightened tourists starting down the trail on mules, tired tourists coming back. I even painted the funny hats women were wearing at the time.

A couple from back East who were staying at El Tovar used to come in and visit while I was painting, and we became friends. They started coming down every evening about five-thirty when I was ready to quit. We'd have a drink in the bar and then eat. Sometimes when I'd be finishing up a figure, a waitress would come in and say, "Hey, Fred, that man you're doing, he's in the dining room right now!"

I had fun with those walls. When I ran out of tourists I painted a Hopi imitation of a Navajo dance.

"That man looks like he's carrying everything but the kitchen sink," one of the waitresses said.

"We call it the Merchant Dance," I told her. "He's a Navajo, and he's just come out of a trading post. He even has his soda pop."

When I Discovered Pluto

Clyde W. Tombaugh

   In 1894, when famed astronomer Percival Lowell set out to substantiate his theory concerning the probable existence of intelligent life on Mars, he focused on Arizona because of the climate and elevation. Seeking the ideal site, he wanted the highest possible location with clear atmospheric conditions to ensure maximum observation time. Various sites from Tombstone to Prescott were investigated, but the atmospheric conditions were not quite good enough. Finally, at seven thousand feet on the Coconino Plateau a few miles south of the San Francisco Peaks, the elevation and the purity of air were right. There Lowell built his observatory.

   Although Lowell's sensational theory concerning extraterrestrial life has never been substantiated, his prediction of the existence of so-called Planet X proved accurate. Before Lowell died in 1916, he left his young assistant with the admonition never to abandon the search for Planet X. Nearly a quarter-century later, Clyde Tombaugh, a 24-year-old amateur astronomer from a farm near Larned, Kansas, located the planet—now known as Pluto—about six degrees from the position Dr. Lowell had calculated.

   In the following memoir Tombaugh recounts his tedious task of searching for the unknown planet. He examined hundreds of fourteen- by seventeen-inch photographic plates, each teeming with tens of thousands of star images.

   The discovery of Pluto was tangible proof of Lowell's intellectual vision and his tenacity. Because of men like Lowell and Tombaugh, Arizona became known worldwide as a center of excellence in astronomical studies and observations. And that tradition continues with the University of Arizona's distinguished program at the Kitt Peak Observatory near Tucson.

The year 1980 marks the fiftieth anniversary of the discovery of the ninth planet, Pluto. Only two other major planets have been discovered since the invention of the telescope.

• • •

During the first decade of the twentieth century, Percival Lowell of Boston became interested in the possibility of a planet beyond Neptune. He had established an observatory near Flagstaff in 1894 to study the planet Mars. From a study of some very small calculated perturbations of Uranus, Lowell realized that a new planet, if it existed, would be at least one hundred times fainter than Neptune. It would have to be singled out from hundreds of thousands of faint stars. The search for it would have to be a photographic one, conducted by comparing pairs of plates for one tiny star-like image that shifted position in the one- to two-week interval between the plates of each pair.

For two years (1905–1907) Lowell's assistants took a few hundred three-hour guided exposures of star regions in the Zodiac, where the other plates are to be found. Lowell tediously scanned these pairs of planets with a hand magnifier, holding one plate over the other in a nearly superimposed position. Frustratingly, he found no new planet.

The Lowell Observatory launched another planet search (1914–1916) with a more powerful, wide-angle field camera of nine inches aperture. To facilitate the tedious examination of these plates, the observatory purchased a "Blink-Microscope-Comparator" from the Karl Zeiss works in Germany. About one thousand plates were taken along the Zodiac belt. One pair of plates taken in

From Clyde W. Tombaugh, *El Palacio* 86 (Summer 1980): 10–18. Used with permission from the Museum of New Mexico.

244

1915 recorded images of Pluto, but they were missed. For one thing, the astronomers were expecting to find a planet about ten times brighter than Pluto appeared when at last it was found.

Lowell died in November 1916, bitterly disappointed in not having found his predicted "Planet X." However, he had charged his younger assistants never to abandon the search.

Eleven years later the Lowell Observatory purchased the unfinished disks for a thirteen-inch aperture camera. The new trustee, Roger Lowell Putnam (Lowell's nephew), wanted to get the more powerful sky camera built and renew the search for his Uncle Percy's Planet X. He had difficulty finding the money for the project, because of little general confidence that a trans-Neptunian planet existed. Finally, Putnam approached his uncle, Lawrence Lowell, president of Harvard University, who gave ten thousand dollars for building the telescope, mounting and dome. The project ran on a very tight budget. Finishing the complex triplet lens alone cost nearly five thousand dollars.

All the construction was nearing completion when I entered the scene. The Lowell Observatory staff consisted of three middle-aged astronomers, one machinist, one secretary, one general flunky, and one part-time janitor. The budget was strained to the utmost; they could not afford to add another trained astronomer to operate the new telescope and conduct the new planet search. Indeed, Dr. V. M. Slipher, the director, was dubious that any young Ph.D. would care to take on such a tedious task with such doubtful outcome. Slipher began looking for a devoted amateur astronomer.

At home in Kansas in the spring of 1928, I finished making my third reflecting telescope. For six weeks I had tried to obtain a precise curve on the nine-inch diameter mirror, and finally achieved a good parabolic figure. The seven-foot tube was made in a tinner's shop. My father and I built the equatorial mounting from discarded farm machinery. It proved to be an excellent telescope, yielding sharp detail on the moon and planets, with magnifying powers as high as four hundred. In the fall of 1928, I started making pencil drawings of Jupiter and Mars at the eyepiece. These I sent to the Lowell Observatory. They could check the accuracy of the drawings against their current photographs.

Very soon, I received a letter from Director Slipher, who expressed much interest. He asked a number of questions, among them, "Are you in good physical health?" I answered immediately.

245

Then came a second letter with more questions. "Would you be willing to work with our new photographic telescope in a cold, unheated dome? If so, would you be willing to come to Flagstaff in January, on a three-month trial basis?" Promptly, I answered that I would.

After Christmas, I made ready for my trip to far-away Arizona. Early in January 1929, my father drove me to Larned, Kansas, thirty miles from our farm, to board the Santa Fe train. I had earned some money running a wheat-cutting combine for a neighbor the previous summer, but I didn't have enough money left in my wallet for a return ticket. I was armed only with a high school diploma, good grades, and a fair amount of self-taught astronomy and observing experience. I spent the next twenty-eight hours in a chair-car, intrigued with the western scenery.

Dr. Slipher met me at the Flagstaff depot, and took me up the snow-covered, steep, winding road to the observatory. I have often wondered about his first impression of this raw, twenty-two-year-old farm boy from the plains of Kansas. More remote from my mind was that I would discover the ninth planet thirteen months later. Not until a few days after my arrival did I learn that I would be involved in a search for a new planet.

When I arrived at the new dome, housing the new thirteen-inch telescope, Stanley Sykes, the machinist, and his son were drilling holes and attaching some of the telescope controls. Little did I realize then that I would be responsible for keeping this instrument busy for the next fourteen years.

In the meantime, until the telescope was ready, I was assigned various tasks: stoking the big furnace with pine logs, learning darkroom techniques, guiding spectograph exposures with the large twenty-four-inch refractor for Dr. Slipher. Again, I made sketches of Mars when the twenty-four-inch was free. (E. C. Slipher, the Mars man, was serving as a state senator in the Arizona Legislature in Phoenix, and I did not meet him until several weeks later.)

On February 11, the thirteen-inch triplet lens arrived from Massachusetts. Three special fourteen- by seventeen-inch plate holders were made in the observatory shop, built to bend the photographic plates slightly concave to conform to the curvature of the twelve- by fourteen-degree field. The focus was critical, to within one two-hundredth of an inch over the entire plate area! Each plate had to be bent in the plate holder by five thumb screws on a testing

246

table before it was placed in the telescope. For a few weeks I assisted Dr. Slipher with making various critical tests and adjustments. For a few nights he checked me out on procedure. Finally he told me I was on my own.

But there were several other vexing problems with the instrument that I had to solve. Slipher instructed me to photograph the regions in Gemini favored by Lowell in his prediction for Planet X and proceed eastward through the Zodiac as rapidly as possible. The western half of Gemini was in the thick of the Milky Way. I can never forget how overwhelmed Slipher was with these plates, which recorded one-third of a million star images each! Picking out a faint planet amid the myriads of star images would be literally like finding a needle in a haystack. The understanding was that I would take the plates at the telescope and develop them in the darkroom. But more experienced personnel of the staff would examine the pairs of plates under the Blink-Microscope-Comparator.

The two Sliphers spent about two weeks "blinking" the Gemini pairs of plates, which was too fast for a thorough search, and they missed detecting the faint images of Pluto. There was a sense of dismay. Their hopes were that the more powerful telescope/camera would be the panacea in finding Lowell's Planet X. It presented instead a formidable task because of the presence of so many stars.

By the middle of June I had taken over one hundred plates. Only a few pairs had been blinked. The thirteen-inch instrument resolved the rich Milky Way regions in Scorpius and Sagittarius into about one million star images per plate. Dr. Slipher was getting desperate. One day he came to my office and asked me to start blinking the plates. This awed me, because the one doing the blinking carried the responsibility for finding or not finding the long-sought planet. I had inspected each plate with a hand magnifier the past few months for image quality, and had seen the teeming myriads of star images. I winced at the grim task he had set for me. Some two months earlier, after seeing some of the first Gemini plates, I had commented that I was glad that I did not have to go through the starry mess. Now it was dumped right in my lap!

After blinking two pairs of the large plates, I was thoroughly discouraged. Each pair of plates recorded several dozen asteroids which also moved. How was I to distinguish a trans-Neptunian planet from these bodies? My morale was at its lowest point.

247

One day in June 1929, an astronomer from an eastern observatory stopped at Flagstaff to visit us. Dr. Slipher and I had taken him out to the new thirteen-inch telescope dome and explained its program of work. The visitor, in his early sixties, at one point leaned over to me and said, "Young man, I think that you are wasting your time looking for distant planets. If they existed, they would have been found long before this."

In spite of my discouragement, I was not going to admit defeat to an outsider. So I said to him, "I don't think anyone has searched for planets to the faint limit provided by the thirteen-inch. I am going to give it all that I've got." Then the thought flashed across my mind: Oh my, I have made a terrible commitment! I would like to have seen the expression on that astronomer's face nine months later, when the news of the Pluto discovery reached him.

Nevertheless, that astronomer had voiced the current consensus of astronomical opinion, backed by the negative results of several earlier planet searches.

I knew I must find some sure-fire way of distinguishing asteroids from a distant planet. During the rainy season in July and August, I studied the geometry of apparent planetary motions by plotting the daily positions of distant Uranus and Neptune to contrast to those of Jupiter and Mars. I soon saw the solution to my problem: I must take the plates at close to the "opposition point" in the sky (180 degrees from the sun) and thus avoid the near stationary sectors of the asteroids that lie between 36 and 64 degrees on each side of the opposition point. All bodies external to the earth's orbit appear to retrograde (move backward) at opposition, the nearer bodies moving most rapidly. Moreover, the earth's daily orbital motion would be tangential and thus provide a parallax effect for an immediate estimate of the distance of a planet suspect. This, then, would be the key strategy in the planet search. Strangely, this precaution had never been presented to me in my instructions. With these realizations, I felt enormously encouraged that the planet search could be conducted thoroughly and with finality. Also, the thousands of false planet suspects produced by chance plate defects could be quickly checked off by the use of yet a third plate taken of each region.

After the end of the rainy season I started photographing the "opposition" regions in the constellations Aquarius and Pisces in September 1929, and marched eastward in the Zodiac thirty degrees each succeeding month. During the full moon period, when long exposure plates could not be taken because of "sky-fogging," I would work in the daytime examining the pairs of plates on the Blink-Comparator. The plates of every pair had to be exactly matched for stellar magnitude limit and identical focus; otherwise, the blink technique wouldn't work. Many precautions had to be taken to achieve perfect matching.

The plate regions in Aquarius, Pisces and Aries were the thinnest star regions searched, recording approximately fifty thousand star images per fourteen- by seventeen-inch plate. I could thoroughly blink such a pair in three days. In November, the search regions entered the constellation of Taurus. The number of stars increased to over one hundred thousand, and the blinking of a pair of plates required one week's work. Several times Dr. V. M. Slipher would come to the Comparator room and ask if I was finding anything.

The plates taken in latter December in eastern Taurus and western Gemini were in the Milky Way galaxy and recorded about four hundred thousand star images each. It required three weeks to blink a pair. I was getting behind in this tedious examination. One had to confine attention to no more than a dozen stars during a few rapidly alternating views of the two plates on the Blink-Comparator. Each tiny star image was a candidate for a planet, and one had to be conscious of seeing each image. Any star image that showed a displacement of one-half millimeter or less per day would indicate to me that it was a planet beyond the orbit of Neptune. So I knew exactly what to look for.

Since I was already behind in the blinking work, I decided to postpone the two very star-rich regions in western Gemini. On February 18, 1930, I placed the Delta Geminorum (at the eastern edge of the Milky Way) plates on the Comparator and started blinking. These plates were taken in January. The January 23 and 29 ones were the best matched. By four o'clock that afternoon, I had covered one-quarter of the plate area. Upon turning the plate carriage to another small area about one inch east of the guide star, Delta, almost instantly I spied a fifteenth-magnitude star winking at me, and disappearing when the comparator shutter shifted the view to the other plate. Looking slightly to one side of it about one-eighth of an inch away, I saw another fifteenth-magnitude star image doing the same thing. I stopped the automatic clicking shutter, and turned the alternating shutter slowly by hand, back and forth.

249

It was immediately evident that the two winking images were on different plates. The image of the January 29 plate was one-eighth inch to the west of the one on the January 23 plate. The apparent shift in position was retrograde as it should be. That's it! I exclaimed to myself. A most intense thrill came over me.

I measured the shift with a plastic millimeter ruler—3½ mm in six days! These images still could be two independent variable stars in alternating phases, by rare chance. I removed one of the plates and placed the third plate—the January 21 plate—on the Blink-Comparator. The images on this plate were soft and expanded because the atmospheric conditions turned bad after I had started the exposure that night. But there was the shifting image, one millimeter east of the one on the January 23 plate. The shift in position was consistent. Now I was nearly one-hundred percent sure.

Then I got out the three eight- by ten-inch plates taken with the 5-inch Cogshall camera simultaneously with the thirteen-inch. With a hand magnifier, I inspected the small configurations of stars in that immediate area. There were the planet images on all three plates exactly in the same corresponding positions. Although very faint, they were unmistakable.

Fortunately, I thought to look at my watch a few minutes after I first spied the images, right at four o'clock. I studied the images some more. For three quarters of an hour, I was the only person in the world who knew exactly where a new planet was located. Then I notified Dr. C. O. Lampland in his office across the hall, showing him the images on the original pair.

I was so excited I was shaking. Leaving Dr. Lampland to study the images, I went down the hall to the other end of the building. I saw that V. M. Slipher's office door was open. I paused a moment, trying to regain my composure. Then I walked in. "Dr. Slipher, I've found your Planet X!" Slipher was electrified. He rose up from his desk chair, with a combined expression of elation and doubt on his face. "If you care to see it, I'll show you the evidence," I said.

Immediately he came out of his office and hurried down the hall to the Comparator room. Lampland stepped aside for Dr. Slipher to look. I explained that the shifts in position were consistent for an object beyond Neptune's orbit. Both men agreed that the object was very promising. "We must keep this a strict secret within the staff for a few weeks and follow its motion," Dr. Slipher

250

said. The plates were three weeks old, where was the planet now? "We must rephotograph the region immediately," he said. We looked out of the window. The sky was very cloudy, and much snow was on the ground.

It was now 6:00 p.m., an hour later than my usual departure to drive down Mars Hill to eat dinner in a cafe and pick up the observatory mail at the post office. The sky was still hopelessly cloudy. Instead of driving back up to the observatory, I decided to attend a movie. It was Gary Cooper in *The Virginian*. The sky was still cloudy when I left the theater. I drove up the Hill and tried reading, sitting up for possible clearing, until about 2:30 a.m. It would now be too late to get the discovery region with our instruments.

The next day other members of the observatory staff were shown the Pluto images.

On the evening of February 19, the sky had cleared off fairly well. I loaded one large plateholder and set the thirteen-inch telescope on to the guide star, Delta Geminorum. After finishing the one-hour exposure, I developed the plate and put it up to dry. A few hours later, I placed it on the Comparator to blink it against one of the discovery pair. The planet image on the new plate should have been about ten millimeters west of the January 29 position. It required only about ten seconds of blinking to pick up the image. And there it was—in the right position.

On the evening of February 20, 1930, Slipher, Lampland and I went to the dome of the twenty-four-inch refractor in great anticipation. The question uppermost in our minds was: Would the new object show a planetary disk under high magnifying power? Slipher set the telescope to the proper star-field coordinates by the use of the equatorial circles. Then with the use of the film as a field guide, the small configurations of faint stars were identified. There was the planet, shifted slightly in position from the photograph taken the night before. With a deep sense of awe, we realized it was man's first direct look at the new planet. Perhaps never again would astronomers be able to share such a moment. There was also disappointment, because no disk was perceptible. Indeed, this new planet presented a most unimportant appearance.

Pluto was only one-tenth as bright as Lowell had predicted and there was no one-second of arc disk visible. Yet, it was within six degrees of the position indicated by Lowell, and approximately at the distance he assigned. Was this object really Lowell's Planet X?

251

For the next several weeks, Lampland took four-by five-inch plates with the forty-two-inch reflector on every possible night. The larger plate scale would permit more precise positions. Also, Lampland made several long exposure plates with the large reflector, reaching into the nineteenth magnitude, in a desperate effort to detect a satellite. If a satellite could be found, the mass of the new body could be determined with the use of Kepler's Law. But no satellite was then found, for at that time Pluto was nearly one thousand million miles beyond the orbit of Neptune. Even Pluto itself was four thousand times fainter than the faintest star visible to the unaided eye on a clear, moonless night, away from city lights. Visually, Pluto was at the very limit with a twelve-inch telescope.

Of course the trustee, Roger Lowell Putnam, in Springfield, Massachusetts, was promptly notified of the find; also Lowell's brother, Lawrence, at Harvard, and Lowell's widow, Constance. At first only a few others were so informed of the discovery. Putnam was particularly elated, not only for his deceased Uncle Percy's sake, but also because he had induced his Uncle Lawrence to provide the money to build the thirteen-inch sky camera. The cost was now justified.

Over the next four weeks, as the region veered away from the opposition point, the new-found object began to slow down in its motion, by an amount that only a body considerably beyond the orbit of Neptune could possibly do. There was no longer any doubt that the object was trans-Neptunian in nature.

During these ensuing weeks, everyone on the Lowell Observatory staff was making preparations, including writing special reports, to meet the expected demands and furor once the news of the discovery was out.

On March 13 the news was released from the Harvard Distributing Center. This date was of special significance. It was the 149th anniversary of the discovery of Uranus as well as the 75th anniversary of Percival Lowell's birth. The storm of intense interest by both the astronomical world and the public greatly exceeded all our expectations. Headlines blazed in newspapers and magazines all over the world. An avalanche of telegrams and letters poured in. The Lowell Observatory staff was overwhelmed. I recall this response most vividly, after fifty years. I am now the only living member of the Lowell Observatory staff who experienced this extraordinary episode; I had just turned twenty-four two weeks before the discovery.

I had kept the secret of the discovery, and did not even tell my parents. News of the discovery was picked up by the Associated Press, and the publisher of the Pawnee County weekly paper, *The Tiller and Toiler*, Leslie Wallace of Larned, Kansas, phoned my parents near the little town of Burdett, and said to them, "Did you know that your son has discovered a planet?" The news spread like wildfire. My little high school of about seventy-five students, from which I had graduated four-and-a-half years earlier, went wild with excitement. They felt that they were the most famous high school in the country.

One might have expected the interest to die down after a few weeks. Quite the contrary. Because of the unique properties of Pluto, it seemed to be in a class of objects new in astronomy. Heated controversies ensued among professional astronomers, challenging the validity of Lowell's prediction.

Within a few months after the announcement, there arose apprehension that the "real" Planet X was yet to be found, if Lowell's actual prediction had any validity. Several astronomers pleaded with Dr. Slipher to have the planet search continued. "You have the instrument and the expertise," a group of them implored. "What else is out there in the far regions of the Solar System?"

I thought that my tedious task was finished, but it had only begun, and would go on for another thirteen years. In May of 1930, Dr. Slipher instructed me to resume the search. The staff now had complete confidence in my work. As it later came out in records of observatory correspondence, they felt they would be hard put to find another observer who would put forth such devotion and perseverance. I had become the expert in planet search technique and skill.

Ranching During the
Great Depression

Nel Sweeten Cooper

The decade of the 1930s meant hard times for Arizona as well as the rest of the nation. Relying primarily on agriculture and mining, Arizona was especially vulnerable when the national economy stagnated. The first stages of the depression unfolded in predictable patterns. The price of all agricultural produce declined, while debts appreciated and farm and ranch foreclosures multiplied. Arizona cotton producers suffered major losses, but cattle and sheep growers felt similar hardships as the price of beef and wool spiraled downward. Citrus growers also grieved over their losses; grapefruits, oranges and other fruits ripened and fell, left to rot in the groves.

Most ranchers, like the Cooper family in the following memoir, managed to hold on, however dispiriting the situation. Government efforts designed to reduce production and thus push prices upward seemed reasonable in theory, but painful in the actual implementation, which meant destroying crops and slaughtering animals rather than marketing them.

This memoir vividly illustrates once again how women contributed to the life and economic development of Arizona and the country. As a young bride, Nel Sweeten Cooper homesteaded her own land and worked as a full partner in building her family's ranch holdings. After her husband's death, Mrs. Cooper struggled to retain the land and livestock despite society's prejudice against women entrepreneurs, legal stumbling blocks, and the skepticism of her fellow ranchers.

This ranchwoman's account of her family's bewildered and anguished reaction to the government's herd reduction program is ironic and heartrending. Nel Cooper's recollection is a reminder that, despite good intentions, national policies often have unforeseen and painful consequences as they affect individual lives.

Compared to most pioneer ranches ours is a "newcomer," being only fifty-six years old. For it was in February of 1923 that I filed on a grazing homestead. I had gone into Prescott from Skull Valley where I was visiting my aunt and her family, the Gists, in company with Roy Cooper, my intended husband, to obtain our marriage license as we planned to be married three days later.

We got the marriage license and the official said to me jokingly as he handed the paper to Roy, "In three days you will be a married woman and all business transactions will be in your husband's name."

We thanked him and left. But I was thinking about the homestead I had been contemplating filing on. I had become interested in "homesteading" since the summer of 1921 when I had first visited the Gists. . . . From time to time I thought about homesteads and homesteaders. It all seemed "romantic" to me. Romantic! It turned out to be far from the interpretation I had of that word then.

As we left the courthouse, I mentioned this to Roy, asking, "I can't have a homestead now, can I?"

He laughed, "Not unless you file in three days."

"Then I am going to do it," I said. "But, I don't have the least idea what to do, do *you*?"

"Yes, I filed last year. It was the last open land within our range at the headquarters in Williamson Valley. There is open land on the desert near our kidding and lambing headquarters. You went with me last week, remember? It will be a good thing for Cooper and Sons to have patented land there." Cooper and Sons consisted of John Thomas Cooper and his sons Will and Roy. At

From Nel Sweeten Cooper, *Arizona National Ranch Histories of Living Pioneer Stockmen*, compiled and edited by Betty Accomazzo, 2 (Phoenix: Arizona National, 1979), 129–165. Used with permission from Betty Accomazzo.

256

that time they had ten bands of goats and five bands of sheep. They moved about over the country much as did one of the nomads of Eastern Europe.

I was born and raised in the hill country of West Texas, Angora goat country. My father had owned Angora goats—all my people did. I loved them.

Roy explained, "I'll call my lawyer in Phoenix and see what can be worked out." He did call the lawyer and after a lengthy telephone call, he turned to me pleased. "He'll have everything ready and the proper papers for you to sign first thing in the morning."

On Sunday, February 18, 1923, we were married and boarded the train for Congress Junction, Arizona. . . . It was imperative that he be in Congress Junction Monday morning.

We stayed at the Henderson Hotel for two weeks—until the shearing was completed, the mohair and wool sold and shipped. All this time, in the midst of the hectic shearing, a place for me to live was being prepared. It was a lovely camp, which was to be temporary. It was two tents, eight feet by ten feet, walled up with lumber two feet high. Our bedroom tent was floored with one-by-twelves. The kitchen tent faced the bedroom tent with a space between, shaded by a large palo verde. There I began my cooking "career." I knew how to cook, but I didn't know how to cook in great quantities, for after my father's death in January of 1910 when I was eleven, we had lived in town and there had been only my mother, my two sisters and me. Now there was the kidding and lambing crew, the herders—twenty to twenty-five men. I made many mistakes, but I finally learned to put enough chili tepines in the beans to burn the bottom out of any herder's cast-iron stomach.

At first I enjoyed the desert. The wild flowers were budding, a faint green haze shimmered over it all, and I was learning an entirely new way of life. Then, the wind started to blow, and soon I felt tension in everyone.

Our first child, Roy Jr., was born June 1, 1924. He was the fourth grandchild and first grandson of Martha Brannan and John Thomas Cooper. When, less than two years later, our second son, Robert Dee, was born February 5, 1926, my father-in-law told his friend Barney Smith that we had hurried to have a second son so that we could balance the pack on the mule. Our third son, John William, was born September 25, 1927.

• • •

Roy and I hadn't been established on our Spring Creek Place many years until other homesteaders were attracted to the area by the abundance of good water and good browse. Since the other homesteaders all had only cattle, and we had goats as well as cattle, we were due for conflict. Although their livestock ranged everywhere, they objected to our bands of goats that were all under herd and each herder instructed to keep them off the homesteaders. One year Roy was arrested twelve times for trespassing and although he stood trial and was acquitted each time, it was expensive! Roy began buying out the homesteaders. He bought six before he died.

• • •

Cooper Ranch is one of the best watered ranges, that is, natural water. The Hassayampa River is our eastern boundary. There are numerous creeks, Spring Creek, Cottonwood, Blackwater, Arrastra, Mocho, some others as well as many permanent springs.

• • •

It was about this time that Will Cooper took over managing the sheep while Roy and I kept the goats. Will had enough pasture for the sheep after he no longer had the goats. I think everyone liked this arrangement. We built shipping pens on one of the homesteads Roy bought, and we moved there during "shearing."

Our boys were growing up. They would soon be of school age. There was still a school at Wagoner and although it was three miles from the "shearing" corrals, we decided to stay there at the "shearing" place and send the boys to school. The boys rode horseback; each boy had his own horse. They rode with another boy from the west side of the Hassayampa. They tied their horses to mesquite trees near the schoolhouse. Horse racing was forbidden, but several times someone had to back-track the schoolboys to recover lost articles—saddle blankets, school books, lasso ropes! Once Bob's was missing and he was heartbroken. It was found, but for punishment for disobedience, his father kept it hanging in the dining room a whole week.

258

Mr. Roosevelt and his Drouth Relief Shipments set us back considerably. They were awful! Heartrending to people who loved their cattle as Roy and his boys did. There were four "shipments" in all and what they really accomplished, I have never understood. There was nothing we could do to prevent them. A rain might have, but it would not rain, watch the skies and pray as we did—no rain.

From the beginning, Roy looked terrible. He had no appetite, lost weight. After the fourth shipment, I told his father that if we had to make another shipment, I'd push Roy in after the last cow and shut the freight car door. Roy must have lost twenty-five pounds.

We were ordered to ship a band of goats. These must be she-stock, two to six years old—the prime producers—mothers. They must be driven to the nearest railhead—Congress Junction in our case. The goats were in good condition and were no trouble to drive.

The goats were corralled in the Santa Fe shipping pens and counted onto freight cars and sent to Tovrea Packing Plant in Phoenix where the goats were slaughtered, the meat processed and given to the people on Relief. Cooper and Sons were paid one dollar and fifty cents per head. We were lucky to receive this generous amount for animals worth many times this sum. We heard that mohair growers who owned goats in Mojave County were to receive one dollar per head, all she-stock. They were advanced thirty cents a head, [and] the animals [were] shipped to California for processing. Thirty cents was all they were ever paid.

My father-in-law had a great desire to taste the canned goat meat and although he and all of us searched the shelves in the grocery stores, it could not be found. Finally we learned that it had been sent to Relief Centers, but when we located one of these places, we were told we could not buy even one can! We had to be on Relief! My father-in-law said he'd be danged if he'd go on Relief just to get a can of his own meat. Still, being a determined man, he wanted to taste that meat! One day a sly look came into his eyes, "I'll go out to Tovrea's and get me a can of that meat!"

Roy explained, "I've already been to the plant. They say, 'Only if you are on Relief!'"

My father-in-law answered, "I'm not going to the plant. I've known Ed Tovrea a long time. We've always been friends."

259

"Ed Tovrea can't get it either. Can't you understand, Dad? The meat belongs to the government!"

"We'll see," said John Thomas in a mild tone.

I don't how it was accomplished. I didn't ask, but one day, soon after, I came in to find my father-in-law and my sons eating meat from a knife-opened can. When John Thomas saw me, he smiled triumphantly and held out his pocket knife with a morsel of meat on the point. "Have a bite. It's good. Not as good, perhaps, as fried goat chops or roasted ribs, but not bad. In fact good. What do you say, boys?"

Enthusiastically they agreed with Granddad.

The cattle shipments were another matter. A heartbreaking thing! Early in life our sons had shown that they "took after" their father. They know cattle. Almost from infancy Roy Jr. was a near genius in distinguishing at a glance one cow from another, knowing which calf belonged to which cow. In fact, he was so good that his father and our men "paid their bets" on Roy's word. For instance one man or the other would point out an animal and remark that that heifer or bull or steer was the calf of such and such a cow. Someone would disagree! "Bet you five dollars," the other would say. "You're on! We'll ask Roy Boy." And if Roy Boy wasn't with them, the animal was described to him and on his "say so," the loser "paid up."

Bob is almost as good. In fact, in general, he is the best cowman of the three. Not only is he better than his brothers, he has no peer. He can ride up to a herd of cattle, and at a glance, tell if there are any strays—if so, to whom they belong. And he is an excellent roper. Also, he knows his horses.

John is a good all-around cowman, too, but not spectacular like his brothers. Being the youngest, he did not have the teaching of his father as many years, for Roy Sr. was killed when John was eleven.

I am not bragging about my sons and their cow-sense. It came naturally from their father and his teaching and from our foreman Ingersol Heckle.

As I said, those Drouth Relief Shipments were awful! The first was in the summer of 1932, when we were ordered by the government to have all our cattle gathered by a certain date. We were to hold them in an accessible place for the man they would send to inspect them and tell us "what would be done." The young man who came at last—he was to have arrived in the morning, and it was well into the afternoon by the time he drove in—all "Importance and Authority," and he hadn't been there ten minutes until even I knew he didn't know much about range cattle. "Not dry behind the ears," our foreman, Ingersol Heckle, told me in a low voice as he came by me.

We were not to corral the cattle, but to "Hold them in a loose herd," and it had taken all hands and the cook, [and] me, to hold the hungry, hot cows.

In a curt voice, the young man explained that he would determine the condition of each animal and tell us which ones would be able to be driven to the shipping point, Kirkland, Arizona, thirty miles to the rails. We would be paid twelve dollars per head, but only for those that walked all the way. If an animal fell by the way, the brand was to be skinned out and taken along. We would receive eight dollars for it. The cattle in the worst condition were to be cut out from the herd, driven a short distance and shot. Yes, we would receive eight dollars per head for these. Some of the cows had small calves. "What about them?"

"They can be hauled," the condescending young man conceded.

"Typical shave-tail lieutenant!" my husband, who was a World War I veteran, said to me as he turned a cow back near me. He looked sick as the young man began "cutting the herd," and he looked sicker and sicker as the work went on.

Roy Hays, a ranchman from Peeples Valley, was with the government man. He had been asked to accompany the—I don't know what title the young man had. Ever after we referred to him as the "shave tail." Mr. Hays had seemed ill-at-ease when we greeted him. We felt reassured to have a good cowman there. Our hopes were dashed when he stayed on the sidelines, saying nothing. We had thought he was the person who would select the cattle. He told me years later that he had expected, when he agreed to take the job, that he could be of help to the ranchers. Instead, all that was required of him was to guide the government man to the different ranches. The whole thing proved so frustrating that he quit.

The government man took advice from no one. As he hurried through our herd designating just one animal then another, I think he daubed different colors of paint on them. Soon he had finished and demanded that certain cows be cut out. He went to his car, took out a high-powered rifle, and proceeded to drive the doomed cattle over a hill.

261

Our children, who, of course, had helped in gathering and in holding the herd, were bewildered, and their father, and indeed all of us, were so numbed by shock we hadn't properly explained to the children what was happening.

When the man left with his gun, driving the condemned cattle, no one noticed Roy Jr. had followed. There were cows of his in that group, and soon after the first rifle shots were heard, he came at full gallop back to us, crying—to his father: "Daddy, do something! The man is shooting our cattle!" We tried to console him, explain to him, but it is hard to explain to an eight-year-old boy why the government had decreed such a thing, especially if you don't really understand yourself.

That first slaughter, about thirty head were destroyed. For days on end, buzzards circled the dead cattle, and for many years the bones bleached. Another thirty cattle were driven to the rails. This depleted our herd, but when three more such shipments were ordered and made, we were almost wiped out. I hadn't thought it possible, but after each shipment, Roy Sr. looked worse. He must have lost twenty-five pounds. But Mr. Roosevelt found something else to occupy himself—a war was brewing. He left us alone. We were beginning to recover when Roy Sr. was killed in an accident at the ranch. This was August 17, 1939.

I never had any intention of selling the ranch although many people were surprised and advised me to sell, saying that I would surely go broke. A woman and three young boys just couldn't make it. We have, though. At times it hasn't been easy. And, always, it is a gamble.

From the first, cattle buyers had me bluffed. Not at all like selling the mohair. One reason, I think, I knew more about Angora goats and the selling of the mohair, having been raised in the Angora goat country of Texas, and, too, most of the mohair in Arizona was taken to a central place where the buyers and ranchers met and the mohair sold at auction bid.

Cattle buyers come to each individual ranch, look at your cattle and the deal is made if each agree. The first year after Roy Sr.'s death, the man that Roy had dealt with the year before sent word that he was interested in our cattle, and that if I would have them in, he'd be there on a certain day. We had most of them gathered and in a holding pasture. Then, I studied the *Arizona News Letter* (the cattlemen's Bible, one buyer termed it) for prices.

Early in the morning we corralled the cattle. The instant the man went into our corral, he pulled a "long face," and began to whine about the condition and quality of the cattle. When I told him the price I wanted, he sounded as if he would weep.

"Didn't you buy from Roy last year?" I asked.

He admitted that he had. "But, these are—uh—they don't conform, and the price. . . ," he whined on.

I didn't know what "conform" meant, and anyway, whining just isn't in my book. I can't stand a whiner. "Then you don't want our cattle," I said. I called to Roy Jr. to open the gate into the holding pasture and to Bob and John to drive the cattle out. "Thank you for coming, Mr. -----." I left him standing in the middle of the corral with a strange look on his face.

Then a man named King sent word that he would like to buy the cattle. He, too, had bought from Roy. He, too, asked would I have them "in?"

"Yes, early in the day."

He set a date and I notified him we'd have the cattle ready. Again we gathered the cattle and corralled them in the holding pasture. We waited and waited—all day. And the buyer didn't come—nor did he notify us why. Later I asked Tom Richards why Mr. King hadn't come. Tom was embarrassed; then he mumbled that Mr. King, when he heard he'd have to deal with a woman, turned around in the middle of the road when nearly at the ranch and went back to Wickenburg.

When my sister-in-law, Learah Morgan, heard about my failure with cattle buyers, she was scandalized. "Nel!" she said, "They want to dicker! It is a sort of game!"

"I don't know how to dicker," I told her, "and, besides, I have no time for games. I have the cattle ready for them to see and tell them what price I want."

"You'll never make it," she said sadly.

And I almost didn't a few times. Once I took a ten percent cut on the herd, then ended up with a ten percent cut on the cut! On top of that there was always a three percent shrink. I have never been able to figure that deal out, but I almost lost my shirt on that one.

I had been told over and over how men hate to deal with women, and after Mr. King, I believe it. I was scared, but I let no one know.

In the last forty years there have been many changes. Now high trucks come to our corrals, and we weigh, load and send them on their way. (The cattle belong to the buyer when they walk off the scales. I learned that the hard, expensive way, too.) My son, John, installed our own shipping pens a number of years ago. Before that we drove the cattle about five miles to a neighbor's scales where we met the trucks. We paid ten cents a head for the privilege of using the scales, and we were grateful that we could. I learned that first year not to corral the cattle for the buyer. If he couldn't ride a horse or was afraid of my jeep driving, he was out of luck. But, no dickering—I never learned that.

Today my son John manages the ranch—he meets with buyers, but I am afraid he is like me. He doesn't dicker either. I heard him say once that he has never sold cattle when the "price was right." Oh well, we all know there is no gambling game of chance that can compare with cattle raising. If the price is up, we are in a drouth and the cattle are thin, may have to feed—always something, but interesting, always challenging. Never a dull moment! And, although there have been days on end when I saw no one except my family and our workers, no phone rang (there wasn't a phone), and no mail came, [I] have never been lonely. Always a crisis to meet, some problem to solve. Even though jeeps and four-wheel drives have supplanted the pack mules, we never "get the slack taken in."

• • •

One morning in the spring of 1946 I was ready to mount my horse to go with the roundup crew when a car drove up. A man got out and asked for Mrs. Cooper, Nel S. Cooper. He emphasized the name. I rode back to him. He told me he was from the Federal Land Office and he wanted to know what I intended to do about the fine I had not paid the Federal Government for trespassing on their land!

I was flabbergasted. I told him it was the first I'd heard of it. When I convinced him I had not received a bill, he presented me with one. It was a staggering amount. When my head cleared a little, I saw that its location was the Stock Driveway, and I had been "in trespass" since 1919. When I informed the man that I had not lived in Arizona until February of 1923, he said that made no dif-

264

ference, Cooper and Sons had been there then and, "What arrangements do you intend to make to pay your fine?"

I tried to explain that the Coopers were not the only users of that land. At that time the land was all unfenced and cattle as far away as Peeples Valley were gathered there each year.

"That does not concern me," the man replied. "I want an answer at once. What are you going to do?"

"Nothing," I told him. "Not until I know more about it." I didn't have the money to pay even a fourth of the fine. I don't remember now, but it was something like $1.50 an acre! And since 1919 to 1946? And we paid the leases, too!

Howard Smith took care of my land leases at that time, so I took my trespass fine problem to him for advice. He was startled. It was the first he'd heard of it. He advised me to wait until he made further investigation.

There was nothing I could do. I didn't have the money, and I doubted that the Bank of Arizona, to whom I was mortgaged, would lend me the money. Three times more the man came to see me, asking when I would pay the fine.

Each time I told him, "I don't intend to pay it if I can get out of it. I consider it unfair, and I don't have that much money."

In the meantime Howard Smith was doing all he could. First he telephoned the district office in Albuquerque. He found that some people had paid their fines at once rather than fight it and have something like that hanging over their heads. I didn't pay for more than a year. Then, one day I was notified that all my Federal Leases were cancelled! Just like that—cancelled! Howard was an excellent mathematician. He figured, prorated, taking into consideration all the users of the Stock Driveway through all the years, and he came up with the sum of $73.29! "Make out your check for this amount," he told me, "and be sure you write on it: Paid Under Protest!" I did, and I mailed the check. My Federal Leases were restored. Incident closed.

Japanese Relocation: Recollections from the Poston Camp, 1942–1945

Marry Masunaga

In fewer than nine months after the stunning dawn attack on Pearl Harbor, more than one hundred thousand men, women, and children—almost the entire Japanese-American population of Arizona, California, Oregon, and Washington—had been rounded up and confined in ten "relocation" centers. Most of these camps were in bleak and remote areas selected primarily for security. Three camps were established in Arizona—at Poston, Gila River, and Luepp. Located within Indian reservations, the Poston and Gila River sites were barbed-wire enclosures maintained by a small detachment of military police. The isolated camp at Leupp in the Navajo country was a maximum-security facility for "malcontents."

Marry Masunaga, a young Japanese wife awaiting the birth of her first child, was sent from her home in California to the relocation camp at Poston, on the Colorado River. Eighteen thousand Japanese-Americans eventually were imprisoned there, making Poston the third largest population center in Arizona in 1942. Mrs. Masunaga remained at the Poston camp throughout the war, bearing three children and raising her family in a crowded enclosure. Like the majority of Japanese-Americans, she and her family went quietly to the camps in the sincere belief that this was "our very best constructive recourse to prove our . . . loyalty to this country."

The Relocation and Enemy Aliens Act, which excluded persons of Japanese ancestry from the West Coast, remained in force until January 2, 1945. At the end of the war, the Masunagas returned to California. But, like so many people who were in Arizona during the war, they returned to make their homes in the Arizona desert and to find jobs in the flourishing postwar economy around Phoenix. More than three decades after the war, Mrs. Masunaga agreed to a lengthy interview about her experiences. This memoir is an edited version of that oral history.

267

Life in these camps was primitive and harsh but not nearly as brutal in the physical as in the spiritual sense. Mrs. Masunaga vividly recreates the physical setting, the food, the amusements, and the gossipy details that made up daily life. The absence of any bitterness or anger in her recollections is truly remarkable. The experience of Japanese-American citizens who lost their liberty because of the accident of ancestry must have been a kind of deprivation and torture which no lack of food or physical pain could equal. It was particularly ironic during a war which their fellow citizens were fighting in the name of individual liberty.

By April we were all put into different camps. We had to dispose of the nursery. A government official came. There were great big government posters put up on telephone poles about our having to leave. I remember seeing these black prints on white posters on a telephone pole near our place. My husband then had to dispose of everything. We had two big warehouses and a storage area for groceries. He also sold rice and chicken feed to the chicken farmers, so he had a huge warehouse full of chicken feed. All of this had to be disposed of, and these rather unscrupulous dealers would come and offer you nothing just for the privilege of hauling it away.

We had a German butcher who had been in World War I and that man was so outraged because both Harry and I were so young. He was so protective. I remember the day that a dealer came and emptied the grocery store of merchandise. Oscar [the name of the German]—got drunk. I remember he simply cussed out the dealer every minute that the man was there; every time he loaded something on, he was there. He was totally drunk.

[The store was called] Masunaga Takayama Company Stanton stores. It was their firm for twenty years. It was a kind of a focal point for people buying Japanese food because they were one of the few stores that carried it. And so everything was disposed of and we had two cars. All of the cars, trucks, and everything had to be disposed of except for our one car that [my husband] had bought before he was married. So he took the tires off and in the empty great big grocery store, he put the new car up on blocks and hoped to goodness it wouldn't be vandalized any further.

Then we were told to pack two suitcases—only what we could carry. We left on April 15 [1942], so you [can] see [that] all of

This is an edited version of a lengthy question and answer interview by Dr. Constance Myers with Marry Masunaga, February 25, 1979, in Tempe, Arizona. The complete transcript of the interview is in the Hayden Library, Arizona State University, Tempe, Arizona. Used with persmission from Arizona State University.

269

this happened from Pearl Harbor to April. I was already seven-and-a-half months pregnant, and they told me I would have to be separated from my family and stay in the prison ward of the general hospital in Orange County. I couldn't go with [my family] because there weren't any facilities in camp for babies or anybody yet. But I told them I would risk anything. I would sign anything so I could be with my family, my mother and my sisters. We became such a cohesive unit. We just clung to each other, I think. So they allowed me to go.

I had one [suitcase] full of the baby's things. Baby [clothes] and everything I had read from Doctor Spock's book that was necessary, from vitamins [to] what have you, for the baby. I forgot to take clothing that I could wear after I had the baby. I had nothing but maternity clothes. I didn't have sense enough, I think. I just had maternity clothes in my suitcase and the baby's things—all the things I had knitted and made and the pretty things that my mother had gotten and my mother-in-law had gotten for the first baby-to-be. So I had to take those things and that was all I could carry.

They told us that there would be rattlesnakes and scorpions and so the first thing I did, all of us, was go out and buy high-top boots clear to our knees, but we never wore them. They were so hot and clumsy.

What took some of the space [was] our books and photographs. We had burned all things. We were made so fearful. They took up all of our knives and scissors, radios, cameras. They were all confiscated. We were given plenty of notice. We must have had at least a couple of weeks to get rid of our household belongings. We were lucky. We asked one of our customers whom we didn't know very well if they would stay in the house for free for however long it would be and so our house, the little tiny wooden framed house, was lived in by someone the whole time. It was an elderly [Caucasian] couple who had a grandchild, and they stayed in it during the war for us.

We all had to congregate at the Anaheim railroad station. We were given written orders. There were a few who dared not to. They had to go through the courts and were jailed. Korematsu, they were lawyers to begin with—young lawyers—and they challenged the fact that *habeas corpus* and all of these legal steps were not taken. But they had to go through a very lengthy trial and were imprisoned during that time. There were a few who challenged it, but for the most part, for one thing, the Japanese American Cit-

270

izens League had gotten together. I was a very young member then, but we got word from them. They had representatives in Washington, D.C., talking to the White House, and we had gotten word, all the different chapters, to cooperate fully. That would be our very best constructive recourse to prove our citizenship because I don't know of anyone who felt anything but loyalty to this country. We had Japanese faces certainly, but . . . our hearts were with . . . we were Americans.

So on the proper day, April 15, [we] went to the railroad station. [We] all met there. We all had to wear those hideous tags. That is the most humiliating symbol to me to this day. That hurt more than any other thing—to have to wear that tag because suddenly I felt like I was baggage. I was no longer a human being. Each family was issued a number, a family number. Do you know I've forgotten it, but it seemed like it was 36660, something like that. The tags were too big for one thing. They must have been about six inches by two inches with this large number at least an inch tall—hanging, just like shipping tags. My mother's family had another number, and we did have to wear them up front in the middle of our chests . . . until we got to Poston, Arizona.

And that was an all-day trip. It took us all day and we were given box lunches. It was certainly the first train ride in the United States that I can remember. All I remember is our being seated. It was kind of exciting. I don't think we had time to be depressed. There was so much we had to keep up with. Knowing what to carry, where to go and what to do. Scared, of course, not knowing—apprehensive, not knowing what could happen to us. All we heard was mainly about the rattlesnakes and scorpions. I think I was more scared of that. I don't think I remember like—it must have been for the Jews who were decimated where they had an inkling of what might happen. I don't think anyone knew what was going to happen to us. There were, I remember, a whole group of people just watching us and I remember writing. I did keep a journal but since then I've lost all those things in so many moves.

I remember we got on a huge bus, extremely hot, and we were processed in a long, long, bedraggled line through a mess hall, a barrack. That's what we lived in for the next three-and-a-half years. They were constructed very crudely, just slapped together. They didn't have time. It was done in so very short order. The desert was simply dug up and these were placed like in the army, very much like in the army.

271

There must have been about a dozen barracks lined up in two sections. Then the latrines—the mens' latrine, the womens' latrine and the laundry in the center. One mess hall at the end was used for mess hall purposes. Rooms measured about twenty-four by twenty-four feet square, and we had to live in them by the numbers that we were assigned. So my widowed mother-in-law, the bachelor man, and the young married couple had to occupy the one twenty-five or twenty-four by twenty-four room.

We were fingerprinted and we had to sign a paper. I remember rebelling inside but by this time—six or seven o'clock at night . . . I remember being angry, though, that I had to sign a paper saying that we would not hold the government liable for whatever happened to us. Somehow I felt like a criminal being fingerprinted. Then we went into these rooms and they were absolutely barren. A bale of hay was there [and] canvas bags. We had army cots, [with] single springs on them. We had to fill in the canvas bags with the straw and that was our bed. No sheets, no nothing, you know. You just slept on them. We were issued two army blankets—no pillow—a canvas bag and the bale of hay. Food was K-rations like in the mess hall, until they got more organized.

I think everything must have been terribly chaotic. I've read Mr. Dillon Meyers' book on the logistics. He was the Director of the WRA—War Relocation Authority and he was truly an understanding man. But this was after all one little thing—one operation during the war when there so many more critical operations—military operations—getting an army together. When you think of what our country was going through at that time with a war that we weren't prepared for, to take care of us had to be a very incidental concern.

There were one hundred thousand of us altogether. There were ten camps, I believe. There were three camps in Poston. Our camp was called camp number one and we were separated by perhaps five miles or so. There again, I really don't know the real numbers. But there were ten thousand I know in camp one, five thousand in camp two and five thousand in camp three located on the Poston reservation, Indian reservation. We didn't see any Indians. Of course we were confined. We weren't allowed to move about outside the camp. Later things relaxed as things became organized.

I remember crying because I was tired, too, but sitting on my suitcases and just crying [and looking at] wooden floors that had holes in them. Great big holes. The wooden floors were laid with the boards a half inch apart so we could wash them down with a hose. There was one spiggot at the end of each barrack and you had to tote your water.

I remember the first winter when we didn't have stoves and the temperature. . . . The food was inadequate. There were so many grievances. I never felt that there wasn't enough [food], but it was just the quality, the dullness of the diet. It was mostly out of cans and having to do with the army rations of a certain category at the beginning. [We ate] lots of beans and canned wieners. No fresh vegetables—canned vegetables. Canned everything, which the Japanese would find most distasteful because the Japanese don't cook like that, you know. Our food is barely cooked and color and texture is a necessity to our eating. The way food is arranged is absolutely part of our eating and so to have everything come out of cans was partly it, I believe. [We] got our own cooks. Then from a very army-oriented food supply and materials why gradually we were able to petition for our own native food because I don't known what proportion were the *isei*, our parents, our mothers, mostly women, few men, mostly and a lot of *kibeis*. We were accustomed to Japanese food, so the food was gradually changed. Then within a year the farmers grew the vegetables and cultivated. We had water for irrigation. The irrigation canals were backed up and made into great big swimming holes. It didn't take but about a year or so before the place became quite civilized. Lawns were put in between the barracks. There were some beautiful Japanese gardens created by these people who had time on their hands.

When we first arrived we saw this big room. And a family was assigned to a room, a room with no dividers. [There were] just as many cots as there were people. No chairs. Nothing. Just an empty room. All of them, all of us had to have something to sit on and to eat on, to write on. There were, fortunately, huge, huge piles of the leftover lumber after building the barracks. They hadn't burned them or carted them away yet. So they were rapidly, like scavengers, just swallowed up by all the different people. You see, there were a lot of volunteers that had gone in prior to our mass arrival to get some semblance of operation going, feeding all these people and taking care of the immediate health emergency problems. There were some young couples—young doctors who had volunteered and had gone in a month or so before. So there were enough extra tools around. I remember my husband taking a ham-

273

mer and a saw. That's why our suitcases were so full. We were allowed to take a hammer I think, and a saw. A small saw. Not the big one. They immediately hammered together benches and tables.

We did have a Sears-Roebuck catalogue very shortly and so we ordered fabric. After I had my baby, my mother sewed my dresses to wear instead of a smock, all by hand. We had some savings. Then we were all given sixteen dollars a month individually. That's what we spent. Sixteen dollars a month might not seem like a whole lot, but between my husband and myself that was thirty-two dollars. The food and the housing [were furnished]. We didn't have to pay utilities. [There was no heat so at first] those of us who had babies were allowed the first stoves that winter. They began gradually putting oil-burning stoves in.

We walked all over. I walked to the hospital, which was two miles, to have my baby—stopped for the pains. I remember we were the lucky ones. Then those of us who had babies were later on issued mattresses, and we got the cotton mattresses instead of sleeping on the straw. We really pioneered, so I'm not scared to go anyplace. If I didn't have certain physical problems today, the Peace Corps [would] really appeal to me because I feel like I can do anything from scratch.

Eventually we had a very adequate diet. It was minimal. They had to adhere to certain standards because, after all, there were people who questioned the validity of our evacuation in Washington. There were many people who were working to change things, but mainly there were strong forces, in the academic world in particular, who felt that it would lead to the same kind of, perhaps, socialization that the Indians had gone through. That we would become devoid of personal ambitions—those kinds of maybe long-range consequences of this. There were also people who questioned the legality of it because we were American citizens. Our men were in the armed forces. We had many things from them except the war had greater demands elsewhere, of course. That's understandable.

I had to get ready for the baby. With the Sears-Roebuck catalogue, we bought the inexpensive chintzes [for curtains and pillows]. But we didn't [get rugs] because it was so hot in the summertime. It was really neat. You know, we'd take turns. We each got a hose—bought a hose and we'd take turns. See, there was only one water faucet at the end [of the barrack] at the beginning to hose down the building. Then the bottom would be cool—under-

274

neath and we slept better. We also wet our towels and put them on the mattresses so we could sleep at night.

My husband made a cooler. They mickeymoused all kinds of coolers. They devised them out of fans and made their boxes out of scrap. Vegetables then were gradually being shipped in boxes—in those days wooden boxes—so there was plenty of extra lumber to make a cooler. Gradually most everybody managed to save enough money to buy a fan and put coolers into the windows. We used our army blankets, which we couldn't stand, as [room] dividers. It got so hot, you see. That summer we didn't need very much to wear or to protect us so that's what we put up immediately.

[We] ordered sheets from Sears-Roebuck and pillows. [My husband] was in the accounting office. They had a store there—gradually a community store. Because of that he had access to a ride on the truck to go to the town of Parker, Arizona, to pick up different supplies for different people.

My husband, because he worked for the canteen, was able to get eight-foot wire fencing, a remnant of it, so he made my children a play yard. He made all their toys—their wagons, their wheelbarrows. Everything was handmade by him and then we had a great big sandpit that he made. I was into Spock and those kinds of child-care books. And so the sandpile was tremendously critical. You need a sandpile, but we were right next to the library, so that all the people who went there always saw my children and they would sing this song, "Don't Fence Me In," as they passed by because of this eight-foot fence he built for them. It was a good deal safer because then I could leave them to go to the bathroom. The bathroom was so far away. We had to walk about half a block to the showers or the bathroom and we would take turns babysitting.

[Mr.] Takayama, he was not a member of our family, but they put him right with our family members and with my mother-in-law also. That's one of the first things we did—we put [up blankets as dividers]. This is probably the most—well, I don't even want to talk about it . . . a young married couple and their sex life. Absolutely no privacy except the army blankets. The agony of it all for me over such things.

Private matters [were] the least of [the government's] concern. They really were unprepared for such a huge enterprise. One hundred thousand people is a lot of people, and we were not like the army—a selected group of homogenous age levels of young men that you could feed and clothe and take care of. There were

275

the very aged to the new babies—[all] different social, economic, educational levels of people thrust together, and we had to go into the mess hall like a herd of cattle, although most mess halls attempted to unify the families. On those army picnic-like tables where there were just benches . . . , we tried to reserve [places for] a family and tried to maintain some kind of family unit. [We] ate together, sat together but there were many barracks that didn't do that. They had greater social problems then with the youngsters, the teenagers.

Those friends on the outside who weren't in camp—our Caucasian friends sent many things. Of course, there was already a hospital in the making. [The hospital was staffed by] Caucasians, and then all the volunteers from the Japanese populace. There were many trained people—you know, we had many doctors, lawyers.

There were a whole staff of people there, but the rooms weren't ready and so, for instance, my sheet was not changed. I had some kidney problems because of not taking in enough water anyway. I was on the same sheet for fifteen days. It was black. My mother took it home one day and washed it because of the dust storms. See, those swirling dust storms that obliterate—literally you cannot see ten feet in front of you—would come and in a matter of minutes you'd be just coated with dust. You would leave your hands down and there would be an imprint there.

[I was in the hospital] about fifteen days. Dawn, my daughter, was the tenth baby born in camp. I occupied a room with the two other women and they lost their babies through dehydration. I was lucky. That was so sad. I could never forget that. One girl was only eighteen years old and her husband was a Catholic. He was in the army, and he wasn't there. I don't know what her name was anymore.

[When I was able to leave the hospital] I went to stay with my mother who lived across the way. She took care of me because, you see, you had to tote the water such a long distance to take a bath. My mother would have to walk almost a block to get the hot water so I could take a bath. She brought food for me so I wouldn't have to go to the barrack.

July—my daughter was born on July 1st and it had registered 124 degrees outside. [She was born] early in the morning, but it was so hot. They didn't have a scale then, but they guessed

276

six and one-half pounds. She was a healthy—she still is a very healthy child—a person—today.

When I could wash [I went back to my barrack]. You had to wash everything by hand on a scrub-board. They had a laundry room with those great, big cement tubs—two tubs that are together. We had those suction-like things we bought from Sears. They're like drums that are as big as a large pot and you push down on them. Plungers, we called them. Our bedspreads and blankets and heavy things—we used that to wash with because they were enormous. [It took] two or three people [to wring]. That was fun because the laundry rooms were all cement floors with the drainage. It was playing tug of war. We were young. You know, [we were] twenty-two, twenty-four, and there were at least a dozen of us young married couples. We really had a good time. We were called the watermelon brigade because we were all pregnant and very, very large.

My husband built a kind of a kitchen—tiny, little kitchen-like corner [in our room]. [He] built a wooden sink and an icebox out of scrap lumber where we could go buy a piece of ice for fifty cents.

Of course, the store soon—oh, within a year—sold fresh things, so we could buy fresh. The vegetables were grown by the evacuees. In fact, it became a major enterprise as far as the improvement of land and usage of land is concerned. They were able to create agricultural areas for the authorities. But they grew all the Japanese vegetables as well as other vegetables, so our diet got better and better.

We had a period, a dreadful period, when there was an unscrupulous director who was pocketing the money and the sugar coupons and what have you. I understand he went to San Quentin. But there was a period where we were served from breakfast to dinner, great big neck bones only, for meals, along with bread and rice. It didn't last very long. There were enough vocal people who protested to the right places and the man was caught. But that's bound to happen.

When my father was released from Santa Fe, he came to Poston to rejoin his family. Most did that. After all, there was no reason to have kept them apart. We were incarcerated, and he was just simply in another camp. So gradually families were united. I think that many *isei* men felt [adrift] because suddenly they were nothing. They lost their positions in a real sort of way.

277

I don't think any of it really went hard after the initial losing of everything—your home, your property, your business, your job. We were together as a family and so it was a time of rest and perhaps finding [ourselves] and finding who [we] were. Most of our parents were in their middle forties and so when I tried to put myself in their position I don't know how I would have felt. Of course [my father] was placed in a separate camp in Santa Fe, New Mexico, and then he rejoined my mother. He wrote every chance he could. In Santa Fe one of the things that he did and I treasure it very, very much is—he made me out of ironwood—he polished it and made me a flower stand out of heavy, heavy ironwood and inscribed my name in calligraphy. He varnished or lacquered it so that I still have that. He also made—they saved all the onion sacks that came in that woven, twisted—it wasn't hemp or anything— but those onion sacks were taken apart and that was a great treasure for my father because when he came back from Santa Fe he had these strands of onion sacks. So he rewove them and he made my husband a cigarette case and he made my sisters each a purse from this onion sack. He rewove it until it was so fine—very finely woven—and from it he wove the cigarette case that I have for my husband with his initials H. and M. throughout. He made us *getas* because we'd have to walk [so far]—*getas* are the footwear that are on clogs—where you put your feet in them. He made those for us at Santa Fe and sent them. He made each of us a pair of those that he hand-carved. They made all kinds of things that they were able to get from the desert. He had polished some stones and sent those. They were to mount or something. There were all kinds of art expression in camp by creative people. Many carvings, for instance, from the roots and the ironwood that they found and then lots of stonework. Later on somebody acquired a polisher and different kinds of jewelry were made. Of course, paintings, sculpturing maybe, but I don't remember. Then some of the most beautiful things were the Buddist altars that were carved out by different people painstakingly put together.

I had a baby so [I] didn't work. It isn't that they made it so mandatory. Then there were camouflage net factories in one or the other camps where they wove camouflage nettings for the war effort. There were all sorts of things—different kinds of enterprises being promoted by, I think, by the Relocation authority. [My parents had] a nursery. [So when my father rejoined us] my mother worked in a nursery and dad worked in a nursery, too. I think they made cuttings of trees and [put] them [in cans] so that they could be transplanted around the barracks and all. [They] certainly [weren't] sold. Teachers taught, nurses nursed, and so on.

I was very self-centered—caught up in surviving for my baby and myself and walking almost a block to meals and to the latrines which were so far away. Trying not—when the baby cried in the middle of the night—I remember wrapping her and walking outside of the barracks so that the rest of the people wouldn't be disturbed, because you could hear all the way down the barracks. All the noises—the coughing, the talking, the laughing, the crying, whatever. And it was just getting the food and preparing grown-up food for my baby. It was just a matter of survival. There was no special food for the babies—the first child. There was a lovely nurse who married into our block. There were romances going on, too, and we were the closest friends. Her name was Mary Yamagada. She married, then had a baby and by that time I had already a child and was ready to have my second baby within a little over a year. Babies came then. You didn't have ways to prevent. I was so ignorant. Later, when I became sophisticated enough to ask about [contraceptives], we could get them at the hospital. They fitted us with diaphragms, for that matter.

Mary had her first baby and being a nurse and having nursed before she knew the steward—the manager of the food, I guess—[who bought] the supplies. So between the two of us we went to this man and asked if we could open up a special office for the babies so that they could have formulas instead of anything that happened to come in until that time. He cooperated fully and before you know it, Mary and I took turns managing the diet office. We were able to order the very best formulas, called SMA, then baby food—all the Gerber baby foods we wanted. Anything. We eventually, because Mary was a nurse and was much more aware, also branched out and supplied everyone in camp who needed it— the ulcer patients and people like that—with baby food. Then we were also able to order powdered milk and dry fruits. All they had to do was sign. Between the two of us we really managed so well because she was an outstanding person.

[My mother-in-law] worked in a canteen because she was in a grocery business, you see. [For those who refused to work] there was plenty to do. They whittled a lot, played cards. They made many beautiful things. A lot of artwork came out of that from ironwood that they found in the desert. You were allowed to

279

wander a little farther as time went on. Well, what was there but the desert? The Colorado River if you went far enough. So lots of that rock was polished. Some of the most beautiful things were made out of the sides of apple boxes—little, tiny birds for brooches were carved out and earrings and painted ever so delicately. I have a few left-over. I wish I hadn't given them all away, but I have a few of the less nice ones left that a friend carved for me. But they are absolutely works of art.

They had school from K through high school. My sister Frances graduated Poston High School. There were enough high-school-age children to have everything going because there were twenty thousand. They had teams all over and stiff competition. I think they had football. I'm sure they had all those things. Like I say, I was so immersed in my own—having two babies very quickly. Eventually golf came into being. But you see that may be the second year or so. They cleared off and made some greens. My husband played golf. There were all kinds of clubs.

Former teachers and leaders organized every kind of club you could probably have in an ordinary life. Especially the lessons. The flower arranging lessons, tea ceremony, singing. All sorts of things. The calligraphy, embroidery, flower making was a rage out of crepe paper. They were so hungry for flowers and then using those for flower arranging. Sewing. Just name it.

I remember taking different magazines. Subscribed to them if we could afford them, but we passed them around—women's magazines—and it was just very, very fortunate for me in my barrack. Later on—you see—I moved into the young married couples' barrack, as my best friend and her husband moved out to go back to Santa Ana at a very early stage, because they owned farmland and they were able to negotiate with the community. They were prominent people there in Santa Ana and so they had enough people who would sponsor them or vouch for them. They were very like charter members of the Methodist church and all of these things helped them. They were well established, so they returned early and, as those so-called apartments were vacated, my husband and I moved in one and that's when we were free for the first time. My mother-in-law occupied next to us, but she had another room with a partition and that must have lasted at least a year and a half or so. Half the time, but this last barrack was right next to the library. We were right next to it, so I had all the magazines and books I could ever want. We weren't allowed to have radios

280

until later. I remember having one, though, later and I remember hearing Arthur Godfrey. I never missed him.

I had three babies in camp. Dawn, the eldest, who was the tenth baby born, about six weeks after I was in. Then Brian came about. [The worst memory for me was] I think the lack of privacy because I was recently married and having to be in one room with a bachelor and my mother-in-law. . . . It was the most torturous kind of experience. My husband's affectionate overtures became nightmares. That and in your private world—taking a bath with so many people, having to go to the bathroom with stalls that are lined up and you're exposed. You never really do become immune to it. There's something in you that wants to cling to yourself as a person. This constant exposure to enormous numbers of people. Of course we always had to eat with people—all three meals—and bathe with them. You really didn't have privacy except in the quiet moments when we did get our apartment, our one room, that is.

I could have left camp about the second year [and gone] to parts east if I weren't pregnant. My husband went to Cleveland, Ohio, because my sisters were going to school there. And several others from our block went and they roomed together in a rooming house. He must have stayed a couple of months at the most. They worked in a furniture factory and most of the people had never seen a Japanese before and were just totally shocked that they could speak English, but they were so like them except for their faces. They weren't the caricatured buck-teeth, horned-rim-glass people. They were just ordinary people and they made some very good friends among the neighbors. Everyone seemed to be most hospitable and helpful and they got along beautifully, but my husband didn't want to settle in Cleveland, Ohio. He said the trees were all black from the soot and that turned him off more than anything else. So he came back to camp and waited for the [end of the war].

A Navajo Code Talker in the Pacific Theatre in World War II

Cozy Stanley Brown

World War II produced a boom in Arizona's economy and a great many changes in the lives of individual residents. Increased demand caused the prices of minerals and foodstuffs to soar. And the combination of good weather and large tracts of federal land ensured the establishment of numerous military training bases and airfields. Patriotic Arizonans, like thousands of other Americans, poured into induction centers in response to the Japanese attack on Pearl Harbor.

As the long and brutal Pacific campaign got under way, the U.S. Marine Corps sought special Navajo recruits to transmit secret radio and telephone messages during combat. The Navajo language was especially suited for use as a code. Its verb forms are extremely complex and the sounds and speech cadences of a native speaker are virtually impossible to duplicate. At the outbreak of the war with the Japanese, the Marines estimated that no more than twenty-eight non-Navajos, American scholars or missionaries who lived among the tribe, could understand the language or speak it with any degree of fluency. Although the Allied Expeditionary Forces had used a variety of Indian languages as codes in World War I, the Navajos were said to be the only U.S. tribe that German anthropologists and linguists had not successfully studied. There seemed little possibility that either the Germans or the Japanese could break such a "code."

In addition to their linguistic skills, the Navajo soldiers' adherence to traditional tribal ceremonies and religious practices had a reassuring effect on their fellow combatants. Ernie Pyle, America's most famous war correspondent, recalled how the Navajo soldiers prepared for the invasion of Okinawa. The Indians stained their faces with paint and improvised ceremonial dress from chicken feathers, seashells, coconuts, empty ration cans, and spent rifle cartridges. Several thousand fellow Marines watched gravely as the Navajos danced and chanted to their *deities. They called upon the spirits to sap the Japanese of their strength, through gestures they placed the finger of weakness on the enemy, and they chanted the Marine Corps hymn in Navajo. After the ceremony, Pyle asked one of the Navajo privates if the Indian soldiers truly believed that these rituals would safeguard them. The young Navajo replied "yes" with assurance and sincerity. He also remarked that they had seen reassuring physical signs: ". . . on the way up here there was a rainbow over the convoy and I knew then everything would be all right."**

At the time of the Japanese surrender, more than four hundred Navajos had served as code talkers. In the following selection, Cozy Stanley Brown, a Navajo from Chinle, Arizona, recalls his service with the Marine Corps in the Pacific Islands. In addition to recounting his experiences as a code talker, Brown speaks of patriotism and duty to country from a Navajo's point of view.

---

*Ernie Pyle, *Last Chapters* (New York City: Henry Holt, 1946), 135.

My name is Cozy S. Brown; [I'm] fifty years [old]. I was born December 5, at dawn, in about 1925 or 1926. It was where Del Muerto Canyon and Canyon de Chelly connect. That was what I was told. My mother is Mary Stewart Brown. My father was Jack Brown, who died four years ago. His Navajo name was Tall Boss (*Naat' aanii Nééz*), and he was a well-known medicine man. He sang the Female Featherway Chant, the Shootingway Chant, the Blessingway Chant and the Evilway Chant.

My clan is the Deer Spring (*Biih bitoodnii*) which is the same as the Bitter Water clan (*Tódích'íí'nii*). I was born [to] the Red Running Into Water People (*Tachíí'nii*), which is the same as the Tobacco People (*Nát'oh dine'é*). I was raised with sheep and goats, and I grew up with my late grandmother's assistance. As soon as I was old enough to realize what was happening, I began to herd sheep and goats. That was how I earned my living in those childhood days.

My grandmother was born at Fort Sumner (*Hwééldi* or *Bosque Redondo*) over at the eastern edge of New Mexico. She was four years old when the Navajos were allowed to walk back to the Navajo Reservation. So, I inherited my character from those people. After I got bigger I noticed my father was working at the trading post called Upper House of Thunderbird Trading Post, which is now Thunderbird Lodge. I grew up near that trading post. My oldest brother and a sister died at the time. I have another sister who is still living today. They were attending school when I became aware of things. In the fall, when school was about to begin, I cried because I wanted to go to school with my sisters and brothers. I

From an interview with Cozy Stanley Brown of Chinle, Arizona, by Jones Van Winkle, in Broderick H. Johnson, *Navajos and World War II* (Tsaile, The Navajo Nation, Arizona: Navajo Community College Press, 1977), 52–63. Used with permission from the Navajo Community College Press.

285

told my parents that I would like to go, but they kept telling me that I was too young. Later, my parents got together and discussed it and agreed to let me enroll.

I was six years old. One afternoon, a saddled horse was brought in front of our hogan. They told me to wash up and get ready to go someplace. I ate my lunch and I was forced to go right away. So we started to travel on horseback. At that time there weren't many vehicles.

I think [the year] was around 1931 or 1932. My father and I rode double on the horse. Before we left, the trader, who was my father's employer, came out of the post and asked us where we were going. My father replied, "We are going to school." Then the trader said, "What will you name him?" At that time Navajo children had no English names. My father looked at the trader and said, "His name will be Cozy." That was how I got my English name. My father registered me with that name at the school.

The trader's name was Cozy. His last name was McSparron. That was how I got my name.

I was taken to Chinle Boarding School, where I attended for six years. I liked school, and they took good care of me. It was like a military setup. They used to [awaken us] early in the mornings, and we ran long distances very early.

We used to form a single line and do calisthenics. There was enough food and medical treatment for us. I attended and did very well for six years at the Chinle school. I was involved in all of the activities. I realized what was really happening when I got promoted in all of the activities I took in school. The way I thought about it was that the Anglos and various other Indian tribes helped me in those activities and in many other teachings. They helped me learn many things and I forced myself to get the best out of whatever classes they offered me. It didn't take me too long to learn the white man's language.

I was one of the boy scouts and dorm leaders. They told us to work for our own clothes at school; so I worked for those clothes. I did all of those things until I finished the sixth grade.

Then they told me to choose what high school I would like to go to—Fort Wingate or Shiprock, but I already had chosen to attend Shiprock. I guess some of my teachers from Chinle had been transferred to that high school, and they wanted me to attend it. Four of us were chosen to go to that school. There were two girls from Chinle, Arizona. I was included with a boy from the Chinle

Valley Store. I will introduce him later, because I went to war with him and he got killed in action.

I started seventh grade at Shiprock. Things went well for me, and I got to know lots of girls and boys. I came home when school was out and spent my summer vacation there. When school started again in the fall, I returned. I attended until it was time for school to be out. Then they asked me if I wanted to stay that summer and work in the fields. That was fine with me; so I spent the summer planting and working crops. I did that for four summers. In early fall, when school was about to begin again, I went home for only three weeks or so before going back to school.

When I reached the twelfth grade and it was close to my graduation, I heard that the Japanese and the United States had gotten into war. It was December 7, 1941. At that time I was old enough to qualify for the military service; so I thought about it. As our parents used to say, "You have to think about things before you get into them."

Later, it was announced that some Navajos would be needed to go into training. They told us we would learn some things pertaining to the war. They gave us two weeks to think about it. I did my own thinking, and I didn't inquire of my parents; and I decided to go ahead and enter the service.

Six of us signed up for the training. I can't recall all of the men. I do remember Raymond Nakai and former Judge William Dean Wilson, because we were in the same class at school.

They told us to go home for a week, which we did; and we were told to return to Window Rock, Arizona, for a physical examination. Navy doctors examined us, and we were physically all right. Raymond, who later became our Tribal Chairman for some years, did not qualify for the Service at that time because he had high blood pressure. However, he went with the Navy later. We left there for Fort Wingate, New Mexico, where we met many others. There we took the oath that marked us as American soldiers. Then we took the Greyhound bus to San Diego. The next morning military clothing was issued to us.

It was May 4, 1942, when we took our oath. We had eight weeks' training at the Marine Corps Boot Training Camp. We were trained for only eight weeks because the war was going on and they were lacking soldiers. That was why we were forced to get the training quickly. There were twenty of us who completed the eight weeks of training and were highly honored. I still remember some of the names of the men whom I was in training with. They came from Tuba City, Shiprock, Lukachukai and Crownpoint. There was a man with a queue (hair), who came to the training camp, and his queue was cut off. Twenty-eight of us left the training camp, and one guy named Mr. Johnson was already at the camp we were headed for. So with him, it made twenty-nine of us. There we learned infantry tactics.

We went to Camp Elliott, close to San Diego, California. Afterward, it was the Navy Training Center. I don't know whether it's still a Navy Training Center. We were at that camp to learn basic things. The main reason for us Navajos was our language. They liked to use our language in war to carry messages. So we were taught how to use the radio. We had to do that in a hurry at that time. I guess that was why they forced us to complete the training in eight weeks. Then, we got together and discussed how we would do it. We decided to change the name of the airplanes, ships and the English ABC's into the Navajo language. We did the changing. For instance, we named the airplanes "dive bombers" for *ginitsoh* (sparrow hawk), because the sparrow hawk is like an airplane—it charges downward at a very fast pace. We called the enemy *ana'i*, just like the old saying of the Navajos. The name *ana'i* also is used in the Navajo Enemyway ceremony. We changed the English alphabet to the Navajo language, like for the letter "T" we used *tashii* (turkey), *tsin* (stick), and *tliish* (snake) in Navajo. We usually used the harmful animals' names that were living in our country for the alphabet. Then a name was written on a piece of paper. Some words were marked off and some were accepted. That was the way we completed our alphabet, which was used against the enemy in our communications.

Then the soldiers started to learn the Navajo alphabet, how to operate radios, telephone and other military equipment. We did that for eight weeks, when eight [Navajo] men were selected. I was one of them. They told us to get ready, but we had no idea where we were going, because they were not allowed to tell us. If they did the enemy would know it right then. So, we walked to the shore and the ship was waiting for us. We got into the ship and started our journey at dawn from San Diego, California.

[We arrived at] New Caledonia. The eight of us got off at that island and spent the night there. The next morning we were divided and assigned to different ships. Three of us were assigned to one ship and the other code talkers were divided among the

288

other ships. I met a General named General Vandegrift. We shook hands with him and we told him our names. He picked me as his partner and the other code talkers were divided among the high-ranked officers. We discussed how we would use the Navajo alphabet that we made. Some [words] we kept to ourselves even though they already were written out on the paper. We did that because we did not know what would be happening ahead of us. I joined that group and I don't know how I was ranked.

[I was with General Vandegrift and] also a man named Dale June. Then we continued our journey on the ship. There were many ships of all different sizes. We called the ships battlewagons, cruisers, destroyers and mine sweepers. I don't remember how many days we traveled because it was many years ago. Anyway, we got to a place called Guadalcanal. At Guadalcanal they divided us again. It is part of the Solomon Islands. Those Islands were different in size and Guadalcanal is the biggest. When we arrived at the island, they placed me in a regiment.

A regiment consists of some battalions, like First Battalion on to Fifth Battalion. Next, was the Eleventh Marine which connects with the Artillery Corps. There were five of us in the regiment. One code talker was assigned to each battalion. I was with the headquarters, which consisted of a general, a colonel and a lieutenant general, with a lot of lesser officers.

The men were divided into groups, and placed in different areas in the jungle. We had discussed again how we would use the Navajo language, and we informed the officers. We were well taken care of. The generals would not allow other soldiers to come near us.

Even the colonels and the captains were not allowed to come near. We were not supposed to take orders from any officers except the high one we were assigned to. That was the way we began our duties as code talkers in the war.

Long ago our elderly people had many bad hardships. Accordingly, I guess we decided to go to war and protect our people from having other hardships. We have done that by the way of our thinking and teaching, just like when we approach things that are new to us. That was when we thought back about our people and our surroundings. I would think, "I'm doing this for my people." I believed what we did was right, and it was worth it. We protected the many American people, also the unborn children, which would be the generation to come. Now, I see young men and women, and

I am glad for what I did for them. Many people reach old age. Not long ago my grandmother from Chinle Valley died of old age. Those are some of the things we should think about. Some of us veterans were proud and glad that we went to war, but I don't know how some of my friends feel now.

We were code talkers for four months at Guadalcanal. That was the time we took advantage of our enemy. It was like the old saying of our elderly Navajo people, "Only the Navajos had the whole world in their hands," or "The Navajos created the earth." According to that, the Navajo people helped the American soldiers, and the enemy never did overcome them. That was why I had faith and believed what our elderly people said.

• • •

We left Guadalcanal for Sydney, Australia. When we got there, our leader, General Vandegrift, was unsatisfied with the place. In Guadalcanal it had rained almost every day and night. There was no dry land there. We never slept much either at night or during the day, except on a few occasions we would sleep a little.

When we got to Sydney, General Vandegrift said, "The place is not good for my soldiers." So we left Sydney on a ship called West Point for a place named Melvin in Australia. It was located in the south part of the country. The place was similar to our Reservation. The Anglos were also similar to the white men on our Reservation, because they had come from the same countries—like England. The people there were very helpful. They treated us like their own relatives, and they chose each of us to be with one family. One soldier would go with one family and another would go with another family. The people had cows and sheep. We were not hungry for mutton because they fed us that meat very often. That went on for eight months.

When we were still in Melvin, a group of American Navajo soldiers arrived there. There were twenty-nine of us that first went into war. We were divided among the Second, Third, Fourth, Fifth, and Sixth Marine Divisions. I guess they had noticed that code talkers were important and very helpful in the war; so they sent us more Navajo soldiers to learn.

I think it was in 1943. We taught them the skills we had learned in our training as code talkers. The new training lasted eight months. After we had completed it we moved to a place

290

called New Guinea. We were told that the American Army was having hardships from their enemies, the Japanese. The main place for us was called the Aru Islands. We helped the Army fight the enemies there. One of my in-laws was with the Army. He and a bunch of other soldiers had set up a group similar to the Marines, but they called themselves "Bushwhackers." I saw only his dead body when we arrived there. They told me that the enemy had killed him that day.

Afterward, the war cooled down in New Guinea; so we moved from that place on Christmas Eve to the New Britain Islands. We arrived on December 25. There were Japanese soldiers on that island. The place was mainly called Cape Gloucester, New Britain Island. We spent three or four months there.

We lost one of the Navajo men that I was with. If you were teaching some boys, one guy usually would act silly or disregard your instructions. He thought he would not get shot in action while being a prankster. One evening, I got all six of my boys together, and we sat at a makeshift table and started to eat our meal. It was in a large foxhole, with canvas to protect us from the rain. A man spoke out, "I'm getting fat, and I eat too much. It would seem like the enemy would butcher me anytime." My father and mother had told me when I left home not to say such words in war. I taught my boys and soldiers that, along with other teachings. This guy was a prankster when he met us in Australia. He used to run away from the training camp.

During the evening we heard the Japanese planes; so we took cover like prairie dogs sitting in the prairies when the sparrow hawk or eagle attacks them—and they run into their holes for protection. We all jumped into the holes. The silly guy was still sitting on the edge of the hole, disregarding the attack. I guess the Japanese turned off their airplane engines a distance away while approaching us. They attacked us with a bomb called "daisy cutter." The daisy cutter usually exploded 50 feet in the air so that the shrapnel would hit us. The silly guy got killed there, just like he had predicted.

It took us a long time to search for his body in the dark. We were under thick jungle trees, but when they dropped a few of the daisy cutters only stumps were left of the jungle. After that had happened, we went over to the hole where the guy was assigned, but he wasn't there. We even dug out the hole and we still didn't find him. Later, we found him a few feet away from the hole. He was all blasted up by the bomb. We gathered some of the remaining parts of the body and wrapped them with the canvas that covered the hole. An Anglo guy he was with also got blasted.

That again relates back to our parents' teachings. They would tell us not to say evil words while in war. They kept those things sacred to this day. Now, old age has come upon them, including our grandparents. People like them still carry sacred blessings for us today. I suppose if the man had not said the evil words he would have seen his parents back home, and he would have had a family and a good living.

After that bombing happened, we started to move, and we won the New Britain Islands from the enemy. The American Army attacked the other side of the Islands, and we were on the opposite side. That was how we easily took the islands. I guess you would say, "Just ran over something in no time." Then we moved to another place from there, but it was still among the Russell Islands (Solomon Islands). The Army raided the enemies in Bougainville, the same time we did. They won the island from the enemy that day. Then we moved to another place in the Solomons. At that time they named the places by Army codes. I guess they have different names today. While we were there a group of Navajo soldiers arrived for training, and we moved out again. At that time I had spent a year and ten months overseas.

It was in 1944. We moved to a place called Palau Island. The Island was long in length and narrow in width. When we got there we started combat with the air enemy. There was an airport and a high mountain peak. There were holes in the mountain where many enemies were hidden, and they used them for protection. That was where we had bad hardships, but we killed all of the enemies that were near the beach, also those in other areas besides the mountain peak. We had a hard time exploding the mountain because it was made of quartz rock. We tried to kill the enemies that were on the mountain. We would kill two or three at a time during the night when we snuck up on them.

We used guns. The regular bombs didn't help much because of the hard rocks. Flamethrowers and napalm bombs helped a lot, though. A napalm bomb was a bomb dropped from an airplane. It bounced twice or several times; then it would roll into one of the holes in the mountain and explode. It produced very hot heat. The flamethrower was the one that we carried on our backs, and the weapon shot fire. We used it when we went out to the tips

292

of the holes and killed the enemies with the hot fire. The enemies really did suffer from that fire.

We spent two months there. One day when I was operating the radio, a call came in from the Hawaiian Islands. At that time we called the Hawaiian Islands "Abalone Shell Water" in Navajo—like the abalone shell water they use in the Squaw Dance ceremony today. The call was for Major General Vandegrift at the Seventh Regiment's Division headquarters. I wrote down the codes in Navajo. After the call, I gave my notes to one of the Anglos who was a de-coder. He changed the codes into English. Our names appeared, and we were ordered to return home because we had completed our war duty in action.

It still was in 1944, during the fall season. I left from here in the fall and returned the same month two years later. So all eight of us that had left started to move back that day. There was one German guy, a radio operator, who came back with us. His people in Germany were having a war in Europe at that time. We had been with him in our fighting. He was born in Britain.

We were told to begin our journey back home the next day. One of my cousins from the Chinle Valley, who was from the Red Running Into Water clan (*Táchíí'nii*), had sent a message for me to visit him before I left for home. I went early in the morning, at dawn, to visit him. When I arrived there, he was covered with canvas. That was where my cousin died. His property was given to me, and I took it to his mother when I got home.

After that, I started back. We had spent two weeks sailing overseas, but I spent only six days on my way back home. I returned home at the same time and the same date that I had left. That meant that I was an active soldier exactly twenty-four months.

I killed some enemies. I was holding one enemy in my hands when I killed him. I held him with my hands and that was when I brought back the scalp of an enemy. I used my knife to cut his head off and I pulled out a bunch of sideburns, which I was taught to do by a medicine man called Stewart Greyeyes. He is still living today. He also performed the ceremony on me before I left for war. I brought one of the enemy's scalps home. The Squaw Dance was performed on me for the enemy scalp that I brought home with me.

I took a furlough for thirty-five days to have a Squaw Dance for me. After my leave was over, I went back to the east coast and from there they transferred me west to a place called Quantico. I

293

took high-speed radio training there. Then I returned to San Diego. I was told to instruct the new American soldiers that had just arrived for training. I worked as an instructor for almost a year.

When I was teaching in San Diego the men I had gone to war with were all discharged. I guess they kept me for the skills and experiences I had from the training. While I was in San Diego they told me to teach one guy so he would take over my duties. I taught a man named Lee Hubbard. After he completed his training with me, I was discharged from military service.

I worked in Los Angeles, California, for three more years. Then I was laid off from that job, and I returned to my relatives on the Reservation. I worked for the BIA (Bureau of Indian Affairs) for a while, but I resigned and went to work for the Arizona State Employment Service. Then I went with the BIA again. From there, I went on to different jobs according to their salaries. I worked for the National Park Service in 1960. During the winter season, when they closed the Park Service, I worked on construction or at the public school. That has been my occupation to this day.

When I returned [from overseas] they again performed an all-night vigil of the Blessingway chant. When I got home things were all ready for a Squaw Dance. So, that evening, plans were made for me to have the ceremony performed. We took the Squaw Dance prayer stick to Chinle Valley, to a man named Mr. Red Canyon. The dance was performed very well for me. From there, my mind began to function well again.

[I believe in Navajo ceremonies] because I was mainly raised with them. I guess my grandfathers, grandmothers, my father and mother used the Navajo ceremonies. I also believe in Anglo religion, like the Catholic religion. The prayers and the stories are similar to Navajo legends and prayers. That is how I think about the two religions. Some parts of the legends are slightly different.

• • •

My main reason for going to war was to protect my land and my people because the elderly people said that the earth was our mother. That was why our elderly Navajos blessed the earth with corn pollen. There are Anglos and different Indian tribes living on the earth who have pride in it. That was my main reason for fighting in the war; also, I wanted to live on the earth in the future. Some of our men are in the military services today for the same reasons. One of my nephews is in the Marine Corps today. He probably thinks the same way I thought when I was in the service. The Anglos say "democracy," which means they have pride in the American flag. We Navajos respect things the same way they do.

The Navajo people get their blessings from the four sacred mountains, our mother the earth, father the sun and the air we breathe.

That idea was told to me by my late father. Our grand-children and our young relatives will carry on those beliefs in the future, if we tell them and if they have knowledge of sacred things. Those are some of the reasons I went to war—and because I had pride in all of those things.

The younger generations need to know the stories and lives of the older people and of the past. I hope that what I have said will be useful in telling the important things done by the Navajos in the Second World War.

295

Barry Goldwater Remembers

Barry Goldwater

Prominent family names always spring to mind when one recalls the early history of a state. The Cabots and Lodges dominated the early years of Massachusetts history; the Berkeley and Lee names are indistinguishable from the Commonwealth of Virginia. Austin and Houston, pioneer families and heroes of Texas independence, are now the names of cities instantly identifiable with the Lone Star State. And in Arizona, the Hayden and Goldwater family names are among those synonymous with commerce and politics from the territorial era to the present.

Arizona was still a territory when Barry Goldwater was born. The grandson of Polish Jewish refugees who hauled freight to army posts and mining camps, Goldwater either witnessed or participated in virtually every development as Arizona progressed from a frontier territory at the turn of the century to a Sunbelt power in the 1980s.

As a young boy Barry Goldwater developed an intimate knowledge and lifelong love of his home state. On camping trips with their mother, the Goldwater children explored remote areas from the Grand Canyon in the north to the Mexican towns at the southern extreme. They became familiar with geology to understand how Arizona's spectacular topography developed; they learned to identify woodland and desert vegetation. They studied Arizona history, hiked through her Indian reservations, and photographed both people and mountains. The lessons and experiences of childhood stayed with Barry Goldwater as he matured. In spite of his various careers as merchant, pilot, and politician, Goldwater is recognized first and always as Arizona's most devoted native son.

W hen I was born, Arizona was still a territory. The automobile was a newfangled invention. Steam locomotives and horses pulled our conveyances. For personal transportation we had the horse and the street railway. There was no federal welfare system, no federally mandated unemployment insurance, no federal agency to monitor the purity of the air, the food we ate, or the water we drank. There were not enough federal marshals to control the outlaws. My grandfather came to Arizona before the cavalry had ended the attacks of hostile Indians on white pioneers.

. . .

My grandfather, Michael Goldwasser, was a Polish-Jewish refugee. He was born in the city of Konin, in 1828, one of twenty-two children of Elizabeth and Hirsch Goldwasser. Under the oppressive rule of the Russian czars, Jews in Poland were denied educational opportunities, their employment was restricted, boys were conscripted into the Russian Army.

When my grandfather was fourteen years old, he was involved in some sort of revolutionary activity serious enough to cause him to believe his life was in jeopardy. He crossed the border at night into Germany and never returned to Poland. He never again saw Elizabeth or Hirsch.

Once safe across the border in Germany, where the political climate was much more tolerant of Jews, my grandfather decided to travel to Paris, where he found employment at the tailor's trade. He mastered the language and saved his money. When the French government collapsed on February 24, 1848, Mike gathered his belongings and crossed the Channel to London.

From Barry M. Goldwater, *With No Apologies, The Personal and Political Memoirs of United States Senator Barry M. Goldwater* (New York: William Morrow and Company, Inc., 1979), 15–43. Copyright 1979 by Barry Goldwater. By permission of William Morrow & Company.

Whenever I encounter some passionate advocate of bilingual education arguing the necessity of offering instruction in both Spanish and English in public schools of Arizona, I invariably think of my grandfather, the French-speaking Polish immigrant boy who cheerfully learned English because it was a social and economic necessity when he moved to London.

Michael Goldwasser was twenty-six years old when he met a seamstress named Sarah Nathan. Two years later, on March 6, 1850, they were married.

In 1851 Michael's younger brother, Joseph, then twenty-one years old, fled from Poland to avoid conscription in the Russian Army. He came to London. Mike and Sarah took him in.

The brothers were remarkably different. Mike was tall and fair, an easy mixer who made friends everywhere. Joe, dark and swarthy, was a head shorter than his brother. Today we would call him an introvert or a loner. It was Joe who talked his brother Mike into seeking their fortune in the New World.

News of the gold strike at Sutter's Mill in California had reached England. In the United States, Joe argued, there was no discrimination against Jews. There they would find unlimited opportunity. Joe didn't propose the brothers should become gold miners—let others dig the precious metal out of the rocks. He and Mike would be merchants.

Finally, it was agreed that Mike and Joe would go to California. Sarah and the two children, Carolyn and Morris, would remain in London. She would support the family [by] working in the seamstress trade. Mike, the thrifty one, had put by enough to enable the brothers to go into some kind of retail business in California.

Mike and Joe Goldwasser arrived in San Francisco in November 1852. They journeyed by stagecoach to the newest bonanza town, Sonora, in the foothills of the high Sierras. Mike had planned on opening a general store. He soon discovered his meager capital would not permit the acquisition of a stock of merchandise sufficient to compete with the existing stores.

Gambling, whiskey, and wild, wild women were an inseparable part of the American West. The Goldwasser brothers opened a saloon on the ground floor of a two-story building which housed the camp's most popular bordello.

In fifteen months Mike saved enough money to pay the passage for Sarah, their two children, and to finance the trip for

299

Sarah's recently widowed sister, Esther. On July 2, 1854, Big Mike was reunited with his wife and children in San Francisco.

Sarah was a city girl. She found the crudities of life in a mining camp intolerable. After three years in Sonora, during which time she gave birth to two children, Elizabeth and Samuel, she moved back to San Francisco with the four children and her sister.

The gold boom in Sonora faded. Miners moved on to new strikes. The saloon business suffered. Joe went to one of the new towns, opened a saloon, and in six months was broke. He moved again, this time to Los Angeles, where he opened a tobacco and notions store in Bella Union Hotel.

In 1855 creditors put a padlock on Big Mike's Sonora Saloon. He joined Sarah and his children in San Francisco and spent the next three years working in a variety of jobs, earning enough to pay all his debts. In 1858 he moved his family to Los Angeles and went to work with Joe.

In 1859 overland travelers brought news of gold discoveries in the western portion of the territory of New Mexico, the area which was to become Arizona. Big Mike brought the Goldwater name (the brothers had anglicized the spelling by this time) to Arizona in a two-horse spring wagon loaded with tinware and Yankee notions.

To reach the placer fields east of the Colorado River, Mike had to cross three hundred miles of desert. Watering holes were few and far between. He ferried the Colorado at Yuma, then made his way north on the Arizona side to La Paz, which was located some fifteen miles to the northeast of the present city of Blythe, California.

The Southern Pacific Railroad completed its line from Los Angeles to Tucson in 1880. Prior to that date most of the supplies for the western part of the area were carried up the Colorado on river steamers and then freighted overland from the port of La Paz.

Joe moved from Los Angeles to join Mike. In partnership with Dr. E. B. Jones they developed and operated the largest wagon freight line in the territory. They hauled supplies under contract to most of the Army forts during the government's campaign against the Apaches. They operated businesses in Tucson, Phoenix, Yuma, Prescott, Bisbee, and Wickenburg.

The river currents at La Paz hampered the docking and offloading of the paddle-wheel boats. A new site was selected a few

300

miles downstream, and Mike Goldwater built an entire new town. He named the new port Ehrenberg in honor of a German mining engineer who had become his best friend. On my uncle Morris's first trip to Arizona he and Mike found Ehrenberg's body near the Dos Palmas Store, which was operated by a character known as Bottle-ass Smith. The murder was never solved, but thanks to Mike, Ehrenberg's name is still on the map of Arizona.

McKenney's Pacific Coast Directory for 1880–81 has only two entries under the heading "Ehrenberg." My uncle Henry was the postmaster, and J. Goldwater and brother were listed as operating a general store.

Ultimately Mike and Joe established a mercantile headquarters in Prescott when that city was the capital of the new Territory of Arizona. They handled general merchandise, hardware, agriculture implements, furniture, and carpets.

Sarah and the children moved from Los Angeles to San Francisco. Joe joined them. He negotiated the freight contracts, bought the merchandise, was the resident agent for the Arizona enterprises.

Mike stayed on in Arizona. He financed and built a gold stamping mill on the Hassayampa River to handle ore from the fabulously rich Vulture Mine. When the owners of the mine ran up a $35,000 debt they said they couldn't pay, Mike took over the mine and operated it until the obligation was liquidated. Then he gave the mine back to the owners.

This fugitive immigrant who traveled halfway around the world to establish a mercantile business was not seeking riches or power or the easy life. He endured hardship and privation. He survived the attacks of hostile Indians. He was separated from Sarah and his children almost continuously for the first twenty-seven years of his married life. What he sought was freedom and independence. He found it.

They called my grandfather Big Mike not because of his physical stature, but because, as my uncle Morris once explained to me, he was big in courage, big in vision, big in heart. He died before I was born. His story is not unique.

In 1877 Mike turned over the active management of the Arizona properties to his sons, Morris and Henry, and joined Sarah in San Francisco.

My father, Baron, was sixteen years old when he came to Prescott from San Francisco in October 1882 to work in the family store. I cherish many pleasant memories of my father, but I never really knew him. What I know about him I learned from my mother and my uncle Morris. He was five feet six inches tall, slender, cosmopolitan in his habits, devoted to providing for his family, but never really one of us. Uncle Morris said my father worked hard at pleasing customers, serving his apprenticeship without complaint, but was often critical of the merchandise and the selling methods.

At the end of that first year in Arizona my father went back to San Francisco to visit Mike and Sarah. When he returned, he brought with him a magnificent square piano, which he promptly sold at a handsome profit. He purchased the piano with his own savings—he never brought it to the store. He refused to divide the profits of that initial sale with his brothers. He made his point. Goldwater's started handling pianos. In the next twelve months they sold fifteen. As a result of this first independent venture, Morris and Henry let Baron expand the lines of the merchandise they handled far beyond the staple necessities originally featured.

About three years before Baron came to Arizona, M. Goldwater & Sons had tried to open a store in Phoenix, a new farming community in the central part of the state. For some reason the store didn't go and was closed. Now Baron wanted to enter this market again. He argued that mines around Prescott would someday be worked out. He said the state's economic future would be built on agriculture. He thought the population of Phoenix was bound to grow faster than Prescott's.

Morris and Henry were opposed to the opening of a branch in Phoenix. Baron was insistent. They finally played a game of casino to settle the matter. Baron won. In 1896, with Baron in charge, a branch of M. Goldwater & Sons was opened in the valley community.

My mother, Josephine Williams, grew up in the sand hills of Nebraska, moved to Chicago, and went through nurses' training. In 1903 her doctors told her she had lung fever and recommended she go to Arizona. She came by herself, keeping her medical problem a secret from her parents. She told them she was going west with a patient and would write when she was established—an explanation literally true. She was the patient.

Not too much was known about tuberculosis at this period, but it was believed the dry air of western deserts had an exceptional healing quality. Most of the "lungers" lived in tents on the outskirts of Phoenix, seeking maximum exposure to the sun and the air. My mother never discussed her illness or her recovery with us, but I do know that within three years after she came, she was doing special duty as a surgical nurse at the old St. Joseph's Hospital.

My father made the Phoenix Goldwater store the leading fashion center of the territory. He traveled frequently to San Francisco and New York on buying trips. He sold high-quality merchandise at high prices. He established the motto which was the guideline we all followed until our family sold the store in the late 1950s. It was: "The Best Always."

Baron Goldwater was one of the most eligible bachelors in the territory. Josephine Williams was "that new trained nurse from Nebraska." My mother says she met my father at the store. They were married in 1907. She was twenty-nine, he, forty-one.

My father had been living with two other bachelors, Dr. George E. Goodrich and Gus Hershfeld, a highly respected professional gambler. They had an adobe house about two blocks from the store. When I was a boy, it had a green door and green shutters. My father's first proposal wasn't an offer of marriage. He invited Jo to move in with him, an offer she rejected scornfully.

According to Uncle Morris, the wedding took place in Prescott during a snowstorm, the ceremony performed by an Episcopal priest. Following a reception at the boardinghouse where bachelor Morris lived, the newlyweds left on the Santa Fe train for a honeymoon trip to New York City. I was the first child of Baron and Josephine Goldwater.

Arizona was admitted as the forty-eighth state of the Union on February 14, 1912. My uncle Morris was vice-president of the Constitutional Convention which preceded that event. He was elected to represent Yavapai County in the first session of the new state legislature.

My father was a very private man, almost solitary. His pattern of life was rigidly followed, day after day. My mother says he wanted children but never knew quite how to cope with us. My brother, Bob, who is fifteen months younger than I am, was born on the Fourth of July; my sister, Carolyn, on April 15, 1912, the day the Titanic went down.

Uncle Morris was gregarious, impulsive, a leader of the Democratic party and a highly respected citizen. He became my friend and my instructor.

Mother loved the out-of-doors, absorbed the culture and the history of her adopted home. My father was a city man. He had his store, his card games in the afternoon with cronies at the Arizona Club, and the companionship of his male friends, who often stopped on their way home to have a drink at Baron Goldwater's house. When Prohibition became the law of the land, my father bought the bar, the back bar, and the brass footrail of his favorite saloon and had them installed in the basement of our house. The country went dry, but that bar was always wet.

My first year in high school I was not a scholastic success. The principal diplomatically informed my father that I probably would do much better in a private school. The following fall I was enrolled at Staunton Military Academy in Virginia. It was probably the best thing that ever happened to me.

Looking back on this period, I now understand the friends of my childhood were all the sons of successful fathers. But to be a success in that period didn't mean you had to be rich or white collar, black or white, Gentile or Jew. To be respectable meant respecting others, keeping your word, paying your way. The kind of work a man did wasn't important.

I realize now the Goldwaters were somebodies in the social and economic circles of that dusty little frontier town. But when I was growing up, I never thought I was different from anyone else. I was a poorer scholar than some of my friends, better at athletics. Thanks to my courageous, remarkable mother, I knew a lot more about Arizona than many of my friends.

Before I was ten years old, "Mun" took us on camping trips to every remote corner: to the Grand Canyon, to the Navajo and Hopi reservations, to the border towns of Douglas and Nogales, to the high mountain places—Flagstaff, Show Low, and Springerville. We had a Chalmers touring car with boxes built on the running boards to carry food, cooking utensils, and other camping gear. Mun did the driving and the bossing. Bob gathered the wood and built the campfires; Carolyn washed the dishes. Mother did the cooking. And when we got stuck on those primitive roads, it was my job to take the shovel and dig us out.

Mun told us the history of the places we visited. We had to learn and identify all the vegetation. She read to us from books about geology so that we could understand how the mountains and valleys were formed.

History and literature fascinated me. The military training at Staunton was physical and mental. I accepted the discipline as

304

being necessary, was absorbed by the studies of military tactics and the history of the world's great battles. I graduated as the outstanding military cadet of my class.

My instructors at Staunton urged me to pursue a military career. They said I qualified for an appointment to West Point, and their sponsorship would make it possible for me to enter the academy. The idea appealed to me, but my father was not well. Mun wanted me to come home. I enrolled as a freshman at the University of Arizona in the fall of 1928.

My mother, who, in addition to managing our pleasant household, worked for volunteer charity organizations and served on the medical auxiliary of the hospital, was a talented golfer. She mastered the game and became club champion. On the morning of March 6, 1929, Mun teed off at eight-fifteen in the second round of a women's tournament at the Phoenix Country Club. After eight holes, she was two up on her opponent. Suddenly, without offering any explanations, she walked off the course, stopped only long enough to take off her golf shoes in the locker room, and drove home. Afterward she told us, "I just knew something was wrong."

When Mun reached home, my father was still in bed—a most unusual thing for him. He appeared to be in great pain. Mun called the doctor and did what she could to make my father comfortable. He was dead when the doctor arrived.

The Goldwater store was under the capable management of our longtime associate Sam Wilson, but the first breezes of that economic windstorm, the Great Depression, were being felt in Arizona. It was time, I thought, to go to work.

My apprenticeship in the business world commenced the spring my father died. I was twenty years old. Goldwater's had fifty-five employees. The annual sales were about four hundred thousand dollars.

The fact that my name was Goldwater didn't cut any ice with Sam Wilson. I started as a junior clerk. Over the years my father had dropped most of the general lines. Goldwater's had become a high-fashion store catering to a clientele in the middle- and upper-income brackets.

In the piece goods section I learned the different fabrics, how to tell them apart and what they were used for. As soon as Sam thought I had mastered one line, he moved me to another department. With the exception of ladies' undergarments and shoes, I did it all. My salary was fifteen dollars a week, and I had to live on it. Bob and Carolyn both were away at school. Mun didn't charge me anything for room and board. I had been used to more spending money when I was at college, but this was different—this was earned money.

During my first campaign for U.S. Senate, my opponent referred to me in a belittling manner as a "ribbon clerk." I responded saying that I was a damned good ribbon clerk and proud of it. I said, "The people I know who work at this trade are honest and enterprising, determined to give their customers value received for every dollar spent. I want the gentleman to know that's the way I intend to conduct myself when I'm sitting in his old seat in the Senate." I don't claim that working in a store, dealing with customers, employees, manufacturers, and brokers, is the equivalent of an academic degree, but I do think that in this real world of commerce I learned some things not taught in any college.

The Depression wasn't really felt in Arizona until 1932. I have never found a satisfactory answer to explain this time lag, but 1932 was the year of most business failures. We cut the inventory, skimped on advertising, switched off lights to save electricity, and reduced deliveries. Everyone in the store, including me, took a cut in pay, but we didn't fire anybody. We never sued anyone to collect an overdue bill. We never missed a payroll.

The hard times which commenced in 1929 and continued until the beginning of World War II reinforced all my understandings of economics. Businesses go broke because they borrow more than they can repay. Interest rates eat up profits.

• • •

Those first years at the store were exciting and rewarding. Our merchandise was higher-priced than that of our competitors, but we had better quality. Our customers recognized this. Lots of them with comparatively small incomes appeared to prefer to have one or two dresses a year from Goldwater's rather than three or four less expensive garments. With the slogan "The Best Always," our store not only kept afloat during the Depression but gradually increased our volume of sales.

The store didn't claim all my attention, and I became intensely interested in Arizona history. I went again to those out-of-

306

the-way places we had visited with Mun when we were children and found some new ones. I ran the rapids of the Colorado River in a wooden boat, hiked or rode horseback over much of the Navajo Reservation.

Phoenix in this period was a small, semi-isolated western city. The summer heat was intense; only a few theaters and some of the stores had central air conditioning. We called the winter visitors snowbirds and rejoiced when they left in the spring, even though this would mean a lessening of commercial activity.

It may have been the Depression, or isolation, or perhaps our limited population, but there existed in those years a spirit of community which I have never encountered elsewhere. This was a part of our frontier heritage when survival depended on our neighbors.

I can remember a group of businessmen coming to our house to discuss the need for a better hospital when my father was still alive. They talked about where it should be built and how much it should cost. The next day they started raising money. In the teens and the twenties, the institution they built was the equal of anything in a city ten times our size.

In 1930 I decided to learn to fly. My instructor, Jack Thornburg, had a Great Lakes biplane with an inverted four cylinder air-cooled engine. It was the only time I ever kept a secret from Mun.

Because there is considerable turbulence in Arizona the year around, especially during the hot summer months, the best flying conditions for a neophyte pilot are just at daybreak. I would slip out of the house and meet Jack at an unpaved airstrip east of the city.

Flying has been a major part of my life. Perhaps it is the splendid isolation of being alone in the air which fascinates me, or it might be the perspective which comes from looking down on every part of the world—rivers and oceans and cities and hamlets. I prefer night flying to day flying. I see the lights, and I wonder where they are burning—in a young couple's home where they have just put the babies to bed, in a widow's lonely house, or perhaps in a store like Goldwater's when I was a boy. In the daylight hours the landscapes change, are marked by rivers, by luxuriant growth in areas of heavy rainfall. At night even the mountains are blurred. Only the lights indicate the presence of other human beings.

307

• • •

I wasn't breaking any law when I sneaked off to learn to fly, but Mun knew I wasn't going to the store at that early hour. She didn't ask any questions. I didn't offer any explanations.

After my first solo flight, the owner of the ground where the strip was located decided it would be more profitable to plant lettuce than to serve aviation. The airplanes which had been using the strip moved to a new field on the west side of town. Some years later the Twenty-seventh Pursuit Squadron from North Island, San Diego, was named winner of the Frank Luke, Jr., trophy for aerial gunnery. Luke, one of the aerial heroes of World War I, was a native Phoenician. The squadron wanted to fly into Phoenix and receive the trophy. The owner of the ground where I learned to fly had given up on lettuce and was ready to reestablish an airport, but the strip hadn't been graded.

When the city was slow to act, I borrowed a tractor and a drag from a Japanese gardener I knew. With the help of Lee Moore, a local mortician, who had learned to fly about the same time I did, the strip was graded. The runway which resulted from our efforts is now eight left, two-six right of the international airport operated by the city of Phoenix, named Sky Harbor.

In 1978 more than five million passengers arrived and departed from that field, which is only twenty-four blocks from City Hall. The only other major city in the United States with an airport so close to the downtown area is San Diego. When I visit other cities and have to spend forty-five minutes to an hour in a cab or a bus traveling from the airport to downtown, I think how lucky we are in Phoenix. It gives me considerable personal satisfaction to remember my part in the location of Sky Harbor.

When I earned my private pilot's license, there was a one-paragraph story in the *Arizona Republic*. Mun clipped it out and handed it to me at breakfast. "If you had told me," she said, "I would have learned with you." I believe she would.

Since that day I have logged more than 12,000 hours of time in 165 different types of aircraft, helicopters, and gliders. I was the first nonrated test pilot to fly the U-2. I have flown the B-1 bomber, the F-104, the French Mirage, the German-French A-300. I have flown the SR-72 at a speed of Mach 3 at an altitude of 83,000 feet.

308

Shortly after I qualified to carry passengers, my friend Harry Rosenzweig persuaded me to take his current love, an attractive young lady named Strauss, for a ride.

In those days pilot instruction did not include spins and recovery. I had been told that if I ever got an airplane into a spin, I should let go all controls, and the aircraft would right itself.

Harry's girlfriend and I were in the Great Lakes at about 2,500 feet over her house. To attract attention, we were doing some tight 360-degree turns. The aircraft stalled; we went into a spin. I let go of everything, said a prayer, and we recovered. Not long after that, fledgling pilots had to learn how to put their craft into a spin and recover before being permitted to solo.

When my brother, Bob, graduated from Stanford in 1932, we held a kind of family conference. Sam Wilson had married a wealthy widow and retired. I was running the store and enjoying it. It was decided Bob would go to work at the Valley National Bank and learn how bankers made money. By this time I knew we would never become millionaires running a store. Incidentally, Bob wanted to learn to fly, and Mun encouraged him.

I first met Margaret Johnson when she and her mother came into the store to do some shopping in December 1930. Her parents, the Ray Prescott Johnsons of Muncie, Indiana, had leased United States Senator Carl Hayden's home on the Country Club grounds for the winter.

The Johnsons were snowbirds. They had come down hoping the mild climate would benefit Peggy's mother, who suffered from some bronchial complications. I remember thinking she was a rather pretty girl, with very deep blue eyes and a beautiful complexion. She told me later she was depressed by the thought of missing all the good Christmas parties in Muncie. She thought Phoenix was a hick town, and I didn't make much of an impression on her. She said she was going to Mount Vernon Seminary in Washington, D.C. I told her I had graduated from Staunton in Virginia.

Herb Green, a friend of ours, brought her over to the house on Central Avenue for one party that Christmas season; but it was a big affair, and I didn't pay any particular attention to Herb's date. When I saw her again in 1932, the little girl from Mount Vernon Seminary had become a ravishingly beautiful, mature woman. She had come back to Phoenix to be with her father, who was desperately ill. I tried to see her as often as possible, but she had other things on her mind.

When her father died, Peggy and her mother returned to Muncie, and I became something of a commuter. She was fun to be with. I liked her sense of humor, her independence, her throaty laugh, her eyes. I was in love.

The Johnsons spent the summer of 1933 at their summer place in Charlevoix, Michigan. In that two-year interval between our first and second meeting, Peggy had worked as a designer for the David Crystal organization in New York City. Because they were in the apparel business, I had some contacts with the Crystals, and the people I knew there told me that Peggy had exhibited exceptional talent. About the only thing we had in common was an interest in style and fashion. Her father had been president of the Warner Gear Company. Borg-Warner is the result of a merger of Warner Gear and the Borg and Beck Clutch Company. Ray Johnson became executive vice-president, a post he held until his death.

I first proposed after a two-week visit in the summer of 1933. Peggy said she wasn't ready to get married. She wasn't sure about Arizona, and she wasn't sure about me. But I was sure, and I told her so.

Christmas is "The Season" in the dry-goods business. Holiday sales can make the difference between profit and loss for a full year. I went to Muncie the day after Christmas 1933 to spend the rest of the holidays. New Year's Eve Peggy and I were at a dance. She wanted to call and wish her mother a Happy New Year. When we were in the telephone booth, I told her I was running out of money and out of patience. For the umpteenth time I asked her to marry me. She said yes.

We were married in Muncie almost ten months later on September 22, 1934. Peggy and her mother had been scheduled to embark on a long-planned world cruise in January 1934. I couldn't ask her to give it up, but I didn't want her to go. I was tormented by the thought she might meet someone on shipboard or on shore, so I made sure there was a packet of letters waiting for her whenever the cruise ship docked. She still has them.

There are many moments of triumph in a man's lifetime which he remembers. I have been to the mountaintop of victory— my first election to the Senate, and my reelection; that night in Chicago, in 1960, when the governor of Arizona put my name in nomination for the office of President of the United States; and another night in San Francisco when the delegates to the Republican Convention made me their nominee. But above all else I rate that night in Muncie, Indiana.

Peggy and I have had four children. We have known joy and sorrow together. We have encountered pain and illness. We have suffered separation for long periods of time. Through it all she has been my strength, my companion, a part of my private world where no other human beings, not even our children, have been allowed to enter. Peggy doesn't like flying or camping, but she has done a lot of both with me.

By 1937 most of the other nations in the world had recovered from the 1929 Depression. The United States was lagging behind. Things at the store were going very well. My brother, Bob, had been named to the board of directors at the bank. My sister, Carolyn, had married her childhood sweetheart, Paul Sexson, and Mun was in reasonably good health. But I was disturbed.

I had read Hitler's *Mein Kampf*. My grandfather had been forced to flee Poland, and the Jewish community was probably the first to recognize the full horror of the Nazi program.

When Lindberg went to Germany to make his appraisal of Hitler's Air Force, I was pleased. When he attempted to tell the American people about the real purpose of the Nazi glider schools and detailed the technological superiority of the new aircraft the Germans had developed, I hoped it would awaken our nation to its peril. The official reaction, supported by the media, was the exact opposite. Lindbergh was categorized as a Nazi sympathizer. His loyalty to the United States was questioned. We know now that President Franklin D. Roosevelt put Lindbergh on his personal enemies list.

Perhaps World War II was inevitable, but there are some unanswered questions. If the Western allies had maintained their military strength after World War I, could Chamberlain have made that trip to Munich? If a strong West had made it clear to Hitler and to Mussolini and to all other conquest-minded world leaders that the use of military force against a neighbor would be met instantly with superior force, would Hitler have crossed the border into the Low Countries? Perhaps my commitment through the years to maintaining weapons systems superior to any potential enemy is only the natural outcome of my frustrations and disappointments in this period just prior to World War II.

I don't mean to imply that all my attention or even a major portion of it during these years was occupied with world strategy. I

311

had the store, I had Peggy and our family, and I had all the wonderful attractions of outdoor Arizona to occupy my mind.

Our first child, a girl, was born on January 1, 1936. We combined the names of her two grandmothers and called her Joanne. Our second child, a boy, Barry, Jr., who now serves in the Congress from California, was born July 15, 1938. Our third child, a boy, was born in 1940, and we named him after his great-grandfather, Michael. I was overseas in the Burma-Indian Theater when little Peggy was born in 1944.

Despite the war clouds gathering over Europe and our confused domestic situation, these were good years. There hadn't been enough elapsed time to prove that all of the New Deal's social legislation was the true answer to our discontent, but they weren't yet demonstrable failures.

On December 7, 1941, Japanese carrier-based aircraft attacked and virtually destroyed our Pacific fleet at Pearl Harbor in the Hawaiian Islands. While millions of Americans were genuinely surprised by the bombing of Pearl Harbor, which precipitated our legal entry into World War II, they shouldn't have been. Ignorance, or perhaps wishful thinking, had closed our eyes to events in Nazi Germany, Fascist Italy, Imperial Japan, and Communist Russia. Hitler's Germany had absorbed Austria and threatened Czechoslovakia. Mussolini's Italy had invaded Ethiopia. Japan had been waging war on China. Communist Russia, Nazi Germany, and Fascist Italy had been deeply involved in the so-called civil war in Spain.

• • •

It was obvious that air power held the key to the new military strategy. In 1940 and early 1941, the U.S. began training pilots on a scale never attempted anywhere before. Arizona's dry, cloudless skies provide the best flying weather in the nation. In February 1941 the Air Corps opened a single-engine advanced training school at Luke Field, about thirty miles west of Phoenix.

Primary schools operated by civilians taught new cadets how to fly in two-place Stearmans. Three of these schools were in the Phoenix area.

In July 1941, as chairman of the Armed Services Committee of the Phoenix Chamber of Commerce, I paid a courtesy call on Lieutenant Colonel Ennis C. Whitehead, commandant of Luke.

312

My purpose was to inquire if there was anything we could do, as the business community of Phoenix, to make the colonel's job easier. A new base, a new program, a staff composed of officers who had never heard of Arizona until they got their assignment orders—what Colonel Whitehead needed was an officer who knew his way around Arizona.

In 1932 I had attempted to enter the Air Corps as a cadet. My eyesight didn't meet the military standards, and I was rejected. Now I was overage for the Air Corps, and my vision hadn't improved. But I told Colonel Whitehead that I was a reserve first lieutenant in the infantry—if he could use me in any way, I was available. I said I thought I knew something about how to get things done in Arizona.

Colonel Whitehead took me to a typewriter, handed me an application for active duty, and told me to fill it out. I typed out the form and signed it. It was for a term of one year. I believed that, barring a miracle, we would be involved in a war, and I would be in for the duration. The important thing to me at the moment was that Colonel Whitehead needed me.

When I told Peggy what I had done, she approved. She predicted I would find a way to move from a desk job into an airplane. Four weeks later I was back on the base—this time in uniform as First Lieutenant Goldwater, assigned to the ground school—an Officer's Club officer.

One of the great and lasting disappointments of my lifetime is that I never made it into combat. My eyesight and my age were against me. But I didn't sit out the war as somebody's PR officer in a stateside base.

Every second lieutenant who won his wings at Luke wanted a picture of himself in his airplane—pictures to send to the folks at home, to his girl. I took my camera to the base and traded pictures of these young officers for unauthorized flight time. They wanted more than snapshots of themselves standing beside their craft on the ground. When they flew, I had to go along in an accompanying plane to make the airborne shots. When I did, the pilots let me do the flying and log the flying time.

It wasn't a question of learning how to fly. I wanted to become familiar with the military aircraft. I was determined to qualify for some kind of flying assignment in the Air Corps.

After about six weeks I was sent to the Air Corps Supply School at Wright-Patterson Field in Dayton, Ohio, for three

313

months. This permitted me to become acquainted with all the current aircraft being used, not only at Luke but at other fields. Knowledge of the Air Corps inventory was something I put to good use later on.

When I returned to Luke, I went through channels and again requested admission to the aviation cadet program. I was turned down. The training command decided to open a new school at Yuma, Arizona. I was assigned the task of overseeing construction, requisitioning inventory, and doing everything else necessary to put the new school in operation. I was still a junior officer. When the field opened, our assignment was to teach aerial gunnery. The methods of instruction the Air Corps gave us had not been particularly successful. Fewer than ten percent of the cadets were being graduated as proficient.

With the help of Captain Walter Clark, who was assigned to Luke, and Group Captain Teddy Donaldson of the Royal Air Force, we set out to improve the techniques. Clark was a mathematical genius. This was before the age of computers, which could probably equal our efforts in a few seconds. What we developed came to be known in gunnery training as the curve of pursuit, a theory that all bullets fired at an enemy aircraft, starting at 90 degrees and following through to zero, would hit the target. Ninety-four percent of the pilots in our first graduating class at Yuma were declared qualified for gunnery.

The training command in Washington was so skeptical of our reported results they sent a colonel out to investigate us. I think they thought we were cheating or lying. After a short classroom indoctrination, I showed the visitor the accuracy of our theory. It was made standard practice. It is still used.

When the function at Yuma was changed from aerial gunnery to twin-engined pilot instruction, I asked for and received assignment to the Ferry Command in New Castle, Delaware. This was a new group composed of overage pilots organized to deliver aircraft and supplies to every war theater. It wasn't a very glamorous job, but I was still trying to pull strings to get into the four-engine Bomber Command. At least I got to the war zones.

I think I was among the first to qualify as a service pilot because of my familiarity with the AT-6. I took a test ride and passed. Later in the same year I received my regular Army wings which made it possible for me to become a command pilot eventually.

314

• • •

At Luke and in Yuma we trained many Chinese cadets. Some of them became my fast friends. When I eventually reached the India-Burma Theater, I discovered to my delight that many of the Chinese pilots we had trained in Arizona were flying combat here.

• • •

At the end of my tour in India, I was reassigned to a fighter replacement and retraining unit in California, where I served until the end of the war. I was mustered out in November 1945 with the request that I form an Air National Guard Unit in Arizona. To serve in the Guard, I had to take a reduction in rank from colonel to captain. We organized the 197th Fighter Squadron. I requested that we be permitted to make it a nonsegregated military unit. This request was granted.

• • •

When I came home in 1945, it took some time to appreciate all the subtle changes which had taken place during the war years I was away. There weren't any new buildings. There had been no major expansion in the residential areas. But Phoenix wasn't the same. There was a change in attitude, in spirit. We had lost our isolated parochialism and some of that casual mañana attitude which had been a part of our inheritance. The population hadn't increased. In fact, there were twelve thousand fewer Arizonans registered to vote in 1946 than there had been in 1940.

Activating the Arizona wing of the Air National Guard, getting reacquainted with my family, and trying to adjust to the role of a civilian merchant occupied all my time that first year. In 1946 Gov. Sidney P. Osborn, a Democrat, asked me to serve on the Arizona Colorado River Commission. Our goal was to secure congressional authorization for the Central Arizona Project.

I was thirty-seven years old. Every soldier who has ever served in time of war has cause to speculate about the politics which produced the conflict. Because of my uncle Morris and my admiration for him, I had been privileged to know something about the inner workings of our political system. I had never been involved in a purely political dispute between two factions, in which respectable men of good conscience adopted opposite positions and then employed all the tools available to achieve their objective—money, passion, prejudice, and at times outright falsehoods.

• • •

When I was appointed to the Colorado River Commission, [Carl] Hayden was chairman of the Senate Interior Committee. He provided me with an extensive background on the history of the Santa Fe Compact and our struggle with California. My task was to help mobilize public sentiment throughout Arizona in support of the Central Arizona Project for diversion of Arizona's share of Colorado water into central Arizona.

The California interests, seeking to prevent diversion of any Colorado River water to Arizona, employed gross exaggeration and outright falsehood. For almost twenty-five years their delaying tactics were successful. Then the Supreme Court decided in favor of Arizona. The Central Arizona Project was authorized by Congress in 1967. It is under construction and will be completed in the early 1980s.

This was my first exposure to the world of real politics. It led me to understand that in such struggles equity and truth are relatively impotent. It is power at the ballot box, power in the banking circles, and power in the halls of academia which determine the outcome of such disputes.

My first participation in matters political was on a grand scale, embracing two states directly, the other five basin states indirectly, and reaching into the Congress of the United States. My next step took me into the rather limited theater of municipal politics.

Before the war Phoenix was an isolated desert community. The population was less than fifty thousand. The city covered seven square miles. Municipal government was conducted by five city commissioners, who elected one of their members to serve as mayor. The mayor, with the support of two members of the Council, could hire or fire the city manager, the chief of police, or anyone else. As a result of this arrangement, there was a new coalition coming to power every few months. The average term of a city manager was less than twelve months. There had been some graft and some scandal.

In common with most western cities in the days of my youth, Phoenix had a segregated red-light district. The madams and their pimps were well known to the local citizens and to the police. The community was not scandalized by the presence of these "working girls." There was no connection with organized crime.

Four pilot-training schools were established adjacent to Phoenix at the outset of the war. The whorehouses expanded to take care of this new clientele. An alarming high incidence of venereal disease resulted in Phoenix's being placed off limits to military personnel in 1943.

According to local insiders, some members of the City Council demanded and received under-the-table protection payoffs. Nowadays, when anyone in Phoenix talks about the reform movement we started in 1947, they invariably mention open prostitution. This was only one minor manifestation of the problems that existed. What we set out to correct was inefficient city management, totally incapable of delivering the kind of police protection, fire protection, and sanitary services required by our exploding population.

The mayor of Phoenix, a Democrat named Ray Busey, directed public attention to the instability of civil government and the opportunities presented for graft and corruption. Busey, a likable man, appointed a citizen's committee to revise the charter. Charles Bernstein, a prominent jurist who was later to serve on the Arizona State Supreme Court, was named chairman.

This was the beginning of municipal reform and my introduction to local politics. The forty members of the Charter Government Committee were representative of the community—doctors, farmers, lawyers, bankers, and real estate men. I was named to serve, along with my friends Harry and Newt Rosenzweig.

It didn't take us long to discover the Phoenix city charter was woefully deficient. It might have been adequate for a city of twenty thousand, but our population was rapidly approaching one hundred thousand.

The old charter vested complete control of city operations in the Council. The one we wrote transferred responsibility for the day-to-day activities of the city administration to a professional manager. Under the old charter the manager had served at the whim of the Council. We said he could only be fired for cause. Then we provided for the election of six councilmen at large and mayor to be chosen by the voters. We said no councilman, not even the mayor, could directly approach a city employee with a request for service or for a favor. We established a separate finance depart-

317

ment to oversee tax collections and disbursements. It was a good, solid piece of work. The people of Phoenix adopted the new charter in a special election in 1948. We then elected a new mayor, a new Council, and I thought our job was done. It wasn't.

The new mayor, a competent, principled attorney, tried to implement the provisions of the new charter. His Council would have none of it. They preferred the old political system.

We had been naive. We had thought it necessary only to reform the charter; in truth, no written document is of much value unless the people elected to power are faithful to that document. This conclusion, reached at the beginning of my entrance into the political world, has been reinforced by my experience in the Congress. In the past thirty years, we have, as a result of executive action, congressional inattention, and a passel of Supreme Court decisions, radically altered the intention of the Founding Fathers expressed in the Constitution of the United States.

Dismayed at this turn of events, but not willing to concede defeat, we reconvened the citizen group, named it the Charter Government Committee, and prepared to nominate six new candidates for Council who would be committed to the new charter. The committee approached a number of men and women we thought competent to serve on the Council. Most of them turned us down. The time grew short. Other members of the committee urged me to agree to be a candidate.

The war had been over for four years. I was nominally president of Goldwater's, but the problems of merchandising no longer commanded my interest as they had in those early days. Public questions occupied my mind. I was disturbed by my discoveries that greed and power oftentimes made the wheels go around. Because the decision I made then was the true turning point in my life, I have reflected many times on that moment. I had no intentions of devoting my life to public service. I certainly didn't think I was any more competent than the man next door to serve on the City Council. I was angered at the people who had turned us down. I remembered, "All that is necessary for evil to triumph is for good men to do nothing." I agreed to become a candidate. We won. The city government of Phoenix is now respected nationwide for its excellence, its impartiality, its efficiency and its economy.

I enjoyed the campaigning, and there was considerable satisfaction in winning; but my plan was to serve two years, perhaps four, and then return to the store.

318

Up From the Barrio

Maria Urquides

Contemporary Arizona bears witness to a heritage rooted deep in the Hispanic tradition—a legacy from the Old World and the New. Place names, architectural styles, and language reflect the passage of Spanish priests, explorers, and soldiers. In more recent times Mexican-Americans have made an invaluable contribution to Arizona's culture and economy as farmers, miners, and ranchers. Since the end of World War II, they have been increasingly visible and influential in the state's affairs.

Maria Urquides is heir to the Mexican-American version of the Horatio Alger theme. A descendant of Spanish adventurers, she emerged from the barrio of Tucson to become a national figure in the struggle for bilingual education in public schools in the Southwest. In the following tape-recorded interview she tells of her varied career. First as a teacher and then as a school administrator, she worked to preserve Arizona's Mexican-American cultural identity through ensuring that the children of that heritage would have the opportunity to speak, read, and write in their ancestral language.

*C*onsidering *the tremendous Spanish and Mexican influence on the Southwest, it is paradoxical that there even had to be a fight for bilingual education. The Maria Urquides story is one that bridges the gap between the Spanish, Mexican, and Anglo cultures, and the narration begins with her family's migration from the south.*

"Both of my grandfathers came from Spain, and one of my grandmothers, my maternal grandmother, came from Alamos, Mexico. My father and mother were both born in Tucson. My father was born in 1854. He was born right outside the wall . . . the walled city of Tucson. And my mother was born in 1871 and she was born in a little house that later became the El Charro Restaurant [today that home is an historic site, saved from downtown urban renewal but ironically converted into a Greek restaurant in Tucson's La Placita development].

"Mother used to tell us how her father, Joaquin Legarra, bought a little home where Penney's Department Store is downtown now. And some people talked him into starting a meat market, so he mortgaged the little home in order to send money to Sonora, Mexico, to buy cattle and bring the meat to Tucson. Well, the cattle lost so much weight in bringing them through to here that my grandfather had great difficulty and his venture failed. So he lost his home, bless his heart.

"The family was having a very hard time, and then he died when my mother was about, oh, she was about eight. So it was even more difficult and they used to make candles, they used to

Maria Urquides, "The Roots of the Newcomers," in Abe Chanin with Mildred Chanin, *This Land, These Voices; A Different View of Arizona History in the Words of Those Who Lived It* (Flagstaff: Northland Press, 1977), 66–76. Used with permission from Northland Press.

make starch, they used to make tortillas and sell them to the soldiers at Fort Lowell in order to pull through.

"On my father's side . . . he was left an orphan when he was fourteen, and the Lee family adopted him. The Lee family had one of the first flour mills; it was at the foot of 'A' Mountain. They were the ones that raised him after he was fourteen, and my father used to tell me the very interesting story about the Indians and how the Lees used to have him run up to the top of 'A' Mountain and see if there was any dust on the horizon. If there was dust on the horizon that meant the Indians would probably attack that night, and if there wasn't, why the family went to bed a little early. My father would tell me the Indians would come to—I don't want to use the word steal, but that's what it was—come to steal some flour. So if my father spotted the dust, they'd just take turns guarding whatever there was to steal."

We asked about the struggle in her own home to get along in those early days.

"You know, I never remember feeling poverty in my home, my father always managed to have a pantry. The first time that I am conscious of living in a home was the one we had on Convent Street which is right where the Tucson Community Center is; you know that little gate where you go into the center, that is right where our home was. [The community center was part of the urban renewal of downtown Tucson that wiped out most of one of the oldest of the barrios.]

"And they built the home of adobes—beautiful adobes twenty-four inches by eight inches. It took a bulldozer to knock the thing down, I know. When they went through that downtown urban renewal project I just stood there across from my old home. I stood by the cathedral watching them tearing it down, and it really was with mixed feelings."

They call it "progress," this urban renewal which has wiped out many of the marks of earlier cultures. In Tucson this "progress" obliterated the adobe wall that once surrounded the Presidio de Tucson.

"Mother and Dad had eight children. Three died; one was stillborn and the other two died in infancy. Five of us have survived, and we're still living. In that little house we had a pantry, and I can remember that my father always bought as much as he could, you know, wholesale . . . a bag of beans, a bag of flour

321

. . . because he was a prospector and he used to have to leave that much food for us when he would go out prospecting for two or three months.

"Prospecting was very difficult, very difficult. My father did have some land near where the Twin Buttes mine is now south of Tucson. He homesteaded there so he did have some land there. After school was out we would go down there in the wagon for three months. My brothers' heads would be shaved, and I remember taking, you know, those little boxes of dried prunes and peaches which you could get for a song then, and beans and flour. And then away we'd go into the desert to my dad's land. And the first thing that we would do when we got there is butcher. I can still remember Dad swinging the great, big hammer and hitting the cow or steer that we were to butcher . . . to stun him and then slit the throat and we'd have a pail to catch the blood so we'd have blood pudding. The head was roasted. The kidneys and liver we used immediately, and we jerked most of the meat so we'd have meat for the rest of the three months.

"This must have been about 1913, and we stayed out there in the desert while my father went around trying to find some minerals. Oh, yes, I remember eating rattlesnake. We would go out and search for a snake, and then my father would kill the rattlesnake and then he'd measure one hand from the head, another hand from the end of the rattlers, and the middle part is what we could eat. You see, towards the end of the three months we would run out of the food we had brought along so we had to make do. We would catch jackrabbits, too, and he'd make chorizo [Mexican sausage] out of the jackrabbit to make it a little more palatable. The cottontail rabbits we fried and they were good.

"And we would go out and hunt for *bellotas*. You know what *bellotas* are? Acorns. And we would bring them in, and we kids used to make our money that way 'cause we used to sell the *bellotas* when we came back into town. And we felt sort of badly, because we'd take the trade away from the Indians who used to bring the *bellotas* to town."

Maria began to talk of life in the barrio, the predominantly Mexican section just to the south of downtown Tucson.

"You know, I think the reason that we never felt all of this thing about discrimination is because we all needed each other so much. The Indian would come in with the wood, with the pinole, with the acorns and with the tortillas—the corn tortillas—and sell

322

them. And the Chinese were responsible for the roving fresh vegetable carts. And we—my family—were lucky enough. Dad owned about four lots, and so there was a lot of vacant land around us. There were little stables there, and there would be about four Chinese vendors who would keep their wagons there to have an early start. And they would take their vegetables—and you know how artistic they are—they'd clean the carrots and the onions and the *calabacitas* [little squashes] and they'd arrange them on their wagons, cover them with gunny sacks and wet them. And this was in the evening, and I can often remember going to sleep with the sing-song of their chatter.

"They'd sprinkle the gunny sacks with water, and it was just like an evaporative cooler to keep the vegetables fresh overnight. And then they'd start early in the morning and come back at night with empty wagons. They were a terrific people. I had a very soft spot in my heart for the Chinese. Of course [here Maria smiled like a naughty child], we used to steal a little carrot every now and then from them."

We asked how it was that in a family who had to struggle so much for existence there was such impetus to pursue education.

"People have always asked me that. Father was just rabid on education. In fact, the only time that I really remember my dad and mother having an argument was one time when we got up too late to go to first Friday Mass, and so she kept us from school to go to the second Mass. My father came home and found that we had been kept from school that morning in order to go to Mass. And he said, 'If they missed Mass you punish them another way, but you don't make them stay home from school. They have to go to school.' And he took us by the hand and took us to school."

When did she first get the desire to become a teacher?

"When I was a junior in high school it was because of Mary Balch, one of my teachers, that I turned to education. Before my junior year I was more interested in baseball and basketball and that sort of thing. In fact, I made All-State forward, let's see, that was in 1924. I remember Mary Balch because she talked to me very seriously and said, 'Maria, what are you planning to do?'

"And I said, 'Well, you know I have a job at Steinfeld's Department Store and I just maybe will continue to work there.' Used to work there in the summer, and I also said, 'Sometimes I'd like to be a nurse.'

"And she says, 'What about an elementary school teacher?'

323

"And I looked at her, 'Are you kidding?'"

"She says, 'No, I think you'd make a very good teacher.'"

"And she also said, 'Now I know that your family can't afford it very well, but Tempe State Teachers College is a two-year college, and if we could get you in there and then in two years you'd be out earning your living.'"

"So I told my family, and, of course, at that time *nice*— quote, unquote—Mexican girls didn't go away to school, and my older brother was very much against it. My mother cried, but my father made the decision, after Mary had gone to talk to him, that I should go. And so I went to State Teachers College. There it was that I felt discrimination for the first time. No, actually I felt it a little bit at Tucson High School because when I, the Mexican girl, got leading parts in operettas because I had a nice voice, I remember getting a nasty note.

"It was hard on me from then on, from when I became a leader . . . from then on I had to live in sort of a void. And that, I think, influenced me more than ever in what I tried to do in sponsoring bilingual, bicultural education."

We asked her what she meant by living in a void.

"When I started into the music field, you see, I was moving from the laboring class into the middle class, and both sides avoided me somewhat. The Mexican-American thought I was becoming a *gringada* [an uncomplimentary word for an Anglo], because, you see, I was the only Mexican that would get a leading part in the shows; the rest of the class was all 'gringo'—pardon me for using that word, but that's the word that was used at that time.

"So I lost the friendship of some of my Mexican-American friends, not because I wanted to, but because they believed I was shunning them. They were putting me aside, believing that I wanted it that way. And I couldn't visit the 'gringo' homes, the homes of the friends I went to school with, because that was taboo for a Mexican girl at that time.

"So I can remember sitting on the steps of Tucson High crying my eyes out because I didn't have a date for the prom. The 'gringo' would never think of taking me at that time, and the Mexican-American said, 'She is not interested in me.'

"But I think that what made me overcome that is the terrific love and security that I had at home, 'cause that's the only way I can explain my not being hurt more at that sort of thing."

324

And then when she went to Tempe to college. . . .

"When I went to Tempe I was the only Mexican-American except my cousin who was there, but she had come from an entirely different situation. She had come from Ray [now in the general area of Kearney, a mining district in southern Arizona]. Most of the Mexican-American workers up there lived in Sonora. Sonora was Mexican-American and Ray was *the* community. Well, my cousins lived in Ray. You see, my cousin's father was a superintendent of something in the mines, they were elite. At college I roomed with her, and that is when I began to feel discrimination there. I asked for work and I was given the job of cleaning the bathrooms and the toilets, and that is the job I kept for the rest of the time until I found a job singing over at La Casa Vieja in Tempe, which was Sally Hayden's place. She was the sister of Senator Carl Hayden. And that's the way—singing for the diners—I earned my living while I was in college."

When she graduated, she got her first teaching job in Tucson at Davis School, teaching ancient history, art and music.

"I graduated in '28, and I started teaching in September. My father passed away in November of '28. I had only given him two paychecks. You know, I had given him a little money from my paychecks.

"My dad was a terrific man. He had been street commissioner in Tucson for twenty-five, twenty-eight years and he had held the job under Republican and Democratic mayors. But we used to always have to pray that a Democrat would win, you know, because Dad was a Democrat. But the Republicans would keep him on, so my father used to tell us, 'Look, if you're hired for eight hours a day and you don't give as much as you can, that's just like stealing.' I guess that's why all of us have been pretty good workers.

"Well, my father died very happily with all of us surrounding him; he told my mother that."

There was a faint smile as Maria remembered an odd incident that followed her father's death.

"When he died, the newspapers came out that his father had come from Spain, that his mother, too, had come from Spain. Well, I got a call from the head of Mathews Hall where I had stayed up at State Teachers College in Tempe and he said, 'Maria, why in the world didn't you tell us you were Spanish?' I guess if I had, I would have gotten a job doing something besides cleaning toilets!

325

"Yes, that was in 1928, but I suppose the worst discrimination I felt came later when a group of girls went to Washington, D.C. We went visiting the National Gallery there, and then we went across into a little luncheonette and they gave the girls menus. They gave them menus, but didn't give me a menu. At first I didn't think a thing about it. I thought, 'well, maybe there are only two menus.' So then when it came time to order they asked the others what they wanted and ignored me. By that time I began to realize what was going on. So Chrissy, one of my girlfriends who was a peppery little gal, said, 'Say, my friend wants to eat, too.' And the waiter said, 'But your friend can't eat here.' Right in the shadow of the Capitol!"

Maria then talked about her first teaching assignment in Tucson.

"Davis School was 99.9 percent Mexican and Yaqui Indians. We used to get the Yaquis late, and I didn't notice that at first. I wasn't conscious of their problems because I was busy teaching, and I loved it. My goal was to have those kids learn that first-grade vocabulary so they could go into the second grade. But then I became conscious of the poverty, of the problems of the Mexican-Americans and the Indians, and the fact that they couldn't learn if their noses were running, if they needed tonsillectomies, if they hadn't had breakfast. So that's where my social work came in . . . in visiting families and seeing that they were in the best condition so their children could learn.

"I realized, too, that those children would come to school from one drab situation into another drab situation. At that time our schoolrooms were all painted in battle-gray or browns, you know, like they paint the ships in order to last. And it was very dreadful to teach, so I kept asking the district to please paint my room: Would they paint it a nice green or a nice yellow, something bright? And they refused for three years. So one day, one weekend, I got some paint and I got some of my sixth-grade boys, and we painted my room green.

"And I guess that was the first thing I did wrong as a teacher; I did something on my own.

"Well, then I decided we needed shade for the windows— it got pretty hot in those rooms for many months of the year—so I decided to put some shade trees down outside. To raise the money we sold hot dogs. I used to beg, borrow, steal; got day-old bread, and Swift Company was very nice, they'd give me the hot dogs. So we bought trees and planted them. When I came back the next

326

summer, the trees were dead. And I asked the janitor, 'You lazy so-and-so, why did you let the trees die?' I really was getting after him and he said, 'Maria, I had orders not to water them.'"

The incident did not subdue her. She planted an oleander hedge to get shade. Shortly afterwards she was transferred out of the barrio area school and shipped across town to teach at Sam Hughes, then an Eastside Tucson school in a pure white district.

"Well, that was a revelation to me, going to Sam Hughes School to teach. It was the best thing that ever happened to me, by the way, because I really got to know the other side and those people got to know me. Of course, children were children to me, and I loved them, too, at Sam Hughes, and they loved me; and evidently I was successful there too. At Sam Hughes I just marvelled at what I saw. Here there was grass on the ground and here were trees and library books. The difference in schools was not the fault of the district. If there was any fault with the district, it would be that they would let an affluent group of parents do things at one school that couldn't be done at a school where most of the parents were poor.

"And all this was going through my mind: What is it . . . just poverty that is making education of kids at Davis School different or is it methodology? What are we doing to these kids? So then when I went to Pueblo High School [on Tucson's south side], I realized what we were doing to them. Something struck me and I said, 'Here we are. We used to punish kids at Davis School. We told them they couldn't speak Spanish; that they had to learn English.' And then we turn around and give them Spanish in high school.

"And you see, by the time these kids got to high school, well they were so indoctrinated in speaking English and not Spanish that they were prostituting the pronunciation of their own names, anglicizing them, and, worse, they did not even know English properly."

Maria explained that the Mexican-American youngsters had anglicized their own names to avoid criticism. And she knew something had to be done to turn things around. She spoke to Spanish teachers at Pueblo and soon things were turned around in an experimental program that included an honors course in Spanish.

"It was a beautiful job those teachers did there. You could see what it was doing to the kids. They were going back to correctly pronouncing their names. They were holding their heads high. They knew for once in their lives who they were, and they were very happy with their language. And not only that, we noticed, too, the kids that were taking these courses in Spanish were getting higher grades in English, too."

And that was the beginning of Maria Urquides's battle to put bilingual education into the schools. As a representative to the National Education Association she had fought alongside black leaders in the desegregation fight. Mainly through her efforts, the Arizona delegation succeeded in the desegregation of local NEA Associations. Then she turned to her own cause.

"So they were desegregated and the whole focus turned toward the black. That was the time of Watts, you know. After that I went to Monroe Sweetland, who was the NEA representative for the southwestern states and I said, 'Monroe, we have worked hard in the NEA for the black. Now I want the NEA to do something for the Mexican-American.' That was in 1965. So he said, 'What do you want?' I said, 'I want you, the NEA, to give us enough money for a group of teachers to go into the southwestern states and see what is happening to the Mexican-American student. I want to see if they're using any different methodology, because I think that we're doing the kid a disfavor when the only potential that he brings into the first grade that the Anglo does not have is his potential to become bilingual.

"And we're saying to him, 'You can't use this language,' and we're destroying him inside psychologically, and we're producing half of what he could be. We say they're bilingual; they're not bilingual. You're not bilingual until you can hear a language, you can write it, you can read it, and you can speak it. And these kids graduate not even bilingual, not even mono-lingual sometimes. So I said, 'Please get me some money.' And we got the money, and we visited, I think it was fifty-eight different schools around thirteen districts in the state, and then we wrote the book, *The Invisible Minority.*"

There were many meetings, symposiums and hearings in Washington, in Los Angeles, and in other cities. She pressed the leadership in Washington saying, "Now, look, it's time you paid attention to the silent minority." The big push toward federal funding of bilingual education came after a symposium of congressional leaders in Tucson. Bilingual education, although still not properly funded, became a reality and now Maria looked back. . . .

328

"They used to accuse us of being narrow, of believing that teaching Spanish to the Mexican-American child was a panacea, that it would solve all his problems. Absolutely not. It wouldn't solve all his problems, but neither would teaching him English and whipping him for speaking Spanish solve all his problems. So neither is a panacea, but I think that being able to keep your own language, that means that you can keep your own culture and you're not ashamed of it.

"And you know what you are."

329

A Black Magistrate's Struggles

Hayzel Burton Daniels

The story of the national struggle to end segregation in the public schools which culminated in the 1954 landmark Supreme Court decision Brown vs. Topeka Board of Education *is now familiar. Less familiar but just as significant were the concurrent efforts in various state legislatures and courts to challenge the doctrine of "separate but equal." In Arizona, two black lawmakers, Hayzel Burton Daniels and Carl Sims, were influential in securing legislation and a subsequent court decision to end school segregation. The Arizona ruling of 1953 preceded the U.S. Supreme Court opinion, and revealed the young state's increasing maturity in responding to racial issues without violence.*

In the oral interview reprinted here, Hayzel Daniels' personal history follows the pattern of many blacks in American society. His mother sensed that a university degree offered her son greater opportunities than a military rank. So Daniels used his athletic prowess to obtain an education. As a public-school teacher in Texas, he concluded that equal educational opportunity was a matter of law not education, and he returned home to prepare for the Arizona bar. From private law practice he advanced to legislative politics and then to the bench, serving as the first black magistrate in Phoenix.

Although the history of blacks and the struggle for civil liberties in Arizona both await a chronicler, these recollections help provide another glimpse of the rich texture of the state's cultural, ethnic, and political heritage.

*H*ayzel Burton Daniels, Phoenix City Magistrate, sat in the living room of his modest house. He looked to the mementos
around him as he searched back to his beginnings.

"My grandfather and father used to tell me how they left
Florida and traveled into Mexico and then how, after agreements
were reached, they came back out of Mexico to Fort Clark, Texas.
That's where I was born. These people were Seminole scouts; you
see, there had been some inter-marriage between the blacks and
the Seminole Indians in Florida. It was 1907 when I was born down
there in Texas. In 1913 they broke up the scouts and my dad came
out here to join the Tenth Cavalry at Fort Huachuca.

"My dad was a bugler in the scouts and a bugler in G Troop
of the Tenth Cavalry. When the First World War broke out he went
overseas and afterwards he was transferred into the Twenty-fifth
Infantry.

"Well, I grew up around the fort when I was a kid. But
when it came time to go to high school, my mother moved the kids
to Nogales so I could get better schooling. She was my real inspiration to pushing ahead in education. You know, she never wanted us
to be soldiers. Now don't ask me why; she just never wanted us to
be soldiers. Maybe it was because my father never got to be an
officer or anything like that.

"But I think my mother had ambitions that my father didn't
realize in those days. There were five of us children and she had
this terrible desire for her children to have education."

*Actually Hayzel Daniels had twin ambitions: an education
and a career in football. After a disagreement with the football
coach at Nogales, Hayzel went to Tucson High School.*

Hayzel Burton Daniels, "The Blacks Who Pioneered", in Abe Chanin with Mildred Chanin,
*This Land, These Voices; A Different View of Arizona History in the Words of Those Who
Lived It* (Flagstaff: Northland Press, 1977), 194–201. Used with permission from Northland
Press.

"You see I had asked the coach down there at Nogales to put me in the backfield and he said, 'No, you're going to play end.' And I said, 'No, I'm not going to play end. I'm going to Tucson.' And I went to Tucson. My mother said okay and I moved in with a Mrs. Hart in Tucson. Now Syl Paulos was the coach at Tucson High. He was a good coach and I wanted to play for a good one. How did I get along by myself? Well, my mother and father took care of me until my senior year; then I began to earn my own livelihood. And people began to help me because they knew me from my football.

"Well, then I started at the University of Arizona in '27, but it took me until—what was it?—'37 to complete a bachelor's degree. You see, my older brother, and another fellow and myself were living together, supporting ourselves through college. But when the Depression came along, well, that threw me out of school and I went back to work in Nogales as a jackhammer man for the W.P.A. After I saved up enough money, I came back up to the university, and I was determined to play football and finish my education, too.

"It wasn't easy making it, but I would get jobs, not easy jobs, but working as a waiter, or janitor, yard boy, errand boy. Working and going to the university, and, in the first place, being black, was tough. The professors at that time weren't as liberal, as considerate, as they are today. They were clouded by discrimination and the segregation that was rampant throughout the community. So they gave you a bad time and it was discouraging.

"Well, as you might remember, I had been an All-State halfback for Tucson High School and, in fact, All-American honorable mention in my senior year. So the university just couldn't say, 'We don't want you. Go away.' They had to give me a uniform, even though I was black. I remember what Mac [University of Arizona Athletic Director J. F. McKale] told me, bless his heart. He said, 'Now I want to tell you I'm not going to treat you any different from anybody else. You go out there. You do what the rest of them do. If you get hurt, you stick it out.'

"When I hurt my knee, I couldn't go to Mac. I took the doctor's advice to give up football."

And so Daniels missed a chance to become the University of Arizona's first black to win an athletic letter. That "first" had to wait until many years later; in fact, it was 1950 before the U of A awarded its first varsity letter to a black person.

"Anyhow, I stuck it out with school, finished in 1939 and then I went over to the law school to register. J. B. McCormick was the dean at that time and when he saw that I was working—I was cleaning up at the Thomas-Davis Clinic at that time—he rejected my application and told me to get a full-time job and then come back when I had some money. Well, then I got my master's degree and went down to Texas as a teacher in a little country town out from El Paso. It was a little school—one teacher and about fifteen or twenty students. You taught them from the first to the eighth grade. Now the furniture was cast-off from a white school. And the books were cast-offs. The room itself was an oblong sort of thing about twenty feet by twelve. When it rained, it rained inside the building and it leaked outside. And come cotton-pickin' time you didn't have anything to do because all the children were gone cotton-pickin' or cotton-choppin'.

"All those children in a one-room building like that, and with one teacher . . . how the hell do you teach?

"Well, that experience had a lot to do with my understanding of discrimination in education. Later when I was teaching at the high school at Fort Huachuca I saw more of that. The white children at the fort were being transported to another school, but the black children were kept in a crowded little situation with the elementary and high school together, and that's a mess. At that time I was doing some advanced work at the University of Arizona in education and I wrote a couple of nasty seminar papers on this business of segregation at Fort Huachuca. I remember the dean calling me and saying, 'You mean to tell me you're teaching in this school and still you would write these papers? Do you want to lose your job?'

"I said, 'Yes, I want to lose my job so some kids can get some education.' And in my mind I was beginning to get the idea that I really couldn't help the situation by teaching. I said to myself, 'I have to know what the law is. That's what our problem is: we don't know what the law is, whether they are actually administering the law fairly.' You can't tell me that down there in Texas where I had taught, they were supposed to treat children that way. There should have been a truant officer or someone who took care of the Negro children and kept them out of cotton patches. They were entitled to their education as well as the whites. I mean there were, in those days, differences in everything, and the blacks always came up short."

334

Daniels was determined to turn to the law, but before he could return to school World War II came and he served overseas. The G. I. Bill helped him return to the University of Arizona.

"My wife Grace—by the way, I met her when she was doing graduate work at the University of Arizona in 1937—she suggested I go back and try again to get into law school. I went to see Dean McCormick and asked if he remembered me. He said, 'No, I don't.' I said, 'Well, I'm the fellow you told to come back when I didn't have to work while studying law. Well, now I don't have to work because I've got a very rich man (Uncle Sam) that's going to pay my way.' Well, he laughed, and I laughed, and we were good friends up to the day he died.

"Why was I so persistent in trying to get into law school? Well, I don't know. I do know that as a youngster I saw a movie in which there was a black lawyer and the story was that this community was not very well represented, and I was impressed with what that lawyer did to try to help his people. Later as a teacher I found out that blacks were not getting equal education and that they never could get equal education until something was done with the laws. And I knew I wanted to do something to help.

"In fact, when I finished law school I was planning to go to Texas where I had seen those problems in education. But my friends in the law school—Mo and Stew Udall, and Raul Castro and Shelley Richey, who is now a lawyer in Douglas—convinced me that I was needed in Arizona, that I should practice in Phoenix where I was needed. And so I became Arizona's second black lawyer. There was another black lawyer who had come from Oklahoma. He was admitted by motion back in Oklahoma and he came to Arizona during the time you were able to be admitted by motion. So actually I was the first black lawyer who passed the bar in Arizona and practiced in Arizona."

It was not very long before Daniels realized he could do even more for his people by getting into the state legislature and changing the laws.

"At that time old man Wade Hammond was the big honcho in the black community of Phoenix. He was what they called a 'backdoor lawyer,' who, if some black got into trouble, could go downtown and maybe resolve the problem without court action. My dad had soldiered under Hammond down at the fort when Hammond was bandmaster. And Hammond knew me as a little kid and he just couldn't understand why this 'little boy, this bare boy' wanted to run for the legislature. Mr. Hammond, you see, wanted to be the first black legislator in this state. Well, he got a lot of people worked up against me because I had had the audacity to challenge desegregation in the schools. But I won anyway and I went in as a representative in 1950, and Carl Sims and I were the first two black legislators in the state.

"You see, I felt that by going to the legislature I could get the laws changed. Earlier I had read a case where the judge had declared it unconstitutional to segregate Mexicans in the schools in Glendale. I made friends with that judge and he explained to me that it was different for blacks. There was a specific law that permitted the segregation of blacks in the schools and he said if that law could be changed that would be another thing. So I tried to do that; that was my purpose in going to the legislature.

"And in the legislature we did get the law changed; we got the wording of the law to fit the language used in the Glendale case and now we had to go attack the entire thing. And I led that attack. Let me say this, I didn't make friends of every black in the state. Black teachers, you see, feared they would lose their jobs if the schools were desegregated. But that didn't stop me. I knew there was a big job in front of us.

"But I remember how the opportunity came. Representative Jim Ewing from Tucson came to see me and Carl Sims on a Sunday morning. It seems they needed two votes from Maricopa County to get the speaker they wanted re-elected. We were the two votes they needed, so Ewing asked us, 'What do you guys want? Do you want some good committee appointments?'

"I said, 'I'll tell you what. I'll come in, if you're interested in integrated schools.'

"He said, 'Don't want to hear about that.'

"But finally I got to him when I said, 'I want your assurance that we can introduce a desegregation bill on the floor and that your administration will at least give it a chance to pass.'

"He said, 'Well, let me talk to Raymond Langham.'

"Langham was the speaker they wanted to get re-elected and he told Ewing. 'Yeah, let's promise him that. Let's give him that. And we'll do better; we'll give him a vice-chairmanship on the Judiciary Committee.'

"I don't imagine they really intended to go that far. But I did have some strong people on my side—Nielson Brown, the representative from Santa Cruz County, and Hubert Merriweather,

the senator from Santa Cruz. I knew them personally when I was
working at the Old Pueblo Club, working there as a waiter in Tucson. They knew me and liked me; they were proud that I had come
so far.

"Well, I wrote up the bill and we submitted it to a committee, the Committee on Highways and Bridges. I don't know what
that committee had to do with a bill like that, but they said that was
the place to put it. The real reason was that Frank Robles of Tucson
was chairman and he could bring it out of committee. Then we got
it out of two other committees and on to the docket of the Rules
Committee. And believe it or not, there was enough pressure from
the public, enough pressure on the representatives that we were
able to pass the bill in the house in modified form and send it on to
the senate. I think the house was saying, 'Let the senate be embarrassed with this bill.' But they hadn't reckoned with my friend Senator Merriweather. He was the one who got it carried through the
senate, I think, nineteen to one, or eighteen to one.

"The governor signed the bill and we had this modified
thing with the words 'they may separate.' On that basis we filed the
action, seeking to declare the law unconstitutional. But our action
in federal court was aborted because the Los Angeles lawyers who
were working with me came and said they wanted it filed before a
three-judge court and that would put us together with the five
other segregation cases coming up across the country. That would
allow us to go right to the Supreme Court.

"One of the lawyers from Los Angeles was a big labor lawyer and the other two—they came into it through the NAACP—
were outstanding constitutional lawyers. But they overlooked the
one point that you have to have the state declare this constitutional
before it could get to the federal court. Well, there had not been a
state court decision on this new legislation and we were thrown out
of the three-judge court and told to go seek remedy in a one-man
court. So we came down and Judge David Ling heard the case and
he ruled the same way, deferring us to the state court. I guess this
big lawyer who had wanted the three-judge court had been so anxious to get up before the Supreme Court and argue the case, that
he was disappointed that it didn't go that far.

"Well, the California lawyers abandoned us and Herb Finn
[a Phoenix attorney] and I were left. So we filed in Superior Court
and Judge Fred Struckmeyer declared the new law unconstitutional, but he did it from the narrow point that there were new

standards set and therefore it was unconstitutional for that reason. That put us back under that Glendale school case and that didn't satisfy us. So we decided to file against a little elementary school out at the edge of Phoenix and brought them into court. This time it was Judge Charles Bernstein on the bench and he met the issue. He said the law was unconstitutional, a violation of the Fourteenth Amendment. That was a year before the Supreme Court handed down its decision in the Brown case of 1954. I was told that Bernstein's papers may show that the Supreme Court clerk had written and asked for Bernstein's opinion on school desegregation as a guide for the Brown decision."

Hayzel Daniels had been the first black to practice law in Arizona under the Arizona Bar standards. He and Carl Sims were the state's first black legislators and he was Arizona's first black assistant attorney general. Now came still another first in 1965.

"Well, when I came out of the attorney general's office I applied twice for the position of city magistrate in Phoenix. There had never been a black on the bench in the state, and they just wouldn't appoint me. Well, finally, as things changed in the city, they figured they needed a black man. The mayor of Phoenix agreed to that and I was offered the job.

"At the time I had a good practice so I thought seriously about giving it up and going on the bench. I discussed the offer with my wife and she said, 'Here we go chasing windmills again.' But she added, 'You can do some good for your people there.'

"So I took the bench in 1965, and I am still there. I'll be there until I retire."

Remembering Arizona

J. B. Priestley

J. B. Priestley, British novelist, playwright and essayist, spent the winter of 1937 at a guest ranch near Wickenburg with his family. Although the United States was still in the grip of depression, rumors of the impending war in Europe hardly disturbed the American consciousness. As Priestley and his family journeyed across the country to the West Coast and sunshine, the grimness of the European economic and political situation dimmed and gradually receded from their minds. Within a few short weeks, the Arizona sunshine thawed their chilled English bones and "the desert crept into all our hearts."

Priestley's passion for Arizona never waned. More than eleven years later, still feeling the mellow glow of that winter sojourn, he wrote the following selection for Arizona Highways.

Priestley is, in many ways, like the thousands of other Arizona visitors who recall the state's beauty through the photographs and articles of this magazine. In a few pages Priestley gave voice to the thoughts and recollections of thousands of modern travelers who recall and savor their own memories of Arizona.

It is now more than eleven years since I last saw Arizona. This is a long time—much too long. And nobody must imagine that the Priestley family have fallen out of love with Arizona. First, there was the War, with duties that kept us here. And now there is the currency problem. We British must not spend dollars, not even the dollars we earn. This may seem outrageous, until you remember that those dollars enable us to buy things we need urgently. I will admit (come closer, will you?) that by arranging to have some important business in Hollywood, I could probably conjure enough dollars out of His Majesty's Treasury to give me a glorious little stop-over in Arizona. But I could do this only for myself, not for the rest of the family, and if I went sneaking off by myself in this fashion, they might not speak to me when I came back.

Yes, feeling runs as high as that. The desert crept into all our hearts. Every month we take a peep or two through the tantalising little windows of *Arizona Highways*, and although this house high above the white cliffs of the Isle of Wight has its own glorious views, as we take our peep through those little windows, we have a few sighs and curse this new world of the economists and the passport officials. And we begin to remember again. What do we remember? Well, here I shall speak for myself.

My mind returns first to Remuda Ranch at Wickenburg, where we stayed so long. There was the shack near the river that Jack Burden (whose early death must have been a great loss to the whole Wickenburg community) built for me to work in, a shack that may still be seen not only at Remuda but also on the cover of the English edition of my "Midnight On The Desert." I think, too, of that fine circular fireplace in the living room of Remuda Ranch, and I can only hope that, in spite of many improvements and en-

From J. B. Priestley, "Remembering Arizona," *Arizona Highways* 25 (December 1949): 5–7. Used with permission from A. D. Peters & Co. Ltd., London.

340

largements around there, the fireplace, which could not be improved and could hardly be enlarged, still dominates the room. Then various favourite spots in the neighborhood are remembered. Vulture, for instance, and that place up the river where we had so many picnics. They tell me that Wickenburg itself, which was growing fast in our time, has shot up and spread past our recognition.

I remember highways. The first of them is the familiar stretch between Wickenburg and Phoenix. When my wife and I, without the children, paid our first visit to Remuda, we left our baggage at Phoenix and were astonished when the Burdens said casually they would send in to Phoenix for it. Fresh from England, we were surprised by the Arizona conception of distance, which regarded fifty miles as we regard five. Then, as I often had to go to Hollywood, there was the almost equally familiar trail to Los Angeles, U.S. Highway 60, which took us to Salome, where we had many a long, cool drink. Not quite so familiar, though sufficiently well-remembered, was the other road North, on the way to the Grand Canyon or Boulder Dam or the Indian Reservation, which went through Prescott. But we never saw this pleasant town at the right time, for we were always going through it in winter and we usually found ourselves shivering a little up there.

Now I have found a large cardboard box, packed with old road maps, booklets, and photographs of us at Remuda, Phantom Ranch, going up and down the Grand Canyon. Looking at the maps, I realise with deep regret how much of Arizona we left unexplored. For instance, all the Coolidge Dam country and the desert both East and West of Tucson. (But we did definitely prefer the rough and rolling country near Wickenburg to the more conventional desert territory further South, and so belong to the Phoenix and not to the Tucson party.) And I think we took the Yuma trail to California only once. On the other hand, we did a good deal of wandering—in a station wagon—around the North of the state. My wife and three of the daughters, very young then, went twice as far as Rainbow Bridge; and I was up there once. But unfortunately, owing to a change in the weather and the danger of being badly held up, we all missed visiting Monument Valley, which is about the top of the list of places to be seen on any future trip.

Among my most enchanting memories of Arizona is the time—alas, all too short—we spent in Oak Creek Canyon, which to me especially had a peculiar magic of its own, like some fabled

341

garden of the Hesperides in classical legend. Before I die I should like to live some weeks in that bright hidden oasis, out of this world, meditating and dreaming in the sunlight of its early Spring, storing up thoughts and impressions for a book. I have a suspicion that Oak Creek is perhaps under-rated, but Heaven forbid that it should suddenly become popular and become a resort filled with swimming pools and cocktail bars.

Although I am far removed from being a globe-trotter, it happens that in my time I have hit a few high spots of travel. I have sailed up the Nile as far as the Southern Sudan; I have been to the South Seas; I have visited Lake Louise in the Canadian Rockies; I have seen both from the ground and high in the air the grand romantic scenery of the Caucasus. But I have yet to see anything that challenges the fantastic Northern Arizona. Most famous places fall below our idea and expectation of them. They are good but not as good as all that. But the Grand Canyon just goes on taking your breath away. Some of the recent pictures of it in *Arizona Highways* have been among the best specimens of colour photography that I have ever seen; but no camera can capture that huge miracle of shifting light and shade. And it shines in the memory like an old well-tested friendship. Just to remember that it is still there, and far too large to be messed about and spoilt, makes me glad. And if I were back in the Southwest, I should soon be heading for Flagstaff, Williams or Ash Fork, to gape again into the vast glowing abyss.

Yet some of the country east of the Grand Canyon proper, the country reached through Cameron, has perhaps a more romantic strangeness and a more delicate beauty than anything to be seen from the familiar tourist spots along the Rims. Who, having once seen them, could forget the Vermillion Cliffs and the Painted Desert and the Petrified Forest? Or the stupendous landscape that unfolds itself for the guest up at Rainbow Lodge?

But Arizona is something more than a collection of natural marvels and multi-colored landscapes. Thus, I remember with delight the diamond air itself, through which whole ranges of amethyst mountains, a hundred miles away, can be clearly distinguished. And what fun it used to be, travelling the highways on a hot morning, to watch the mirages, to see the hills melt and dissolve and then re-shape themselves! How can I forget the glorious sunsets and the nights that followed, cool, and crisp as a nut? We occasionally run across people here who have followed these same trails in their time, and you should see the way in which our faces light up when we compare experiences.

Then there are the people. I am not going to mention names if only because some who ought to be in the list would inevitably be left out, so that more harm than good might be done. But what a horrible business it would be, visiting this magnificent state and being enchanted by its scenery and climate, if the people themselves were unpleasant! Imagine returning from one of the canyons or a desert sunset and then having to face a lot of sour, sneering, unfriendly types! But of course it was never like that. Wherever we went in Arizona, we always seemed to meet the kind of people we like, sensible and friendly, quiet at the right times, but ready for fun and games, too. During the Thirties, with lecture tours and various journalistic jobs on hand, I travelled extensively in the U.S., particularly throughout the Middle West, and in spite of rumours to the contrary, I always got along with most Americans I met on these journeys; but I do not hesitate to declare that it was in the Southwest—and especially in Arizona—that I found myself most at ease with everybody. They were our sort of folk. And as a playwright and radio speaker, I am perhaps unusually sensitive to the pitch and cadence of the human voice; and I always enjoyed listening to the deep drawl of the honest-to-God Arizona man. It was just the voice you wanted to listen to at the fireside after a long day in the sun.

Voices, faces, blue birds and scarlet birds, cactus and pine, mountains dissolving in the morning mirage or glowing like jewels in the sunset, the sweet clear air, the blaze of stars at midnight—they all return to memory and come haunting our dreams. I would not live outside Britain these days even if I were offered a king's ransom, for not only do I love this battered old island of ours but I believe wholeheartedly in the great social experiment we are making; but to have another long holiday in Arizona, with the whole family along—ah!—that would be happiness indeed.

Index

—All place names are in Arizona unless otherwise identified.

345

347

349

351

353